OFFICIAL REPORT

OF THE

TWENTY - FIRST INTERNATIONAL

CHRISTIAN ENDEAVOR CONVENTION

HELD IN

TENT ENDEAVOR AND MANY CHURCHES

DENVER, COLO., JULY 9 - 13, 1903.

First Fruits Press
Wilmore, Kentucky
c2015

First Fruits Press
The Academic Open Press of Asbury Theological Seminary
204 N. Lexington Ave., Wilmore, KY 40390
859-858-2236
first.fruits@asburyseminary.edu
asbury.to/firstfruits

LOCAL COMMITTEE OF THE TWENTY-FIRST INTERNATIONAL CHRISTIAN ENDEAVOR CONVENTION.

F. B. Spalding. J. W. Barrows. W. B. Shattuc. Rev. J. D. Rankin. G. M. Link. Dr. W. J. Harsha. W. M. Danner.
Rev. J. G. Kennedy. F. B. Gibson. W. E. Sweet, Chairman. H. B. Smith. F. P. Woolston.
C. M. Weyand. F. D. Stackhouse.

THE STORY

OF THE

DENVER CONVENTION

BEING THE

OFFICIAL REPORT

OF THE

TWENTY-FIRST INTERNATIONAL

Christian Endeavor Convention

HELD IN

TENT ENDEAVOR AND MANY CHURCHES

DENVER, COLO., JULY 9-13, 1903

UNITED SOCIETY OF CHRISTIAN ENDEAVOR
BOSTON, MASS.

1

Stanhope Press
F. H. GILSON COMPANY
BOSTON, U.S.A.

TABLE OF CONTENTS.

3

ILLUSTRATIONS.

4

The Committee of 1903.

EXECUTIVE COMMITTEE.

Mr. WILLIAM E. SWEET, *Chairman.*

Rev. J. D. RANKIN, *Vice-Chairman.*

Mr. HENRY KOEPCKE, *Secretary.*

Mr. F. B. SPALDING, *Treasurer.*

CHAIRMAN OF SUB-COMMITTEES.

Mr. FRANK B. GIBSON, *Finance.*

Mr. W. M. DANNER, *Entertainment.*

Mr. F. D. STACKHOUSE, *Decorations.*

Mr. H. B. SMITH, *Press and Publicity.*

Rev. W. J. HARSHA, *Pulpit Supply.*

Mr. JOHN W. BARROWS, *Meeting-Places and Grounds.*

Mr. WILLIAM B. SHATTUC, *Reception.*

Mr. C. M. WEYAND, *Music.*

Mr. F. PEYTON WOOLSTON, *Excursions.*

Rev. J. G. KENNEDY, *Publishers' Display.*

Mr. GEO. M. LINK, *Pages and Ushers.*

Miss NELLIE M. WILLIAMS, *Junior Work.*

Mr. H. R. CHAPMAN, *Ex-officio Member.*

Musical Directors and Associates.

Mr. C. M. WEYAND, *Chairman.*

MUSICAL DIRECTORS.

Mr. F. H. JACOBS, Brooklyn, N.Y.
Mr. PERCY S. FOSTER, Washington, D.C.
Prof. W. J. WHITEMAN, Denver, Col.

ASSISTANT DIRECTORS.

Mr. HINES HIMSWORTH, Denver, Col.
Mr. H. RICHMOND, Denver, Col.
Mr. H. P. SPENCER, Denver, Col.
Mr. T. H. IRELAND, Denver, Col.
Mr. L. B. SKINNER, Denver, Col.

ACCOMPANISTS.

Miss Ethel McDowell, Denver, Col.
Miss Minnie L. Sprague, Denver, Col.
Mrs. Robert Collier, Denver, Col.
Mr. Franklin Cleverly, Denver, Col.
Mr. Milton P. Givens, Jr., Denver, Col.
Mrs. Sidney M. Crane, Denver, Col.
Miss Alice Kopplin, Denver, Col.

CORNETISTS.

Mr. S. M. Crane, Denver, Col.
Mr. W. B. Keyt, Denver, Col.
Mr. L. B. Skinner, Denver, Col.

INTRODUCTION.

A CHRISTIAN ENDEAVOR CONVENTION A MILE HIGH.

"This stone is exactly one mile high," was the inscription borne on a stone on a street corner in Denver.

Christian Endeavor is helping young people to climb to the skies and pull the world up after them, hence there was something especially fitting and suggestive in holding the Twenty-first International, and the first Biennial Convention so much higher in the air than any previous one had been held, the altitude of Denver being over 5,000 feet.

Denver will be remembered as

THE GREAT SCENIC CONVENTION.

Not that the claims of Washington, San Francisco, Detroit, and other places can be forgotten. But never before have we met in an atmosphere so marvellously clear and pure. Never before have the snow-capped mountains looked down upon our convocation in such majesty. Never before have the East and West, the North and South, met at so strategic a centre after traversing half the length and breadth of this vast land, in a three or four days' patriotic, moving-picture panorama.

Many of the young people from the seashore and plains had never before seen a mountain peak, and two of them, in the innocence of their hearts, proposed to take a little walk before breakfast to the mountains and back. They did not seem to be more than two or three miles away, so transparent is Colorado air, though the nearest foothills are twelve miles distant, and Long's, Grey's, and Pike's Peaks, whose snowy caps were clearly visible, are fully 150 miles away.

Like the Washington and Detroit Conventions, that at Denver was housed in

A MAGIC WHITE CITY

that sprung up beside the magnificent City Park, with its 320 acres of artistic landscape gardening, its inviting shade and splashing fountains.

Tent Endeavor, the capitol of this snow-white city, never looked fairer, was more conveniently arranged, or had better acoustics. Every one remarked on that. Even the Juniors' voices carried to the rear of it. The general scheme of decorating the big tent was good, and the effect highly satisfactory. Red and white bunting in numerous bands were caught at the centre of the great canvas roof and swung in a graceful curve down to the side walls. On each of the supporting

7

poles four flags in cluster ornamented, without breaking the view from any seat of the platform.   The row of big center posts were draped in plain white, making a more effective decoration than if colors had been used.   The edge of the platform was draped and some flags flew back of the choir, but the decorations were carefully guarded to prevent a disturbance of the acoustic properties of the auditorium.   The grounds had been made to wear something of a tropical appearance by the palms, yuccas, and other tropical plants that in a measure took the place of greensward.

The white, cool cots of the

The Spick-and-Span Hospital Tent,

and the obliging manners of the spick-and-span attendants made one almost want to be ill.   But few claimed attention of physician or nurse. Colorado heat doesn't prostrate as heat does in the humid East.   Denver mountain water is nectar, and Denver air is elixir.

"Are *you* dizzy yet?" was one of the expected questions, soon after arrival.   But all soon recovered from any unpleasant effects of the high altitude, and the stimulating air and fine water put every one in the pink of condition.

The Literature Tent,

in charge of Mr. Thomas Wainwright, Superintendent of the Chicago Christian Endeavor offices, was an attractive book-store under canvas, with a bevy of Denver's most charming Endeavor girls selling Christian Endeavor literature, and giving silver and smiles for change.   Near this was

The Press Tent,

which looked cool and inviting enough to woo reporters to graphic pen pictures.   Typewriters clicked, stenographers sat waiting by arrays of artistically sharpened pencils, and Chairman H. B. Smith and his busy assistants at their business-like roll-topped desks made ready the proof-slips of the addresses, and looked after the comfort of the press men with cordial good will.

Never was the work of the press committee better done.   An official stenographer made verbatim copies of all the addresses the manuscripts of which had not been furnished in advance.   The Denver newspapers had tents for receiving subscriptions.

The Excursion Tent

was for the convenience of those who wanted information about side trips or railroad tickets.   The Denver way was to make it so easy for every one to do exactly the right thing that no one had any excuse for making a mistake.   A number of churches had set up

Restaurant Tents

in which appetizing lunches were furnished, so that no one need travel to his boarding-place in the heat of the day.

The lunches might be eaten in the "White City," or they might be taken to the beautiful City Park, a square away. At the

Information Tent

facts about Denver's streets, hotels, railroads, and almost everything under the sun were kept on tap, and flowed as freely as did the "purest water in the world" from the iced jars sandwiched in everywhere, between tents, under shady booths. It was into this information tent that all the ladies' hats, pocketbooks, combs, hymn-books, and other articles saved from the wreckage of Tent Endeavor were taken that they might be restored to their owners. Besides all these, the streets of the "White City" had

Rest Tents

furnished with cozy rocking-chairs, comfortable couches, dainty lavender screens, magazines, fans, and attendants with smiling faces and willing hearts. There were numerous booths at which were sold souvenir postal cards, pictures, Colorado minerals, etc. There were tents for public convenience, tents for storing bicycles, and for every use that can be conceived of pertaining to such a gathering.

But this "White City," like other cities, had its suburbs. In various parts of the city were

Sixty Church Headquarters.

Every one of these churches was assigned to one or more States, Territories, Provinces or foreign lands as headquarters. Usually a great white banner overhung the street, telling who were to register and enjoy hospitality there. Inside, the churches were beautifully decorated.

Take as an example the Central Presbyterian Church. Great festoons of red and white were drawn from the galleries to the centre of the lofty dome, the gallery fronts were hidden by interwoven bands and long streamers sweeping upward to the gilded organ pipes and looking like sun-rays from the focal emblem, a large monogram of the letters C. E. was written in electric fire against a cross-barred field of society colors.

The brilliant electric C. E. surmounting the dome of the Central Christian Church was a conspicuous object-lesson to the whole city.

There was a friendly rivalry between the churches as to which should display the most indiscribably bewitching effects and delightful surprises. There were booths for registering, and for information, rest rooms, writing rooms supplied with stationery, toilet rooms equipped

with toilet necessaries, ice-water fountains, telephones, and everything
that the delicate thoughtfulness of Denver Endeavorers could devise.
Here were held the State and other sectional rallies, and obliging attendants gave their time and services to keep the rooms open day and
night and serve the visiting hosts with Oriental courtesy. At the Calvary Baptist Church refreshments were served free to arriving delegates.

DENVER WEATHER AND WHATNOT.

The first hot wave of the season struck in as the Endeavorers were
on their way to Denver. In the valleys and on the plains the travelling delegates sweltered and perspired, but sang and laughed just the
same. Climbing up the plateau to Denver they found it cooler, though
the sun shone hot in the middle of the day, and it shines there 357
days in the year. It was always cool on the shady side of the street, and
in the brick and stone buildings of which Denver is so largely built.

The nights and mornings were delicious, and after the first two
days Denver weather was paradisaical compared with what the newspapers reported for the East. However, the first day was hot for
Denver, and a great many ejaculated,

"Ugh!"

"Oh, my!"

"Whe-e-ew, but it's hot!"

The following lines by a Denver poet give an idea of the situation:

> "They have come and still are coming,
>   From the North, South, East and West;
> And the whole town is a-humming,
>   With their ardor and their zest;
> E'en old Sol has surely never
>   Shone, as now, with fervid zeal,
> In his unchristian endeavor
>   All our noses for to peel."
>
> — *Walter Juan Davis.*

But there's never a time when Endeavorers can't be happy, and
the cheerfulness of the visitors proved the saying. Such laughing,
such jubilant hand-shaking, such amiability, as, begrimed, travel-
worn and hungry, the arriving delegates bumped against one another's
luggage in the crowds, apologized, became instantly acquainted, and
smilingly helped each other.

THE COMMITTEE THAT OVERLOOKED NOTHING.

Never was a Convention more thoroughly and painstakingly prepared for. Every little detail was worked out with mathematical
nicety, and the whole preparations were sandpapered and polished
off days before a delegate put in an appearance.

Mr. Sweet, chairman of the Convention Committee, said, at the complimentary dinner given the committee by the United Society trustees, that there had been no need of a committee meeting for about a week. And Dr. Clark complimented the committee still farther by saying that the machinery had been running so smoothly that no one had heard the slightest creak or jar.

It was a common remark that the ushers showed surpassing urbanity and discretion in handling the audiences, and in dealing with unintentional violations of rules governing them. One usher requested a delegate not to stand before others, and next day apologized to him for being obliged to do it.

The reception committee had no easy task in meeting trains. Some of them went fifty miles and more, and stayed out all night, to be ready to board trains in the morning.

One committeeman, through a mistake, was put off his train, and had to camp out for the night and foot it the rest of the way. But all this was done cheerfully, smilingly.

The only slip, so far as was known, was the failure of a florist, through serious illness, to fulfill his contract to supply five thousand fresh specimens of the great, blue, Colorado columbines every morning for free distribution at the State headquarters, a fragrant work of superogation, the conception of which in the hearts of the committee is enough to put every one thus included in their gracious thought under a lasting obligation to them.

DECORATIONS.

The whole city put on holiday attire for the Convention. State capitol and city court house set the fashion for business blocks and residences by decking themselves in the Convention and national colors, while the brow of the commonwealth, the dome of the State house, with its encircling, many-colored electric lights, looked as if the diadems of Eastern kings had been brought from royal treasure-houses to honor the coming of the Endeavorers.

Some of the leading business houses spent a great deal of money in decorating their stores for the occasion. The main entrance of Joslyn's dry goods store presented a beautiful arch wrapped in the Convention colors, with monograms in the pedestal of each pillar, "Welcome" over the arch, surmounted by another monogram, the words "Christian Endeavor," and a handsome cluster of national and convention flags.

Daniels & Fisher, the Denver Dry Goods Store, and many other similar concerns displayed taste and generosity in decorations.

STREET CARS AND POLICEMEN.

The street-car service was excellent. Denver's system of transfers is liberal. Her cars are roomy and fast. There was little crowding or waiting. When the storm came up on Monday, and the tent went down, extra cars were rushed to the scene that the people might not have to stand in the rain. The conductors were obliging and even sympathetic.

The policemen with whom the writer came in contact might have been trained in the school of a Chesterfield.

"I am very sorry to have to tell you," politely said one in the railway station, "that this room is exclusively for ladies." Contrast that with the brusque "G'wan wid yez, now," of the average policeman.

While no especial civic or municipal courtesies were shown the Convention, as was so signally the case with the mayors of Montreal, Boston and other places, yet the public spirit and hospitality of Denver amply met all demands.

MESSENGER SQUAD STARTING FROM HEADQUARTERS AT THE RAILROAD
STATION.

A SQUAD OF RECEPTION COMMITTEEMEN GROUPED IN THE C. E. MONOGRAM.

CHAPTER I.

An Afternoon of Welcome and Responses.

TENT ENDEAVOR, THURSDAY AFTERNOON.

As on every railroad that radiated from Denver the crowds had come, from Maine to California and from the great lakes to the gulf, so did all the street-car lines converge at the big tent, on Thursday afternoon, where the Convention opened at two o'clock.

The almost torrid heat of the afternoon had been modified by cooling drops from gray skies, giving the air a deliciously cool and fresh scented smell. Inside the white canopied church, which was dripping moisture sufficiently to bring into play an army of black umbrellas, 8,000 Endeavorers were ready to join in the opening praise service, led by that stalwart, worshipful musical director, Mr. F. H. Jacobs, of Brooklyn. Just as the audience was singing the words, "The sun gone down," in "Nearer My God to Thee," the sun came radiantly forth, as though promising not to be naughty any more.

When the melody of the old-fashioned hymns, sweet to many because of early associations, had died away, one arose whom Endeavorers love to honor, and, with a gavel presented by State President Chapman, and made of Colorado products, exercised the well-earned privilege of opening the Twenty-first International Christian Endeavor Convention. The gavel which Dr. Clark received was thus described by Mr. Chapman: —

The core of polished granite represents the young Christian life of the world. The polished silver bands encircling it, and the quartz and gold nugget at the ends of hammer and handle, the refined products of Colorado labor, represent the Christian Endeavor product after twenty-one years of service. A beautiful symbol of a beautiful fact.

Dr. Clark, holding it in his hand, said:—

Let our first word in this convention be from the word of God. As we have journeyed from different States to this exalted privelege, we have looked off unto the hills, and let us say together the first verse of the one hundred and twenty-first psalm. Will you say it after me, — "I will lift mine eyes unto the hills from whence cometh my help. My help cometh from the Lord, which made heaven and earth."

Dr. Clark struck the platform rail with the gavel and said: —

I am very glad to declare the Twenty-first International Convention of the Societies of Christian Endeavor now open.

Dr. B. B. Tyler, of Colorado Springs, whose initials might well stand for "Best Beloved," conducted the devotional exercises, and then there burst forth from the chorus of 700 voices, led by Professor W. J. Wightman, of Denver,

A WONDERFUL WELCOME IN SONG.

How better describe it than in the words of a poetically-inclined reporter of one of the Denver papers: "Against the walls of the great tent the mighty music beat in waves of golden sound. It rose and receded, then soared again to the canvased apex, sank once more to worshipful whispers, and at length died away into silver silence."

Then stepped to the raised platform beneath the great sounding-board a manly figure surmounted by a head that has more than once proved its levelness, politically, and a pleasant, youthful face, Governor James H. Peabody, of Colorado, who voiced

THE WELCOME OF THE STATE.

It is with feelings of sincere personal as well as official pleasure, that I welcome to the State of Colorado, and to Denver, its capital city, the members and representatives of the greatest interdenominational organization the world has ever known, The National Society of Christian Endeavor, an organization Christian in its character, grand in its conceptions, beneficial in its undertakings, stupendous in its membership, and mammoth in its grand work and good results, surpassing all other humanizing agencies during the nineteenth century, and captivating the attention of millions of young people for its future work in the years to come.

We welcome you to Colorado because your organization is a power that walks through the land, inspiring our younger men and women to a higher plane of life, and encouraging us all to live a truer and better life, and blending all nations into that Kingdom of God which is eternal.

I have stood many times upon the bridge over the gorge at Niagara Falls, and watched the waters as they rushed through, driving, plunging, and leaping, now clear and placid on the surface, now dashed against the rocks, now thrown up in spray to the clear vision of the beholder, now pushed aside into a quiet eddy, totally regardless of their future destination, and the thought came to me that the waters of that mighty river were like the American people of the present day, who are tearing, and pushing, and crowding restlessly forward to the accomplishment of one end, — the acquisition of material wealth.

And I then fully realized and understood the true selfishness of our natures in the reckless rush for a share of this world's goods for the enjoyment of to-day and the immediate present, without giving a thought or care for the future. By the future I do not mean to-morrow, or next week, or next year, but the great unknown future of our after life, for which too many of us make no apparent provision.

We felicitate ourselves, therefore, that your coming among us and shedding abroad the warmth of your Christianizing influence must be felt and seen in the uplifting of our people, and causing them to reflect upon the spiritual as well as the material affairs of life, and thereby prove a benefit and a blessing to our every-day life.

When the applause of the audience had died away, there came a word of welcome, no more eloquent it is true, but with just a little sweeter ring: It was the voice of Dr. Robert F. Coyle, Moderator of the Presbyterian General Assembly, and pastor of the Central Presbyterian Church.

Dr. Coyle made a very picturesque figure, with his flowing locks, almost white, his luxuriant, drooping mustache, and his genial face and eyes twinkling with good humor, all of which gave him a striking resemblance to Mark Twain. His white duck jacket added to the unique effect. He voiced the

WELCOME OF THE CHURCHES.

No other International Christian Endeavor Convention was ever held as high up as this one (*Laughter*) and so the churches and pastors of Denver extend to you a mile-high welcome.

It is fitting that high things should issue from high places, in spiritual as well as other warfare. It is well to plant out batteries upon some conspicuous eminence. There shot and shell will carry farther.

I wonder why the agnostics never held a convention of this magnitude. They can talk, blow their trumpet, but when it comes to doing things, where are they? And if they were to plan for a great convention of this sort, and if thousands of them were to pour into Denver or other American city, I wonder if a sign would be flung out to welcome the infidels. "All hail, the agnostics!" I don't believe it, because deep down in their hearts the people will consider no philosophy and no belief that has no God in it.

And so we welcome you because of what you are; because of what you stand for. The days of the goody-goody, knock-kneed Christianity are gone. The Christianity that we must have now is the Christianity that loves the open. We want plenty of good red blood in it; it must be robust and virile and have on its cheek the healthy tan of the open air. Its color must not be put on by cosmetics, but by conflict with sin, the flesh, and the devil.

We welcome you because you stand for interdenominational fellowship and co-operation. Sectarianism is on the retreat, and we hope it will keep on retreating until hidden behind the shadows of oblivion forever. (*Applause.*) Thank God that the barbed wire fences of sectarianism of fifty years ago, upon which clergymen got their ecclesiastical trousers badly torn if they tried to climb over, are gone. Christian people in all our churches have come to the point where they propose to stand for the things that unite, rather than for the things that divide.

I may be pardoned if I say that I am proud to belong to a church which, though devotedly fond of its blue banner, has no use for Westminster leagues of young people or any other kind of leagues of young people that put an emphasis upon Christian division rather than Christian union. Presbyterians like the Endeavor label, and they like the Endeavor goods, and unless I am much mistaken they propose to stand by them both.

Then again, we welcome you because you stand for the highest ideals of denominational loyalty. Denominationalism classifies us; sectarianism divides us. Denominationalism denotes the particular regiment in the army in which we fight. Sectarianism makes bush-whackers. Denominationalism is illustrated by the political solidarity of these United States, "E pluribus unum," many in one. Sectarianism was illustrated some forty years ago, when that final split came and we had two flags and two governments and our beloved land was overrun with strife and carnage.

In behalf of all the churches, and all the pastors, and all who love our Lord Jesus Christ in sincerity and truth, I extend to you a most cordial welcome.

The committee of '03 had already spread its welcome all over the city, and sent foretastes of it out to meet every incoming train, but from no one did the Convention want more anxiously to hear than the handsome, pushing chairman, Mr. William E. Sweet, who put into charming sentences

THE WELCOME OF THE COMMITTEE OF 1903.

In a little church in one of the seaside resorts of Rhode Island, where people of all denominations are accustomed to worship, is this motto: "The church is many as the waves, but one like the sea."

16   TWENTY–FIRST INTERNATIONAL CONVENTION

No more fitting characterization of Christian Endeavor could be made, than this. It is true also of Colorado's welcome. On the broad plain over which you have travelled, in the fertile valleys and in the mountain fastnesses, whose hills shall rejoice on every side at your coming, are Christian Endeavorers who wait to bid you a most hearty and enthusiastic welcome. Colorado's welcome is "many as the waves, but one like the sea."

I wish to take this opportunity to relate a story, very old and somewhat threadbare in this section, but I tell it in order that you may be warned against a similar experience. It is said that in the early days, before the railroads had penetrated into the mountains, two travellers started to walk to yonder hills.

After walking what seemed to them a considerable distance, one suggested to the other that if he would walk on slowly he would go back for a carriage. He did so, but what was his surprise on catching up with his companion, to find him seated beside an irrigating ditch, scarcely two feet wide, taking off his clothes. He expressed the greatest surprise at such an unusual proceeding, whereupon the one who was disrobing said: "I have the dead wood on this thing this time, this ditch looks like it is only two feet across, but it may be a mile, and I am preparing to swim."

Mr. Sweet painted a glowing picture of Colorado and Denver, and then touched eloquently upon the vital theme of the need of Christian character in public life.

What the business world stands in need of to-day is character, integrity, downright honesty. Men who will refuse to do under a corporate name what they will not do under their own names; men who believe that a "good name is rather to be chosen than great riches, and loving favor rather than silver and gold." Men who in politics will plant their feet squarely on the rock of integrity, and will not be moved by a powerful political press or the promise of preferment. Not, "Is it expedient?" but "Is it right?" must be the standard of our business and political life. It is to such a sublime consummation that the church of God contributes when it succeeds in impressing upon the future business or professional man the likeness of Christ.

He closed his gracious welcome with a beautiful poem by James Barton Adams, one of Colorado's poets: —

"Music tremblin' in the air
    Out in Colorado.
People smilin' everywhere
    Out in Colorado.
Laughter in the merry skies,
Cupids in the wimin's eyes,
Brooks a singin' lullabies
    Out in Colorado.

"If 1 should hear the call to die
    Out in Colorado,
Don't you ever think I'd fly
    Way from Colorado.
Heaven's awful far away
An' although it's nice, they say,
I'll jes' cuddle down an' stay
    Out in Colorado."

SPARKLING RESPONSES.

The scheme of responses from the four great sections of the country, and then from the four quarters of the earth, was a very happy one. Owing to the absence of Dr. George F. Libby, one of the first Williston Endeavorers, the response from the home of Christian Endeavor had to be taken for granted; but this lack was more than made up by the speakers for the other sections.

That big-bodied, big-brained, big-hearted Tennessean, Rev. Ira B. Landrith, LL.D., in an address that was full of solid wisdom and witty epigrams, responded

FOR THE SOUTHLAND.

Pity me, people. When I was asked to respond to the address of welcome, I said I would not write a response, because that would be like a girl making up her mind what she was going to say before she was asked.

I am supposed to respond to this abounding welcome on behalf of the South land, only about one-third of whom are here. The others are coming bye-and- bye, fifteen hours late, eight hours late, too late; but I am responding just the same to the welcome you are going to give them when they get here.

I do not know how to do it in a city where they make their mallets out of silver and the handles of their hammers out of gold, and where their mountains are covered all the year around with stuff we do not see down in the Sunny South at all, and standing where they tell me we are a mile high. I do not know how to do it, and so, pity me, people. (*Laughter.*)

I may respond to your welcome, to your wonderful scenery. If we like it we will take it with us — in the carload of kodaks we brought. And I think we like it. We like the sample.

We hung to the brass bars of the Pullman cars, looking out at the matchless scenery along the cañon, and waiting for that sublime point where the Almighty did his supremely wonderful bit of work with that wonderful hand of His, which left the deepest wound on the face of the earth — The Royal Gorge.

And when the moment came, I would have had no one speak to me for anything I could think of. There, sheer half mile above, hung the granite, and I said, "God is here." And a lady came out of the car — she had been in the Pullman, sitting on a soft cushion all that while — and as she looked up where the porter told her to look, — and she thought it was a good dinner, — she said, "Isn't it just perfectly lovely," and I could have hit her, and almost wished I had. If it is all as lovely as that we will take it with us.

I think we will stay. You have got us a mile high, and have the most delightful Coyle around us I ever had anything to do with; then you have welcomed us with such enticing, Sweet words as I have listened to nowhere else, and you cannot put a two foot ditch in front of us and keep us from adopting Denver's motto "Forward."

After describing what Christian Endeavor had done for the South, and alluding to his experiences on the "Nashville, '98" Convention Committee, Mr. Landrith wittily said: —

We were a little slow to take on this Christian Endeavor movement. It came from a section which sent us something we were not looking for. We take everything you give us, even a licking. But they do say the licking you gave us some thirty-five years ago was pretty expensive for the rest of you. We have gotten over it, and I hope you are getting over it. Come again and bring us a blessing that is not so disguised as that one was. It was a blessing, but it was so veiled in a cloud of gunpowder we could not quite see it at the time. We like Christian Endeavor down our way because it teaches us Christian fellowship.

Dr. Coyle said Christian Endeavor was driving at the saloon by methods that are sane. That is a fact, but it is driving it out. I want to make this prophecy because I am going to make it again — that the modern saloon is living in its last quarter of a century. I only say what I believe with all my heart. (*Applause.*)

The East's " Scotch Yankee."

New Hampshire's Scotch Yankee Christian Endeavor president, Rev. James Alexander, caught his audience with the burr on his tongue and the scintillations of his wit.

We, in the East, have rejoiced to hear of your enthusiasm and success, not only in planning for this international convention, but in pushing forward the work of Christ among the young people of your commonwealth. The same resourcefulness, dash, and perseverance, which have lifted the city of Denver into a strategic position in the commercial life of our nation, have found an outlet evidently in your Christian life, and we are here to recognize the fact and to applaud your achievement.

You must not think, however, that you are alone in this respect among the tribes of our Israel. You are not alone. The one thing that has been impressing itself upon every candid observer of religious life in America during the past six months is the vitality, the inherent force, and possibility for expansion of our Christian Endeavor movement.

Mr. Alexander uttered a hopeful prophecy of the future of Christian Endeavor:

The man who has been thinking that the sun of Christian Endeavor is setting will have to think again. We are not looking back upon our Egypts, but we are looking forward, with our faces toward the lands of promise.

> "The year's at the spring
> And day's at the morn;
> Morning's at seven."

We of the East still believe in Christian Endeavor. We still feel an ever-deepening obligation to the rare man whom God has chosen to lead its hosts — Dr. Francis E. Clark. We still believe that its best days are to come, that its greatest service to the religious and civic interests of our time has still to be rendered, and in this faith we have come to Denver. Grander even than the physical environment in which we meet, will be the victories for Christ and His church, which we hope shall go forth from this convention, and better even than the good cheer that springs out of your splendid hospitality will be the larger grasp of the spiritual Christ upon the individual life of all present.

He made an effective closing by relating how one of his parishioners had sent him out to look up a piece of land in Denver, one of his investments, — and he had discovered that it is situated next to a cemetery. Therefore he could improve on the poem Mr. Sweet had quoted :—

> "If I should hear the call to die,
> Out in Colorado,
> I have a little lot near by,
> Out in Colorado."

A BREEZY WESTERN RESPONSE.

"It might be thought," said Dr. Hugh K. Walker, of Los Angeles, "that this Convention, being held in the West, needs no response from the West to its welcoming addresses; but I have travelled 1,500 miles to reach Denver, and this city seems the far, far East to me."

There are three R's which are strong characteristics of Western Christian Endeavor — Real Religion, Rare Ruggedness, and Ready Responsiveness.

Christian Endeavorers want the real thing. They want realism in religion. We do not care anything for pretty phrasing; we care nothing about our minister's vest whether it be high, medium or low, if the heart under the vest beats strong, tender and true. We care nothing for forms and ceremonies. We want a realistic religion. The old-time religion is the only religion good enough for us. We want the religion that centres in the cross. We do not care for that kind of Christ which is not the very God. We want the realism of Calvary. We are seeking the realism of Pentecost. We have a large sense of sin in the Western world; too much to grapple with to care now about philosophizing, we want the real Saviour that saves us from sin.

Mr. Walker brought vividly to mind the fact that the West is no spiritual sanitarium, when he said: —

A one-lunged man can go West and live a long time, or he can die in a very short time. We do not refer to that class of the one-lunged kind, for sometimes they make the best workers we have anywhere in the West, but in this open fight to be an out and out Christian, a man needs to be a rugged fellow, and not the one-lunged, debilitated kind of Christian.

We have ready responsiveness with regard to methods. When I was in the East I heard criticisms about methods. In the West we do not criticise — we go to work. Every move has been taken up by Western Christian Endeavorers, and worked out; the Tenth Legion, the Quiet Hour, the Forward movement, and our societies are taking up missionaries all over the State. The Forward movement, the Christian-citizenship movement, have all been worked, and there is a ready responsiveness. You men of the East think you have a soft snap because you do not lead the hard life that some of us have in the West, but we have the most responsive young people God ever made.

The Western Christian Endeavorer with his Real Religion, with his Rare Ruggedness, with his Ready Responsiveness, greets you Coloradans to-day, and praises God for blessings from the North to the South, from the East to the West.

THE NORTHLAND'S RESPONSE.

The North spoke through the lips of Rev. Ernest W. Shurtleff, of Minneapolis, — "the poet of Christian Endeavor," as Dr. Clark called him. His response was not in verse, but was full of the poetry of action, as he told of the inspiring deeds of the wide-awake Endeavorers of the Northwestern States.

I bring you from Minneapolis and the North this word, that the North is all aglow with old-fashioned fervor and enthusiasm for Christian Endeavor. It has not died out with us. I do not mean that kind of enthusiasm and fervor which is like the passing fragrance of a flower which never comes to fruitage, but I mean that holy thing with the prophecy of the coming fruit. I mean that thing without which no man, no religion, no nation, has come to anything in this world the fire of God, born in the heart and quickening the life.

So in the North we are teaching our Christian Endeavorers to take the Christian roses of their lives up and down the streets of our great city, so that others can breath their fragrance. Clear, distinct, definite work is being done by people who are on fire because they believe in God, and who carry that fire out and set it to work doing something.

These young men and women are all talking and singing through the streets. We are thankful for that. In the Northland I might tell you with all honesty that the ministers generally are teaching the young people that if they have a religion of enthusiasm that is nothing else, it is a reproach to them.

We believe that Christian Endeavor has done its mightiest work—not in the past twenty years but within the last few months, when it has brought to a focus these ideas. We believe in the North that Christian Endeavor is just beginning its life. Christ is coming again, and no man shall crucify him again.

A Hearty Canadian "Amen!"

If ever a Methodist was wise and hearty, it is Dr. W. F. Wilson, of Ontario, who spoke for Canada. You will know how he looks, for he told how on the way one person had asked him if he was not Father Murphy of Peoria. "No," was his reply, "I am Father Wilson, of Hamilton and two children." Then, one of the reception committee had met him miles out, and inquired, "Mr. Bryan, are you to be at the Convention?"

We are children of the same glorious ancestry; heirs of the same priceless liberties, and speak the language in which John Bunyan penned his matchless story, and the sweet-spirited Whittier soared in immortal song. Hence with the heartiest good-will, the Dominion greets the Rebuplic.

Christian Endeavor has done much by its International fellowship to foster this neighborly spirit. You, as Americans, sing, "Sweet land of liberty," while we respond, "Britons never shall be slaves." Thus we are delighted to see the Union Jack and Stars and Stripes twined in peace.

At this juncture Dr. Wilson missed the Union Jack (unaccountably left out of the decorations — an omission soon remedied), but vigorous American applause hailed his reply to Dr. Coyle regarding "leagues," — his announcement of the Epworth Leagues of Christian Endeavor, a union of forces in which he took keen delight.

As Canadians, we greatly admire your splendid Christian President, and we are persuaded that in these United States you respect our noble sceptred King. These two leaders represent the wealth, culture, character, and Christianity of the world. When our late lamented Queen Victoria the Good died, your flag in respect, fluttered at half-mast, and when the gifted, stainless McKinley, passed away, our flag was lowered, and our Dominion bathed in tears.

Canada must always be intimately associated with this world-wide movement. For if Hungary gave to Christian Endeavor Mr. Baer, Switzerland gave Secretary Vogt, and old England gave Treasurer Shaw, why Canada gave Francis E. Clark, the father and founder of this unique and progressive religious organization.

From the Motherland and Other Lands.

The dear old motherland was given a splendid greeting when Rev. F. J. Horsefield stepped to the platform. He is Vicar of St. Silas, Bristol, England, the president of the Church of England Christian Endeavor union, and editor of its admirable Christian Endeavor organ. He is a most lovable, enthusiastic, open-minded man, who brought England's thanks for the Christian Endeavor Society, speaking under commission from a great Endeavor meeting in Spurgeon's Tabernacle, and from the Endeavorers all over Great Britain.

I have been struck with your kindliness. American hospitality has been proverbial. Your enthusiasm has struck me forcibly. I was told, I must own, that the American people were not as enthusiastic as English people. I think I will have to tell a different tale when I get home again. It seems to me behind that star-spangled banner your hearts are filled with enthusiasm. You have men and women full of power; full of force; and full of the promise of a glorious and brilliant future for the world in which you live.

You gave us Christian Endeavor. We can never repay that debt. We have sent you in the days of the past some good things, but you have sent us what seems to me to be a movement that is destined to do more for our salvation in England than ever we have experienced before. This movement gets such a grip on the heart of a man as nothing else can. We thank you for sending us Christian Endeavor.

In crossing the Atlantic with good Captain Potter who was also in charge of the Ultonia that took 186 Endeavorers across three years ago, he said to me: "If you go to Denver, just tell them I gather from those on board my ship that Christian Endeavorers are a good lot from top to bottom." I believe it with all my heart to be true, and I expect to find here, as in my own country, that Endeavorers are every one of them good from top to bottom — good for service; good for worship; good for God's work; good for the elevation of mankind; good for bringing the conditions of Heaven to earth.

After Mr. Horsefield's shining five minutes all rose and sung with might, "God save the King," and then, spontaneously, "Blest be the tie."

India's Answer.

One of the founders of Christian Endeavor in the Empire of India is that young missionary of the Dutch Reformed Church, a son of Dr. Jacob Chamberlain, Rev. L. B. Chamberlain, for years the useful secretary of the South India Christian Endeavor union. He told in an eloquent speech of Endeavorers "that hold conventions a mile and a half in the air, where they have a climate hotter even than Denver's."

India, sir, has a peculiar claim on America, for God, in His providence, used the quest for India to lead the early mariner to the New World. And India has much of interest for the Nation that "beats creation."

India, sir, is justly proud of her intellectual achievements. Hindus were revelling in science, art, literature, theology and philosophy, when only savages inhabited Europe. To India does the world owe the so-called Arab numerals, and the decimal system. From India came algebra and chemistry. There, too, lived and wrote Valmiki, perhaps the first great poet of the human race. To-day India's sons compete with Great Britain's at Oxford, Cambridge, and Edinburg Universities, and not seldom surpass them.

But India is paramountly, *sadly* great in her moral and religious need. The thraldom of caste and custom, the blight of ignorance and superstition, the pall of poverty and famine, the curse of false religion and false morality, make India desperately, piteously, *needy*. The recent government census shows that in India there are more child-wives under fourteen years of age than there are grown women in America. Think what that means in the family, social, industrial, mental, and religious life of the land. And that is but one fact.

Yes, India is in need. She needs your interest, prayer, and money. But she especially needs you, yourselves, vigorous, generous, audacious, young America.

Seeing is believing. Come and see. I do not jest. The opportunity is to be yours. The last India National Christian Endeavor Convention, representing five hundred societies and several thousand members, invited the World's Christian Endeavor Convention to Calcutta, and the officers of the World's Union have the matter under advisement.

So, to the generous welcome accorded us, may I respond, Come and test India's welcome, and see India's need! Then you will say with India's poet laureate: —

> "Take up the white-man's burden;
>   Send forth the best ye breed;
> Go, bind your sons to exile
>   To serve the brown-man's need."

"FROM AFRICA'S SUNNY FOUNTAINS."

It was fitting that a consecrated missionary of the Friends' Church, Rev. Willis R. Hotchkiss, should respond in behalf of the "Dark Continent," for he has experienced its need of Christianity, and carries its burden on his heart.

I have dwelt in the "Dark Continent" long enough to consider myself a resident, and when I am greeted as an African I take no offense whatever. I bring you greetings from the great dark continent, the land of Raymond, Lowe, Livingstone, Moffat, and multitudes of noble men and women who have sacrificed their lives to redeem the waste places of the earth, the habitations that are full of cruelty.

Christian Endeavor does not ask a man whether he lives in Africa, in India, China, or America. It does not ask him whether he be clothed with a black skin, a white, a tawny, or a red one. Christian Endeavor stands, first, last, and always for the salvation of man. (*Applause.*) I read, "in the place where they crucified him there was a garden." Fellow Endeavorers, of this great Anglo-Saxon Convention, there are barren hillsides of human need in Central Africa. There are deserts of human souls in that great dark continent that await your crucifixion and mine, before they become gardens.

JAPAN'S SON.

In quaintly rich Japanese garb, Mr. C. Ogawa, of Sendai, Japan, came forward to speak for what he called "one of the least of the Christian countries, but one full of hope and energy." He is president of that remarkable society of workers in the large government postal-telegraph office of Sendai.

Brethren, among the many kinds of greetings one came very much to my heart, that is that we are greeted just for what we were. We are a country of hope. We have a great field for Christianity, for the Christian Endeavor Society.

The world is one in Christ. Let the world be won for Christ. We are very glad that we are greeted for just what we are, but we Christian Endeavorers would like besides to be greeted for what we shall be in the future.

In broken English that nevertheless could easily be followed, he gave a beautiful message from President Harada:

One hundred and twenty Christian Endeavor Societies in Japan, the land of the dawn, send through two delegates and eighteen banners their fraternal greetings to the Denver Convention.

They flash this message from their sacred Mount of Fuji to the heights of Colorado.

The world is *one* in Christ.

Let the world be *won* for Christ. — Eph. iii. 20, 21.

HARADA, *President.*

OTHER GREETINGS.

In addition to these personally delivered messages, the following greetings came by cable, telegraph or mail; that from the Hawaiian Islands being the first Christian Endeavor message to be sent over the new Pacific cable to the Eastern possessions of the United States. The greetings were from the following unions:

The British union, Costa Rica, Cuba, New South Wales, Finland, Ireland, Brazil, Germany, Hungary, India, Italy, Marshall Islands, Persia, Queensland, Scotland, South Australia, South Africa, Spain, Switzerland, Tasmania, Victoria and New Zealand.

Thus closed a most successful opening service, one of the most successful in all Christian Endeavor history, with fully ten thousand persons crowding the great tent, with impressive and brilliant utterances, and with power and promise in all its minutes. It was brought to a most fitting close by Dr. Carson, of Brooklyn, who conducted a new feature of our programmes, a

PREPARATION SERVICE.

"All things are now ready for a great Convention," said Dr. Carson, "all things, but the greatest of all, the touch of the Holy Spirit of God." He pleaded for the two conditions of His coming, — obedience to Christ, and expectant waiting for His coming. Especially did he urge that "passion for Christ which is power for service," and sent the Endeavorers out with hushed hearts and a deepened desire to be used for God's glory in the Convention and in their homes.

CHAPTER II.

Retrospect and Prospect.

TENT ENDEAVOR, THURSDAY NIGHT.

New watchwords and new men were to the fore on Thursday night, in Tent Endeavor. A wave of sincere sympathy swept over every heart in the audience when Dr. Clark explained that, on account of his recent loss of his wife, Dr. George B. Stewart, president of Auburn Seminary, could not be present to preside as announced. Dr. Stewart has won first place in Endeavor hearts by his cheery, staunch loyalty to Endeavor principles and institutions.

Dr. J. L. Hill, in taking the vacant place, remarked that he had so often served as substitute that he could hardly be held responsible if he should forget and answer to some other man's name when the final roll is called. But Dr. Hill is a presiding officer of assayed and stamped value, and as great a favorite as Dr. Stewart. He was very happy in his introduction of William Shaw, Treasurer of the United Society, who read the general secretary's report.

"Will you authorize me to extend to Mr. Shaw the right hand of salutation?" he asked the audience, "in recognition of his self-sacrificing services in adding to his own work the work of Mr. Baer after the latter's resignation?"

"We will!" responded the audience in thunderous chorus.

Dr. Hill then proceeded to elicit three other deep-toned choruses by asking if the Endeavorers commissioned him to extend the right-hand of congratulation, of covenant, and of fellowship. And to every proposition the tent-full of people rolled out an

"I will!" that shook the tent into billowy folds.

Mr. Shaw's report was entitled

A YEAR OF EXPANSION.

This has been an eventful year for the Christian Endeavor movement. If its strength were in man, it would have been shaken. But because it is in God it has stood firm and unshaken, coming out of each trial with new power and a larger hope.

October 1, 1902, General Secretary John Willis Baer, who for twelve years stood in this place and presented his inspiring reports of progress, in response to what he believed to be the call of duty took up his work as assistant secretary of the Presbyterian Board of Home Missions, thus exemplifying the Christian Endeavor principle of loyalty to our own church. In a few minutes we shall welcome his successor, Mr. Von Ogden Vogt, and a royal welcome it will be. April 12, 1903, Easter Sunday, our beloved Field Secretary, Clarence E. Eberman died like a soldier in the thick of the fight. Of him, as of the missionary apostle, of the first century, it can be said, he fought a good fight, he finished his course, he kept the faith, and has received his crown.

This has also been a year with no great Convention to inspire the workers, and yet it has been a year of growth and expansion along every line.

NUMERICAL GROWTH.

It is true of movements as well as of individuals, now as in the days when Christ spoke the words, that "by their fruits ye shall know them."

Twenty-two years ago an unknown pastor in a little Congregational Church in one of our smaller cities organized the first society of Christian Endeavor. No ecclesiastical court, council, or committee said, "Go to, now; we will organize a movement that will girdle the globe." But to help one pastor, to strengthen one church, and to train one company of young people, the first society was organized. But it was born, not made; it was of God, and He has used it. In purely providential ways it has spread, until to-day there is no land to which it is a stranger, and no tongue in which prayer and testimony in Christian Endeavor meetings are not heard.

From one society in 1881 to 64,020 in 1903, from one denomination to more than eighty, from one city to every country, and from 50 members to 3,822,300, and a million and a half more in societies bearing strictly sectarian names, but patterned after Christian Endeavor and gaining their inspiration from it, — a net gain in number of societies in one year of more than two thousand.

AT HOME.

This numerical increase will be made vivid when, in the closing session of this Convention, the fellowship banners made by Endeavorers across the seas are presented to the States and Provinces that have made at least a ten per cent increase in number of societies during the past eight months. Following is the list to be thus honored: —

Colorado,	Alabama,
New Mexico,	Wisconsin,
Alaska,	Maryland,
Oregon,	Washington,
Louisiana,	Oklahoma,
Georgia,	Utah,
Ohio,	Indiana,
West Virginia,	Missouri,
Assiniboia.	Nevada

JUNIORS AND INTERMEDIATES.

Great success has attended the work for the boys and girls through the Junior and Intermediate Societies. The idea of dividing the Young People's Society into two or more sections of fifty members each, so that all the young people of the congregation can be reached and trained, is meeting with great favor. The Grace Temple Baptist Church, Philadelphia, Rev. Russell H. Conwell, D.D., pastor, has fourteen such societies, and many churches have two or more.

Indiana receives the Chinese banner for the largest proportionate gain in Intermediate Societies, and will hold it until the next Convention.

In Foreign Lands.

The increase in foreign lands has been equally marked. Especially notable has been the progress made in Germany, Finland, France, Spain, Sweden, Japan, Korea, Persia, India, China, and South America.

This has been made possible by the generous financial help that the World's Christian Endeavor Union has been able to render, thus enabling these countries to employ a general secretary who can give his whole time to the work. Germany is now self-supporting, and has two secretaries.

Would that I had time to speak of the splendid work of Rev. F. S. Hatch of India, Rev. G. W. Hinman of China, Rev. I. Inanuma of Japan, Rev. V. Van der Beken of France, Rev. Frederick Blecher of Germany, Carlos Araujo of Spain, and others.

Roll of Honor.

The great Roll of Honor also speaks eloquently of the thousands of local societies that have increased their membership from ten to several hundred per cent during the past eight months, which is but a beginning in the campaign that will be carried on next year.

But while we rejoice in the large numerical increase of the past months, and shall strive to excel our present record during the coming year, yet we feel that it is one of the least of the things for which we have reason to thank God.

Quality of Its Work.

I call your attention to the quality of its work. Organized at a time when the church was coaxing and coddling her young people, Christian Endeavor dared to set up its standard of heroic service. It said, A very few of the right kind of young people are better than a crowd with no purpose. It appealed to younger people not only to have convictions, but to declare them. It made the prayer-meeting its heart, the committees its hands and feet, the Bible its guide, the Holy Spirit its inspirer, Christ its Master, the church its centre, and the world its circumference.

It is a democratic organization, a young *people's* society. No class distinctions are recognized or provided for. Character is the test, not circumstances or condition. It trains young people not simply to work *for* but *with* others, and detests that social or intellectual snobbery that looks down upon, or patronizes, those who lack money or education.

These young disciples took their oath of allegiance, the pledge, they inscribed on their banner "For Christ and the Church," and took for their mottoes, which express the spirit of their service, these: "Not to be ministered unto, but to minister," "We are laborers together with God," "One is your Master, even Christ, and all ye are brethren."

Additions to the Church.

During the past year 175,000 have come from the ranks of Christian Endeavor into the membership of the churches. And thousands more would have come if more pastors had appreciated what a magnificent field for evangelistic effort God had placed at their hand.

This has been a year of great material prosperity and most seductive appeals from the secular side of life. There never was a time when so many things, good in themselves, but bad when given the supreme place, appealed to young people as to-day.

But the letters C. E. have stood not only for Christian Endeavor, but also for Christ Exalted. And because of this fact some who think more of fashion than of faith, of society than of soul, may have been alienated, yet the movement has made a steady gain all along the line.

GIFTS FOR BENEVOLENCE.

But these young people have not only given themselves, they have also given their money. In addition to their gifts in other channels, the societies gave last year for benevolence an average of over fifty dollars for each society by actual detailed reports; a total for all the societies that would have to be expressed in millions.

Three societies deserve special mention. First, the Oxford Presbyterian, Philadelphia, Penn., which gave for missions last year $1,814. Second, the Chinese society in the Congregational Mission, San Francisco, Cal., which gave $1,516, and third, the Presbyterian society, Clinton, Ill., which gave $1,125.

For the Intermediates, the West End Presbyterian society of New York stands first with a record of $311; and the Park Presbyterian society of Newark, N.J., second with gifts of $137.

The banner Junior society in gifts for missions is the First Presbyterian, Omaha, Neb., with a record of $548, and the next is the United Brethren Juniors, Lebanon, Penn., $459.

A number of societies have contributed one thousand dollars or more each for home expenses, parsonage building, etc.

SAMPLE LINES OF SERVICE.

Time will not permit me to enlarge upon other forms of service, so I must content myself with simply referring to a few from thousands of reports received.

I want to speak a good word for the prayer meeting, — the old-fashioned prayer meeting like that in the upper room, where every member is present, and where every member takes part. Not the new style, so-called prayer meeting, where the pastor delivers a lecture, or a few learned men talk on the problems of the day. But a genuine prayer meeting, where the people come to talk with God, and with each other about God's dealings with them. Just such a meeting as many of our churches need more than they need anything else in this world, and which they can have if they will train their young people properly. Millions of these prayer meetings have been held during the past year.

Great emphasis has been laid upon Mission and Bible-Study Classes, and everywhere groups of young people have been doing systematic work along these lines. Especially notable has been the work of the New York, Philadelphia, and Chicago unions. Monthly missionary meetings have been held, and the Missionary Concert revived.

Special evangelistic services like those of the Worcester, Mass., union have been greatly blessed. Cottage prayer meetings and outdoor services have been held.

Mission services and Sunday schools have been conducted.

Fresh-air work with vacation camps and outings for poor children has been carried on, in which the New Jersey county unions and the Baltimore city union have been conspicuously successful.

The societies have covered in their ministries of love the whole range of philanthropic work for the poor, the needy, and the unfortunate, which would require pages to simply catalogue.

MISSIONARY VOLUNTEERS.

During the Boer war, many Christian Endeavor Societies were organized in the prison camps in Ceylon, St. Helena, and Bermuda, with several thousand members. Since the return of these men to South Africa, two hundred have volunteered for missionary work, and the Dutch Reformed Church has opened a training-school for them in Worcester, South Africa. We hold in high honor the little group of five missionary volunteers around the Haystack at Williamstown, Mass. What shall we say of the two hundred Endeavorer missionary volunteers in South Africa?

I would that I had time to tell you what Christian Endeavor is doing on our men-of-war and merchant vessels, for the soldiers in their tents, for the prisoners in our prisons and reformatories. Long before Mrs. Booth thought of the "House of Hope," our Endeavorers had gone to the prisons with the "Star of Hope," and hundreds of men bless God that Christian Endeavor found a place of service behind the prison walls. In institutions for the deaf, dumb, and blind, we have also found a place for loving, Christ-like service.

Its Staying Power.

The staying power of Christian Endeavor deserves mention. At first the critics gave the Society five years to live. Then they called it a fad, and said ten years would see its finish. But, friends, it is alive to-day, and never so great in numbers or so practical in its work as now. I have a list of the first societies organized in each of our States and Territories, fifty-one in all. The oldest one organized in 1881, and the youngest in 1894. Forty-two of these societies are alive and flourishing to-day. Eight were changed to denominational socities, and one was disbanded because the pastor wanted to try some other form of organization.

Any pastor can start a new society, and, if he pushes it hard enough, it may succeed. But will it live and thrive when he goes, and the church is without a pastor? Will it prosper under the new pastor? Will it go on when the new has worn off? Christian Endeavor can answer "Yes" to all these questions.

Its Flexibility and Adaptability.

The flexibility and adaptability of Christian Endeavor is not as generally appreciated as it should be. It works in country church or city; on the avenue or in the slums; in America or Africa. You can have three committees or thirty. You can take the model pledge, or write a better one. You can call it a pledge, or a covenant, a declaration, or anything else that suits you. It is the idea, the ideal, not the mere words, that is of value. You can do anything with it, all that a reasonable church and pastor wants to have done.

It is not a perpetual motor; it will not run itself. It is a method, not a machine. The quality of its work depends upon the quality of its membership. For its largest success it needs the leadership of its pastor, the sympathy of the church, and the co-operation of the home. Its local unions offer an invaluable opportunity to mass the Christian forces of a community, to smite sin and strengthen every righteous cause. It has been used of God to train and develop individual Christians in testimony and service; to show them how to work together; to reveal the needs of the world; to exalt the church and her work; to deepen our love for our own church; to cast out jealousy of other churches; to increase the spirit of interdenominational fellowship; to promote peace by uniting the young Christians of the world in the bonds of Christian love and service; and to hasten the coming of the day when we shall all be one in the love and service of our common Lord and Master.

Another feature on which interest is always focussed in this session of Conventions is the annual address of President Francis E. Clark. This year it was of unusual interest, dealing with questions of the greatest moment to all Endeavorers. The title itself suggests a radical new departure in aggressive work. It is

A TEN YEARS' INCREASE CAMPAIGN.

A definite Increase Campaign to double the number and efficiency of Christian Endeavor societies in a single decade was the theme of Dr. Clark's address at the twenty-first International Convention of Christian Endeavor at Denver. He based his address on the fundamental idea that Christianity is a religion of expansive forces, that "you can no more confine the religion of Christ to its old limits than you can grow an oak in a flower-pot," and that

To Cease to Grow is to Begin to Die.

The marked growth of the Society during the past year in this country, and its larger expansion than ever before throughout all the world, made such an increase seem not only possible, but well-nigh certain within the next decade.

Along two great lines he urged this increase; first, an enlargement of the membership of the local societies. He deprecated the idea, which some had obtained, that a society of Christian Endeavor is simply a little coterie of like-minded young people who could edify one another in the prayer meeting. The fundamental idea of the Society is service, *and service for every one*. The youngest, the weakest, the most ignorant, as well as the best educated and most gifted among the young people, can be trained to serve God and their day and generation.

Enlarge the Membership of Local Societies.

A true society of Christian Endeavor should reach every young person in the community either through its active membership or its associate membership. To this end he urged a special effort to enlist more *active* members, the *working force* of the Society; to obtain more associate members also, those who may afterwards be won for Christ and the church, this being the evangelistic end of the society; and to enlarge the honorary membership for the sake of promoting sympathetic relations between the older members of the church and the young people.

This part of his appeal was happily emphasized by the fact that during the past year thousands of societies have enlarged their ranks, some of them gaining more than a hundred per cent.

Increase in Societies.

Even more emphasis was laid in the address upon enlarging the number of local societies, and in this direction Providence has pointed the way during the past year, for over 2,000 new societies have been formed within eight months, "The ten-per-cent increase campaign of the last eight months has been so unexpectedly successful that only the wilfully blind can fail to see the guideboards of the future. Look at the splendid records of Indiana, Missouri, Ohio, Oregon, Colorado, New Mexico, Oklahoma," he said. "I should have to call the roster of all the States to exhaust the good work of the past year. Lift up your eyes and look upon the white harvest-fields in all the world. India has enlarged her Christian Endeavor boundaries. China with her new secretary is at the beginning of a new year of great expansion. Japan has gained thirty per cent, and just enjoyed the best convention in her history. Great Britain has made steady progress. Germany has made substantial gain. France and Spain have had the best year in all their Christian Endeavor history, while since our last Convention Switzerland, Italy, Portugal, Finland, and Iceland have fairly entered the ranks of Christian Endeavor."

Dr. Clark gave the following summary of the remarkable Increase Campaign.

The Increase Campaign is a concerted movement for the formation of new Christian Endeavor Societies and the addition of new members to the old societies. It was set on foot last November, and its success already marks a new era in the Christian Endeavor movement. A Roll of Honor exhibited at this Convention contains the names of many hundreds of societies that have increased their membership since November from ten to one thousand per cent — an aggregate of hundreds of thousands of new members. The following table shows the number of new societies formed since November in the various State unions, together with the percentage of gain over the number of societies in those States last November.

STATE.	NEW SOCIETIES.	PER CENT OF GAIN.	STATE.	NEW SOCIETIES.	PER CENT OF GAIN.
Alabama	29	11½	Nebraska	50	
Alaska	2	13½	Nevada		
Arizona	1	3½	New Hampshire	27	6
Arkansas	18	8½	New Jersey	46	2¼
California	61	4	*New Mexico*	15	34
Colorado	68	17¾	New York	171	3¾
Connecticut	15	2	North Carolina	25	5¾
Delaware	6	6	North Dakota	9	4¾
District of Columbia	14	9	*Ohio*	335	10
Florida	3	1¼	*Oklahoma*	37	14⅘
Georgia	16	12½	*Oregon*	65	14⅓
Idaho	4	4	Pennsylvania	154	2¾
Illinois	74	2	Rhode Island	10	4½
Indiana	306	16¼	South Carolina	10	8⅓
Iowa	65	3½	South Dakota	6	2
Kansas	40	7½	Tennessee	16	2¼
Kentucky	14	2½	Texas	22	2¾
Louisiana	17	19½	*Utah*	7	10½
Maine	49	5¼	Vermont	24	5¼
Maryland	46	10	Virginia	15	4½
Massachusetts	104	6⅓	*Washington*	63	15¼
Michigan	43	2⅔	*West Virginia*	34	12
Minnesota	31	3¼	*Wisconsin*	91	11¼
Mississippi	6	5	Wyoming	2	6⅔
Missouri	176	13¾	*Assiniboia, Canada*	8	13
Montana	6	7			

GRAND TOTAL 2,460

This list contains all the new societies reported up to July 1. Other new societies are constantly being reported, which will be added where this record is incomplete, especially in the case of Canada, from which few reports have come.

The campaign is to be continued, the aim being to double our number of societies and membership within ten years, by the addition, if possible, of at least ten per cent a year. This can be done, as this preliminary campaign has shown, by a careful districting and organization of the States, by the development of Junior societies, Senior societies, Prison and Floating societies, all of which have proved so useful, as well as Young People's societies.

Many local unions, like Minneapolis, Chicago, Philadelphia, Baltimore, Washington and others, have grown largely and done particularly good work. The following table shows what has been accomplished since November. Read it. Remember that most of the larger States had, already, their thousands of societies. Remember the difficulties of the work in the sparsely settled States. Remember the greater possibilities yet before us. See, in this list, a blessed proof of the virility of Christian Endeavor, and a call to fresh activity for Christ and the Church.

Every State, when it gains ten per cent in societies, will receive a beautiful foreign banner, standing for Fidelity and Fellowship.

Christian Endeavor in Unexpected Places.

But this is not all. Christian Endeavor has appeared in many unexpected places, on the sea and in the camp, in the prison, in the life-saving station and the fire brigades, in a post-office in Japan, in department stores, in schoolhouse districts and neighborhood gatherings. All these different lines of effort which Providence has so plainly marked out as legitimate and most useful lines for the Christian Endeavor Society show how its principles may be extended and the societies expanded.

Care for the Juniors.

The boys and girls should receive special attention. The Junior societies alone within a year may be doubled, and there is now a Correspondence School for Christian workers, which will train superintendents to this most important work.

As a definite proposition to ensure this increase, Dr. Clark proposed that *every State strive to gain at least ten per cent annually for the next ten years, thus entering into a ten years' extension campaign.* As each State secures its ten-per-cent increase, a beautiful foreign banner from some distant land, representing the fellowship of the movement, will be presented to the State, and as for each new State that is admitted to the Union a new star is added to our national flag, so for each ten per cent of gain another star will be added to this foreign banner until the ten show that the hundred per cent has been gained.

How the Record will be Kept.

An Increase Campaign book will also be opened at the headquarters of the United Society, in which a page each year will be devoted to each State, telling the story of its growth in every line of its endeavor. This will be a permanent record of interest, and of increasing and finally inestimable value, for it will be a book of the " Acts of the Young Apostles of the Twentieth Century."

Think of the glorious results of a hundred-per-cent increase in a single decade! Twice as many societies laboring for Christ and the church; twice as many young men and women and boys and girls actually at work for Him; twice as many associate members facing toward the Kingdom, won each year for Christ. Twice as many interested in missions, and twice as many giving to missions. Twice as many who find strength in the Quiet Hour, and twice as many enlisted for Good Citizenship and Civic Righteousness. Can you measure the far-reaching, incalculable benefit of such an effort? It would influence and bless the churches of Christ for all time, and its results will stretch forward into all eternity.

The Campaign Motto.

Dr. Clark proposed for a campaign motto the words "Fidelity and Fellowship," and strongly urged his hearers always to remember that this Increase Campaign is not chiefly for the advance and glory of Christian Endeavor, but always and ever for the glory and advance of the Kingdom of our Lord Jesus Christ. "These efforts," he said, "will, I believe, result in a vast increase of the *spiritual* forces of the Kingdom of Heaven. . . . Let us always, then, keep this in our idea of expansion, that it means upward growth as well as outward, more of those who practice the presence of God, more of those who work well because they have prayed well."

How It Took.

That was a spectacular and impressive scene when, as Dr. Clark referred to the handsome prize banners made by foreign Endeavorers, twenty red-capped ushers stood on the press tables on either side of the platform, and held up the banners for the audience to see.

"Turn them this way," requested a chorus of voices from the singers' seats in the rear.

Another thrilling crisis in interest was when, at the close of Dr. Clark's report, the solid delegations of Wisconsin, Minnesota, South Dakota, and other States responded each in a stentorian "Aye" in approval of continuing the Extension Campaign for nine years more, as Dr. Clark had proposed.

The whole audience caught up the response in a mighty volume, and made it its own. Christian Endeavor evangelism was lifted to the crest of the wave when Dr. Clarence A. Barbour stepped forward and heartily seconded Dr. Clark's proposal, suggesting that the committee on resolutions prepare some fitting expression of this earnest, evangelistic purpose of Christian Endeavor.

The evening was full of pleasant surprises. When Dr. Clark had presented Mr. Von Ogden Vogt, the new general secretary, the Wisconsin and Illinois delegations arose in turn, and sang, and gave their State yells, in token of their affection for and confidence in their former fellow State worker. "It is enough for most men," said Dr. Hill, "to hail from one State."

Dr. Clark made the new secretary's heart warm by his cordial, sincere words.

My duty this evening is as simple as it is pleasant, only to introduce to you our new General Sectreary, Von Ogden Vogt, and also to introduce you to our new secretary.

It is a peculiar introduction, too, inasmuch as it is the introduction not of a stranger to strangers, but of a friend to friends.

It is more like the introduction of a lover to his fiancée, for you have already chosen him, and he has chosen you, and we are here to confirm the bans, and to unite in marriage the Secretary and the Society, the worker and his work.

You have already taken him into your hearts, and some of you have taken him by the hand. I only ask you ever to keep for him in your hearts a warm, true place, and, whenever you have a chance, give him your right hands, to show him that you love him, and wish him God-speed in his work.

I can ask nothing better for him than that you treat him as you did his honored predecessor, Mr. John Willis Baer, as you ever have Mr. Shaw and myself, and the rest of us who are trying to serve you and the cause we love at the headquarters of the United Society.

But my introduction may well take a wide sweep to-night. I introduce you, Mr. Vogt, not only to the thousands of Endeavorers who are gathered here, but to the hundreds of thousands and millions of Endeavorers who are not here, but who are none the less interested in this unique service.

Installation Prayer.

The installation prayer offered by Rev. Teunis S. Hamlin, D.D., of Washington, D.C., was a model of chasteness, impressiveness and adaptation. Mr. William Shaw, treasurer of the United Society, with well-chosen words then extended

The Right Hand of Fellowship.

It is with peculiar pleasure that I perform the part assigned to me in this glad welcome to our new Secretary.

As the oldest member of the Executive Board in point of service, I welcome you, the youngest. I was there when Christian Endeavor as a babe stretched up its tiny hand to the churches and asked to be taken in. I have seen it grow and felt its growing pains through childhood and youth, and helped to celebrate its coming of age in the church of its birth.

We welcome you to a growing cause as the reports just given prove. We welcome you to a movement that is ever broadening and deepening in its work. A movement that dares to change old methods for new and better ones, but that ever and everywhere is characterized by loyalty to Jesus Christ, fidelity to His church and fellowship with His disciples.

I give to you the right hand of fellowship in the name of these thousands of delegates here assembled and the millions more whom they represent. Our right hand is given not only in fellowship, but also in service for the cause we love.

I also give to you the right hand of fellowship in the name and on behalf of the officers and trustees of the United Society. For many years I have tested their patience and had proof of their love. You have come into a circle, the atmosphere of which is sympathy and love. When we give you our right hand, our whole heart goes with it. You are ours and we stand by our own.

In his simple, earnest response to this impressive induction into a great office, Mr. Vogt won his way into the hearts of all present. A clear-headed observer gives this estimate of the new secretary: —

You will find him finished up nicely with recent education, which is a great asset just at this time when the whole world sets its ideals in that direction. He is modest, faultlessly dressed, untiring, adding to his acceptance with me in that he is a fine singer; and so his voice, while deep, carries wide and far. He is oratorical, and is never slangy. It was obvious that his plan was not to attempt to use an influence that he did not have; but, when he has set his mind and heart upon achievement touching some vital issue, as upon the first evening after the love-feast, he is as strong and animated and courageous as a lion.

This was Secretary Vogt's response: —

Mr. Chairman, Dr. Clark, Mr. Shaw, Members of the Board of Trustees, my dear fellow workers, Endeavorers for the Master we have taken up, this is not an hour for very many words; this is an hour for loyal obedience and stern resolves, but before I say another thing I want to tell you my debt to Christian Endeavor.

The first thing that I heard about Christian Endeavor was away back there on the plains of South Dakota. Before I was ten years old I was taught to read the Bible in an open meeting of the Junior Society of Christian Endeavor.

And my next touch with Christian Endeavor was in those great meetings held in Chicago during the World's Fair, just three years after that, in the great world-wide fellowship, as there arose members from Maine, Texas, Manitoba, Canada, England, from all the world wide around, and there I learned what a great thing God had done when he started such an institution as that society, and I am filled with gratitude this hour because in that same society a strong, loving heart got hold of my right hand and lifted me up.

There were men and women devoted to Jesus the Master, men and women devoted to the church. In the first place they brought me the associate membership of the society and then they turned my face out and began to show me the great needs of men. They began to tell me men needed things; that they suffered; that I might help men as they went down in sin and failure.

I thank God because these young men and women there gave me a vision of Christ the Saviour who turned their longing, seeking hearts to Him. Then, after that — the wise institution that is ours — they put my trembling hands to work to do something for those I had been told needed it. It is a wise institution that gives the chance to work. Then I recall one of those dear people got hold of me one day and she said, "Why I am delighted that you are growing." And that was the first indication I ever had that I had been growing. And then I began to understand that my end was not the end to be sought, but somebody else was looking up to me. I was responsible for somebody that was lower down than I was. I had attained something which before I had not been aware of. I love those people that did these things for me.

The platform reception by officers and trustees was almost a crush. Endeavorers love their leaders and prize a hand-grasp as a golden privilege, and so the meeting that began with golden promise closed with golden fulfilment.

MEMBERS OF THE RECEPTION COMMITTEE MEETING TRAINS.

ARRIVAL AT THE DEPOT.

CHAPTER III.

Peep O' Day Song and Praise.

A glorious sunshine greeted the Christian Endeavorers when they awoke on Friday morning, and although perhaps many saw the sun rise it was not long after that hour before the delegates were bestirring themselves to attend the memorial quiet hour services which were scheduled at several of the churches for 6 o'clock, in memory of the late field secretary, Clarence E. Eberman.

The leaders and their respective churches were as follows: Rev. Francis E. Clark, First Baptist Church; H. R. Chapman, Boulevard United Presbyterian Church; Rev. J. N. Jessup, Twenty-third Avenue Presbyterian Church; Dr. V. H. Lyon, Broadway Baptist Church, and George F. Nye, Plymouth Congregational Church.

The general topic was, "Longing for God," but the greater part of the hour was devoted to the life of Mr. Eberman, his work and tours through the South and Northwest. His sunny disposition never failed to be an inspiration to all who knew him.

Each meeting was crowded with testimony to our "Big Brother's" fidelity. One told how he heard of a converted prisoner and took the pains to send him an appropriate text as a personal message. Another told how, facing a long-faced Endeavorer at a dinner-table, he suddenly said with irresistibly comic lugubriousness, "Won't you please smile?" At one place no advertising had been done, and Mr. Eberman on arriving got out circulars, flooded the town with them, and had a rousing meeting in the evening. At another place, arriving faint and hungry, he went straight to the meetings, and worked there four hours without food.

These reminiscences, and many more, come from practically every State, Territory, and Province, and made up not only a noble tribute to a noble man, but a mighty stimulus to better endeavor on the part of all whose task it is to carry on such work as made glorious the life of Clarence Eberman.

Mr. Marcusson, president of the Illinois union, told of Mr. Eberman's self-sacrifice in getting up at two in the morning to meet an engagement in Chicago, rather than travel on the Sabbath. Another related how he had ridden eighty miles in a stage coach, one dark night, driving much of the way himself, because of the illness of the driver, that he might reach and cheer Endeavorers at the end of the line.

It was appropriate to choose the Memorial Quiet Hour as a

service in his honor because it was in this line of work that Mr. Eberman took most interest.

On other mornings the leaders of the quiet hour meetings were State officers from all over the country, skilful and enthusiastic. An introduction, usually sensibly brief, and then — only a chance was needed, and what a torrent of glad testimony!

"*In the name of the Lord Jesus.* We should not allow *anything* that we do for Christ to be done in our own name."

"A boy laid away a stick of candy, hoarding it for another time; but when he went to get it he found that the ants had eaten it all up. *Is your salvation thus laid away on the shelf?*"

"A little girl went to a druggist and asked for 'five cents' worth of glory divine.' 'What does your mother want it for?' asked the puzzled druggist. 'She wants to spread it around in the bad places and make them smell good.' 'O, you want five cents' worth of chloride of lime!' But the little girl was right, for that is just what we must do with whatever measure we have of glory divine, — spread it around in the bad places and make them good and sweet."

These are only samples of the thoughtful, bright, and helpful utterances heard in so great abundance at those inspiring sunrise gatherings.

CHAPTER IV.

Keeping School for Christ.

Eight splendidly manned departments of the Christian Endeavor School of Methods occupied the morning hours between the sunrise meetings and the main sessions. An expert in his line was at the head of each. As a rule the eight different churches were filled every hour, and the students' note-books bulged so that some of them must have had to pay excess baggage charges on their way home. In the First Congregational Church, led by Rev. Harlan P. Beach, educational secretary of the Student Volunteer Movement, was

THE FOREIGN MISSION STUDY–CLASS.

The value of the sessions was rightly voiced by the delegate who said, "I came to Denver from Cleveland, and if I had gotten nothing else from the Convention than what was learned in this class, I should feel abundantly repaid for making the journey."

The leader brought to the class the experience of eight years' connection with study classes in 550 American colleges and universities, as well as of years of experience as a missionary in China.

Each session was divided into two sections. For the first three-quarters of the hour some leading factor in class work was presented, after which came a demonstration of the points discussed, based upon the text-book used, which was Mr. Beach's new book on China, " Princely Men in the Heavenly Kingdom." The remaining portion of each hour was given to an open parliament during which time those present responded readily to questions bearing upon different phases of the Society's missionary work.

On Friday morning the preparation of the leader's study-class outlines was presented. On Saturday questioning in study-classes was the topic discussed. The topic of illustrating the studies was presented at Monday's session. The final half hour was spent in answering the rapid fire of questions pertaining to a multitude of minor study-class details and problems.

THE HOME MISSION STUDY–CLASS.

was conducted by Rev. E. E. Chivers, D.D., Baptist Home Missionary, Secretary in Grace Methodist Episcopal Church. His general theme was, "Leavening the Nation."

"Among the great questions," said the speaker, "which we are called upon to solve is the negro problem. It is a question which must be answered soon for the race is increasing rapidly. Another question is that of Mormonism, for the sect has increased alarmingly in the past decade."

The speaker also took up the Indian question, stating that he believed that the Indian could be made a good citizen instead of a burden to the State. The work of missions must be broadened and that within the United States, for there are thousands, yes, millions, who are not yet in the church and need to be rescued.

Another very important problem is the immigration of foreigners to this country. On all of these aspects of "leavening the Nation" Dr. Chivers was thoroughly informed.

In summing up the number of unreformed, of those of heathen worship, and of those of erroneous creeds, we find that of our 78,000,000 of population, 50,000,000 are outside of the church. Of the 28,000,000 remaining 10,000,000 are Catholic. To sift the chaff from the wheat still further, the Jews and the like must be excluded.

At present there are thirty organized missionary societies in the United States; $40,000,000 are appropriated towards their work. The mission must grow — the workers must understand their work. In conclusion I may give a three-fold need in the successful operation of missions as follows: A well defined sense of responsibilty among the workers; a broad conception of the breadth of the work; co-operation among the workers. These are necessary.

Very practical and suggestive were the sessions of which Rev. Howard W. Pope, superintendent of the Northfield Extension movement, had charge, in the First Reformed Church. They were called

THE PERSONAL WORKERS' CLASS.

Christian Conversation was the first topic, and many illustrations were given of ways by which any Christian can help his fellow men as he journeys along the pathway of life. One should study the art of diverting conversation from the ordinary channels into the spiritual channel.

Again, we should choose an opportune time and place. It is not wise to stop a man who is running to make a train and ask him about his soul. Neither is it a good plan to talk religion to a hungry man. Give him a cup of coffee instead, and make it so hot that it will take him a long time to drink, and then you will have all the more time to talk to him about his home, and mother, and the kind Father. Do not, as a rule, tell people that they are sinners. Rather hold up Christ, and let the Holy Spirit convict them of sin.

Watch for souls as those that must give account. Try to live one day at a time, and that as if it were your last. It is surprising how this habit will deliver you from hurry and worry, and tend to make you considerate of the people whom you meet.

Use little devices for opening conversation. A good illustration of that occurred in the Brown Palace Hotel during the convention. The writer was reading in the lobby when a man sitting next him uttered an oath. The writer quickly laid down a little card on the arm of the chair between them and went on reading. The other picked it up and read, "Why Do You Swear?" On the other side were the words:

"What does Satan pay you for swearing?" asked one man of another. "Nothing," was the reply. "Well, you work cheap — to lay aside the character of a gentleman, to inflict so much pain on your friends, to insult the God who made you, and to risk your own precious soul — and all that for nothing; *you certainly work very cheap*."

"Thou shalt not take the name of the Lord thy God in vain; for the Lord will not hold him guiltless that taketh His name in vain." (Ex. xx. 7.)

The man read it, and put it in his pocket. As soon as his friends left he turned to the stranger who had laid down the card, and said, "Say, my friend, that is the best thing I ever saw on swearing. I know it is a very bad habit and I ought not to do it." He then went on to say that he was a newspaper man in Chicago, and a real heart-to-heart talk followed for about half an hour, and the man promised to settle the question of his relation to Christ. Such a talk would have been wellnigh impossible but for the " Little Preacher " which opened the way and won the man's favor.

"How to Lead a Soul to Christ" was the topic for the second day, and the story of Philip and Nathaniel was used as a basis. The following points were emphasized:

I. Every believer has a message to the world.
II. In bearing that message he is sure to meet objections.
III. He has a sufficient answer, "Come and See."
IV. He is sure of the Master's help.
V. As soon as the sinner begins to talk with Christ the light begins to come. Therefore get him on his knees as soon as possible.

"How to Obtain Power to Make Our Testimony Effective" was the theme for the third day. Every believer has the Holy Spirit, and just as much of the Holy Spirit as he ever will have, for the Spirit is a person. The Spirit, however may not have entire control of the believer, and that is the point to which attention should be directed. An attitude of absolute obedience toward Him will give Him entire control, and then he can and will manifest His power mightily in us. At the close most of the audience were upon their knees before God and many a heart received a rich blessing which will doubtless bear fruit for months and years to come.

THE CHRISTIAN ENDEAVOR SINGING SCHOOL

led by Mr. F. H. Jacobs and Percy S. Foster was quite a magnet. If any one knows how to make the best use of the singing-book in the prayer meeting it should be these two peerless leaders of sacred song.

Mr. Jacobs showed leaders how to harness the hymn-book to the meeting; how to work in harmony with the music committee, "this way" (moving his hands in parallel lines), and not "that way" (moving his hands in opposite directions).

Mr. Jacobs drew a utopian picture of the kind of a pianist he would like to have, and showed a daring fertility of expedients in getting unwilling mouths open in song. Tact and horse sense he believed would accomplish almost anything.

Mr. Foster, who had the second session of the "singin' skewl," illustrated in a practical way, the theories and rules that Mr. Jacobs had laid down. True, he was giving object lessons on this in every session of the Convention, but his work in the school was very helpful as well as interesting.

THE JUNIOR WORKERS' CLASS

at the First Baptist Church was largely attended. The Rev. George F. Kenngott of Lowell, Mass., was leader of the meeting, and made an address on "How to Get and Hold the Boy." He said in part: —

Work with God, work with the child and don't be lazy. The trouble is not in getting the boys, but in getting Junior superintendents who let the pupils share in the responsibility. When you wish drawing done let the boys and girls do it. Appeal to the heart by means of the eye. When you wish to teach your boys or girls to respect the Bible and its age, the best way you can impress it on them is to show them by a chart the different sorts of ways the Bible has been printed.

I wish our Junior Christian Endeavor meetings could be held on week days. We do not want to teach these children a Sunday religion; we want them to learn the religion of every day. A good way to arouse interest in week day religious meetings for the children is to organize the boys and girls into soldier companies. Let them march about; and when they are physically tired, is the time to command attention to the words of the Master.

A rivalry between the boys and girls for the greater attendance in the Junior society promotes enthusiasm. It is a weak boy who has not sufficient influence on some other boy to bring him into the Christian Endeavor meeting; and if the spirit of competition is once aroused in the boy, we need have no fear for his energy.

During the five minutes devoted to questions and an informal discussion of the Christian Endeavor work, Mrs. J. M. Hill made a short address, advocating a closer relationship between the Junior and Senior Christian Endeavor societies. Mrs. F. E. Clark also spoke in favor of organizing "Lend a Hand" committees among the boys and "Whatsoever" committees among the girls. Mrs. Clark believes that a feeling of responsibility is promoted by membership on these committees, and that there is no better way of getting an enthusiastic working membership in Junior societies than by organizing these committees.

At the close of the meeting the Provincial and State presidents of Junior Christian Endeavor societies held an informal discussion of the Junior work.

The Methods Class

was under the leadership of General Secretary Vogt and Treasurer Shaw, at the United Presbyterian Church.

The themes were Correspondence school for Christian workers, Committee work and possibilities and how to realize them, State work, Business meetings, Socials, Literary and athletic features, Getting new members, Sectional societies, Mission and Bible-study classes, and many other up-to-date themes.

The church was crowded at every conference, note-books were everywhere, plans flew thick and fast, questions from the floor fired at the chair, questions from the platform with responses from all over, new ideas and new faces on old ideas — societies over the whole world will be stronger and more enterprising for years because of these meetings.

The Bible-Study Class.

Rev. James M. Gray, D.D., of Boston, conducted three Bible-studies on the theme, "The Gift of Righteousness," using the epistle to the Romans as the basis. The class used their Bibles, reading, marking, and making notes for future use.

Lesson I.

What the Gift Is. — *Romans Chapters i–iv.*

. The gospel spoken of was expressed in the fact that in the gospel was revealed "the righteousness of God." This did not mean God's own righteous character, but as the sequel showed, a righteousness, or rather "rightness," in which He placed the sinner eternally, the moment the latter accepted Christ.

The necessity for this gift, if the sinner were to be accepted, was shown in verses 18 and the following, down to Chapter iii: 19, which express God's wrath against sin, and indict all men, Jews and Gentiles, as guilty of it without exception.

This brought the subject to the consideration of the nature of the gift in detail, Chapter iii: 20–26.

Lesson II.

What the Gift Does for Us. — *Romans v.*

The second lesson showed the effect of the gift of righteousness upon believers in their relation to God.

(1) It brought them into a state of peace with God. This peace might not,

A SCENE IN TENT ENDEAVOR.

at first, be an experience in their own souls, but it was the condition in which they stood before God. There was nothing of enmity now as between them and God.

(2) It gave them access to God. They might now hold fellowship with Him in prayer, worship, illustrated by the access an ambassador enjoyed to the potentate of a foreign country on the declaration of peace following war.

(3) It caused them to rejoice before God. This rejoicing was for three things, the hope of glory, experiences of tribulation, and the knowledge of God Himself.

LESSON III.

What the Gift Does in Us. — *Romans* vi–viii.

As Lesson II. showed the effect of the gift of God's righteousness on man in his relations to God, so Lesson III. showed its effect in the man's own experience.

It brought him: 1. Into a new sphere, where he had become dead to sin in in a condemnatory sense, and alive unto God. Whether he experienced it or not at first he was nevertheless walking before God in newness of life (Chapter vi).

2. He was brought not only into a new sphere, but also a new condition, where he came to experience 'a conflict with sin (Chapter vii), thus emphasized the truth concerning the two natures in the believer, raising and answering the question at its close as to whether victory was obtainable for the new nature in Christ.

3. Finally, the believer was brought not only into a new condition, but into a new possession — the indwelling of the Holy Spirit. It was the office and work of the Holy Spirit to enable the believer to continually triumph over known sin. He did this by means of several things as seen in Chapter viii.

THE PASTORS' CONFERENCES

were under the leadership of Rev. Smith Baker, D.D., of Portland, Me., and Dr. J. F. Carson, Brooklyn, N.Y,. The topics discussed were: —

"How the pastor can lead, not drive."
"How to develop leaders among the young people."
"How to utilize the trained Endeavorers in the larger church work."
"How the Endeavor idea can be adapted to local needs."
"How the pastor can improve the quality of the prayer meeting."
"How the pastor can develop the committee work."
"How the pastor can use the executive committee."
"How the pastor can make the Society an evangelistic force."

Dr. Carson said that he had a number of young people scattered through the congregation who noted auditors that were moved by the sermon, and brought them to him. The method of Dr. Stebbins, of the Central Presbyterian Church, Rochester, N.Y., was cited. He has a Sunday evening repast in the church after the sermon and invites strangers to share it with him, and then he gives them an earnest brotherly talk about Christ.

One minister said that he never held special evangelistic services without the help of an evangelist; a pastor needs another.

Dr. Hallenbeck told how he held a conference with his church officials and induced them to speak personally to the unsaved neighbors nearest them. He was amazed at himself and others that so little emphasis had been put on this kind of work.

CHAPTER V.

A " Forward " Meeting.

TENT ENDEAVOR. FRIDAY MORNING.

Old Sol was playing his heaviest batteries on Tent Endeavor at 9.45 A.M., when the schools turned all their scholars loose to hurry for seats. The flags hung limp. Prespiration oozed from every pore and fans tried in vain to brush the warmth away, but there was joy in the tent that heat could not repress.

"Arkansas for Christ! Hurrah!" sang out some one under the green and white banner of that State.

"Rah! rah! rah!" rang from other parts of the tent, as other State delegations took up their State yells and songs. Sometimes they sang in turn; sometimes all sang together, but they sang and were glad and their enthusiasm was contagious and inspiring.

At ten o'clock President Clark stepped on the platform and made the grateful announcement that Percy S. Foster would lead the singing. This was just what the audience wanted, and "Onward Christian Soldier" began to roll out with a martial spirit and measure that set every blood drop tingling.

Rev. Dr. Power, of Washington, led in an impressive devotional exercise, deftly blending his prayer into praise by breaking forth softly in singing "Old Hundred," followed by the great congregation. The first address was

FORWARD THE STATE AND LOCAL UNIONS.

By Rev. W. N. Yates, Philadelphia.

When God made us, in the very manner of our creation he determined that we should walk by a constant attempt and a successful one, too, of bringing the right foot foremost, that is the way we have to walk. That is the way God intends organizations to make progress, as well as individuals. I know that requires one foot for the time being seemingly to stand still, but while that is true, that still foot is performing a grand work for the time of burden bearing, and it is the only way to make way for that which is further back to come to the front.

Every State and local union has its hind foot or feet and it has a peculiar quality of producing an extra one whenever it is needed. But the only way for a State or local union to make progress, is to take hold of that which seems to be lingering for the time being and, by throwing the weight of the burden upon that part of the work which is in the lead, to help that which is back, to the front.

What are some of the hind feet? Perhaps some of our local and State unions — it may be an official. All I have to say is this, that if an official is too dead to experience a movement he had better be knocked off, for it is a law frequently illustrated in nature that when you cut off a dead branch one that will live and do something will sprout out where you cut the old one off.

It may be a committee. Be careful there. Don't throw a committee — the office of a committee — away in order to get rid of a committee man. Hold on to that committee. It would be just as wise to throw the committee away because it is behind as it would be to throw your left foot away because it is behind your right foot. You will have to get that left foot to the front some how.

Mr. Yates is a powerfully built, businesslike man, and he proceeded in a direct, businesslike way. He has a high, overhanging forehead, and the high-pitched distinct utterance of a commander-in-chief. He was terse, definite and aggressive in his talk and made one feel that what he urged could be done, and easily.

It may be unoccupied territory. In every state and local union there is land and plenty of it, yet to be possessed. We need to throw the weight of our well organized parts into the unorganized parts and go on until every foot of land that lies before us has been reached and organized.

But how is the hind foot brought to the front? First, it is lifted, second, it is pulled, and third, it is pushed. That is the way you get your foot to the front. You have got to get hold of that which is stationary and give it a lift. There are a good many officials, who, in order to do something, have to be lifted.

You will never get a pastor to be a pastor until you lift him once in a while. The presidents, the chairmen of committees of the Christian Endeavor, they must be lifted, and then they must be pulled. There is no other power so forcible to bring out all there is in a man as the power of activity all around him.

One of the most vigorous and successful Junior workers in the country is State Superintendent Kenngott of Massachusetts, to whose work is due much of the splendid increase Massachusetts has made this year in gaining thirty Junior socities. Mr. Kenngott's address was full of practical points, such as a call for more effort to form Junior choirs, even if less must be spent on high-priced quartettes. His theme was

Forward the Juniors.

The Young People's Society of Christian Endeavor was designed originally and is still primarily for the adolescents, for those who are in the period of stress and storm, from twelve or fourteen years of age to twenty-one.

Describing in an interesting way the quirks and krinkles of the boy and girl in the period referred to, and quoting the weighty opinions of Professors Starbuck and Coe, eminent Christian psychologists and authorities on this subject, Mr. Kenngott made a most clinching application as follows : —

The Junior Endeavor Society is absolutely necessary for the safe conduct and continuance of the Young People's Society, it is essential to the life of the church, and holds in its heart the promise of the future. To gather the adolescents into the church, to take advantage of this normal period of conversion, the children need the nurture and care of such a society whose object is "to promote an earnest Christian life among the boys and girls who may become members, and prepare them for the active service of Christ." Our warrant is the example furnished us in both Old Testament and New, and in our own modern experience. The Christian Endeavor idea is not modern though its precise application is.

After a beautiful reference to Jesus' putting the deacon in the kindergarten, and to child training in Jewish homes, the speaker said:—

Much of the training that properly belongs to the home has been delegated to the school, and Froebel, through his Kindergarten, has revolutionized education. The university sends its students into the laboratory and library, into the fields and mines, for original research, using the "laboratory method," because Froebel rediscovered the child whom Jesus set in the midst of the proud elders to teach them humility, and declared that, "the child mind ripens and expands to abstract truth only by and through the concrete." Because the Kindergarten has its colored balls, blocks, and sand-piles that the children may see with their eyes, hear with their ears, handle with their hands, feel with their hearts, and do the things they are taught, therefore, the university has its laboratory method.

The public school, with all its modern methods and appliances, is doing much in the mental and moral training of the children and youth. It does not and cannot properly give the distinctively religious training which is so much needed. The Bible is scarcely read in many schools and is not studied. The lives of Alexander the Great, Cæsar and Napoleon are carefully studied and the lists of their battles memorized, but there is no place for the study of the life of Jesus.

The catechetical work of the Roman Catholic and German Lutheran Churches was referred to as an instance of the tenacity with which early religious impressions stick to the child. Why should not the " Give me the child until he is ten years old," of the Catholic priest be true of the Junior superintendent?

Training in character is the essential product of all training in home, church, and state. The training of a few children may seem insignificant, but it is far more rewarding than preaching to the dull ears and hardened hearts of sinning men who have passed from a childhood untrained in religion into a godless manhood. The church must be a producing force, and she must grow from within; otherwise she can win no conquests without.

The hour-a-week work of the Sunday school for the child was contrasted with the all-the-week work possible through the committees of the Junior society. In summing up, Mr. Kenngott faced with the courage of a broad-shouldered six-footer the biggest lion in the way of Junior Christian Endeavor — how to get superintendents enough.

There is a danger that the church may be considered a Sunday institution if it confines all of its religious services to Sunday. With its doors wide open every day in the week, the children may make a beaten path from the public school to the church for their Junior Endeavor Society, which should meet, if possible, on a week day, because Sunday is already full of religious services, and some time should be allowed for the home. The Junior Endeavor Society is designed for the children who have not yet reached adolescence.

The difficulty in the Junior Endeavor work is not the getting of the children but the finding of a suitable superintendent. Let the pastor himself be the superintendent, if possible. It will give him a great opportunity to know the children personally and to train them in the nurture and admonition of the Lord. It will be his most rewarding work and his highest pleasure.

Then, Forward the Juniors! Why? Because they are necessary as a source of supply for the Young People's Society, they are essential to the very life of the church as a society for Christian nurture, and hold the promise of the future. How? Rally the children around a superintendent, the pastor, if possible, who will love and study the child and the Book. "Well for the child, well for the man, to whom throughout life the voice of conscience is the prophecy and pledge of an abiding union with God."

FORWARD BY ADDITION

was the subject of Harry A. Kinports, New York's State secretary. He is a stalwart layman of large experience in adding both figures and Endeavor societies, being a pushing business man as well as a pushing Endeavorer. He had but one embarrassment which he summed up in his announcement, "Lost, a voice somewhere between here and Chicago, $50 reward to whoever returns it to me."

The thing I am to talk to you about this morning is how to increase numerically. Where are your prospective members? They are in the Sunday schools, in the churches, and in your communities. The question now is how to get them. Let me emphasize some points. One is, have a definite aim. You know a good many of us have gotten into a spirit of self-satisfaction. We are not concerned about addition. It is about subtraction. There are a good many people who have been agitating the idea of how to get rid of some of the young people who have not been faithful to their vows.

With inimitable and cutting satire Mr. Kinports described the society that plodded along year after year with the same dozen or twenty or fifty members that it began with, because it was color-blind to the fact that the community was full of new young people. He described the kind of a prayer meeting that draws young people.

Nothing does me so much good as to have a young men or woman come into the prayer meeting of our church and upon going out say, "That has helped me. I am coming again." Then I know that Christian Endeavor has served its purpose, and I won't have to sit down for an hour trying to persuade that person to join. In that way the numerical increase will take care of itself.

Another way is cordiality. We get our young people into the prayer meetings Sunday nights, and after the benediction has been pronounced you have to see the chairman of the lookout committee and the chairman of the prayer-meeting committee, and you have to confer with Mr. Somebody else, and everybody is conferring, and the stranger goes out and no one has given him the hand clasp of welcome. That is the reason we are not getting them into our societies. We have these little cliques.

That prayer meeting room of ours should have every nook and cranny shouting a welcome to every man and woman who comes there, and then it will not be long before we have a numerical increase.

Just one point more. Personal work and effort. My brother who just left the platform said it meant hard work. We are lazy; we get tired too easy. I wish we had something like Hood's Sarsaparilla for the spiritual blood, that we could buy in bottles, that would give us more earnestness in Christian Endeavor service.

FORWARD BY DIVISION

was the paradox assigned a Kansas pastor, Rev. Charles E. Bradt, Ph.D., of Wichita. But he has handled the question in his own church, and knew just how to prescribe. He spoke with the positiveness of a man who has faced a condition and is not pumping the hot air of a new theory, when he declared that a society of more than one hundred members is too large.

Like Joshua let us advance upon the enemy by dividing our army. His command was, "Forward, by Division!"

This may well be the practice and command of the leaders of our Christian Endeavor forces in many of our churches to-day. Let me tell you why.

DIVISION ADDS.

1. It adds strength, oftimes. "There is that scattereth and yet increaseth." By dividing a society and organizing another out of a part of the original number, increased responsibility is placed upon all. This increased responsibility develops strength in the individual members and hence the societies and the church. Strength we must have to-day if we are to advance successfully against the enemy. "For we wrestle not against flesh and blood, but against principalities, against powers, against the rulers of the darkness of this world, against spiritual wickedness in high places." But we will not get strength unless we get our forces to exercise themselves.

2. Division adds activity. Inactivity is the curse of many a society as it has been the curse of many an army. What is needed is something to quicken their sluggish heart beats and handiworks. Stagnation means death. Division avoids this by creating a wholesome rivalry. In Hebrews x: 24, we read, "And let us consider one another to provoke unto love and to good works." The Greek word for provoke is *paroxysmos*. It means something sharp by one's side, as a spur on the heel of the rider is close to the side of the horse.

Some one has said, "Man is as lazy as he dare be." This may be said even of Christians and some Christian Endeavorers. But let there be a division of the Christian Endeavorers of a large church into two or more societies, standing upon equal footing, and the question how to avoid stagnation and stimulate activity of both heart and hand in furthering Christ's cause will be answered.

DIVISION SUBTRACTS.

It subtracts superfluous members and relieves the society of burdensome material. An army can be so encumbered with numbers as well as impedimenta that it cannot well *attack* the enemy nor *escape* the enemy. This was true with the original army which rallied about Gideon. He organized three Endeavor societies of one hundred members each and with that light brigade he swept the enemy from the field. A society of over one hundred members is too large to do the best work. Two societies with fifty members each is better than one with one hundred members.

DIVISION MULTIPLIES.

Division not only adds strength and activity and subtracts superfluous and unused material, but it multiplies members who become strong and active Christian Endeavorers. This is the inevitable result of organizing the forces so that each and every member shall be given his work and made to feel his personal responsibility. In this way no young people outside, as within, the ranks will be allowed to escape.

This has been the result in my own church. With a society of about one hundred members we divided and organized two societies. To-day we have fully twice as many members enlisted in Christian Endeavor work as previously, and the strength of the members as manifested in love and good work is many fold what it was before the division.

A Kansas cyclone seemed to have burst into the tent when Dr. G. A. Crise, president of the Kansas union, stepped to the front and launched into the

OPEN PARLIAMENT: "INCIDENTS OF PROGRESS."

Endeavorers, without any preliminary on my part we desire to hear from you this morning of some incident of progress, some garnered grain you have brought to the Master's kingdom. In the next ten minutes I want to hear from fifty people. Who will be the first to give us an incident of progress in their respective city, county, or State?

(*Voice.*) Our missionary society doubled in one year.

(*Voice.*) Organized an Endeavor of one hundred in the prison at Atlanta.

(*Voice.*) We support a city missionary.

(*Buffalo.*) Seventy-eight new members. Thirty-one new members in the Junior society. Trebled our missionary work.

(*Voice.*) One member gone to China, and a missionary supported by the church and by the society.

(*Voice.*) We doubled the membership of our society of fifty in the month of March of this year.

(*Voice.*) Gain of two hundred per cent in the Utah State prison.

(*Kansas.*) Presbyterian society of Emporia doubled its society by division.

(*Rhode Island.*) Providence has reached more than 3,000 sailors by personal work.

(*Voice.*) In a little town in Iowa the room is too small for the attendance on the meetings. We need a room three times as large.

(*Voice.*) We organized January 29. Had expenses of $297. We now have $175 in our treasury. We have ninety active members, ten associate members.

(*Colorado.*) Missionary committee made 1,500 visits last year.

(*Arkansas.*) Bentonville organized last month a new society.

(*Voice.*) In Texas we organized a society one year ago under difficulties, with six members. Have increased to sixty members.

(*Hyde Park Division, Chicago.*) Organized a Junior society, and in three months it grew to eighty-one members.

(*India.*) Sunday school committee walking seven and a half miles to conduct Sunday school. Result of the work fifteen baptisms. (*Applause.*)

(*Philadelphia.*) The largest union, I believe, in this country, and yet we have made ten per cent gain. Have now over 33,000 Christian Endeavorers in Philadelphia. First Chinese Baptist Church with a Chinese Christian Endeavor society of eighteen. I have a letter in my pocket signed by the president of that society, sending greetings.

(*Kentucky.*) We want to report from the Junior department the youngest Sunday school superintendent in the world. A boy fourteen years old, who has organized and superintended a Senior society and Sunday school in a district that never had one before.

(*Minneapolis.*) Junior society gain of one hundred and seventy-five per cent in one year. Done by organization and division in our work, and the children did it all.

(*Muncie, Ind.*) Christian Endeavor society in month of March had five conversions. Organized a Sunday school with a membership of one hundred.

(*Nevada.*) First Presbyterian Church, Carson City, gave five times as much money to the foreign missions as ever before.

(*Arkansas.*) Christian Endeavor society has increased fifty per cent during the past five months.

(*Tonowanda, N.Y.*) In one week's meeting twenty-nine conversions.

(*Ohio.*) Organized two societies, first day of May, of sixty. Twenty-two conversions. We have now a Junior society of twenty-one and they have sent delegates and greetings to you.

(*Indiana.*) We started out to make a ten per cent increase, but found that so easy we don't think it counts anything unless we get from twenty-five to one hundred per cent.

(*California.*) I want to say something about the Chinese C. E. Society of the first Congregational Church of San Francisco. One hundred members, less than half non-residents of the city, all men who work for their money, paid $1,500 for foreign missions last year.

(*Nebraska.*) Junior society at Albion with twenty-one members sent fifteen of their number into the church last year. The First Presbyterian of Omaha gave the most money to foreign missions we know of. One of our societies in Omaha had a gain of one hundred and forty per cent. We are not working for banners but for the Master.

(*Missouri.*) Christian Endeavor went down into a town where they had no gospel services, and in less than two years organized a church of three hundred and two good Senior and Junior societies and in one week more than thirty-four people were actually converted.

At the close of this stirring and bracing climax to these practical and pithy addresses, Dr. Clark seized the occasion to emphasize the need of extending the blessings of Christian Endeavor to the whole world, and asked all who had become Christians before they were twenty to rise. It seemed as though the entire audience sprang to its feet.

He then asked Mr. Chamberlain, of India, to speak briefly of India's need, following which Mr. Yates made an appeal for the Clarence E. Eberman Memorial Fund, and the subscriptions began to roll in. The secretary was kept so busy that he wished for two right hands, until the sum subscribed reached more than $4,500 which will form the nucleus of a fund to extend Christian Endeavor around the world.

At the close of this "hilarious" giving, the most suitable speaker and the most fitting topic for concluding the session were introduced, in the person of Rev. Smith Baker, D.D., pastor of Williston Church, Portland, Me., whose theme was,

FORWARD FOR THE MASTER'S GLORY.

Some may say, "Forward for the truth's sake." It is the truth and only the truth that the Christian seeks, but Christ is the truth; all truth commences in Him, all truth ends in Him. "He was in the beginning with God, and He was God; all things were made by Him, and without Him was not one thing made that hath been made; in Him was life, and His life was the light of men." "He is the way, the truth, and the life." He is the truth incarnate.

In our social life, it is not the abstract truth of motherhood that holds and thrills our hearts, but the incarnate, real, living, loving mother. Some men's preaching is like "reading the truth from a tombstone," because there is no living Christ in it, and spiritual truth without Christ is dead. Some persons' lives are like marble statues, beautiful but unresponsive, moral but cold art, not life.

Others may say, "Forward for humanity's sake;" but we go back of humanity to Him who is *the* Son of Man, the only man, the one man above all other men representing in Himself perfect humanity, who came as the only begotten Son of God, and the only perfect Son of man, to redeem lost men, who brought life and immortality to light, to Him for whom, and through whom, and to whom, are all things, — deeper, broader, higher than any nation or race or age, the King of Kings for whom the world was made, and say, "Forward for Christ's glory." He represents humanity.

For whose glory should we live if not for Him who became incarnate for us, who lived, suffered, died, and conquered death for us, our Redeemer, and upon whom our hopes of heaven depend?

> "Were the whole realm of nature mine,
> That were a present far too small;
> Love so amazing, so divine,
> Demands my soul, my life, my all."

What do we mean by "forward for the glory of Christ"?

A machine most glorifies its maker when it best does the work for which it was made. A farm glorifies the farmer when it increases in fruitfulness and beauty. A picture glorifies the artist when it most reproduces his thought, as the "Descent from the Cross" glorifies Rubens, or the "Sistine Madonna" glorifies Raphael. A statue most glorifies the sculptor when it most reveals the thought in his soul, as that of "Moses" honors Michael-Angelo, or the "Greek Slave" honors Powers. A pupil glorifies his master when he most reveals the power of the teacher to awaken thought, as hundreds of men have honored Mark Hopkins. A child glorifies his home when he most reveals the high spiritual influence of that home in his life. This glorifying is not a passive representation, but the power of an inspiration to action. It is as a great picture stirs us to thought and deeds that it glorifies the artist, and we glorify him. To say one thing so as to move to action is better than to say an hundred things which are simply true.

GLORIFYING BY LIVING.

That salesman most glorifies the firm he represents who most pushes forward the interests of the firm. That teacher most glorifies a school who most builds it up in spite of obstacles. That general most glorifies his country who gains greatest victories for it. The man most glorifies any work who most advances that work in its influence through the world. That statesman most glorifies his nation who most advances her power for righteousness and humanity. That Christian most glorifies Christ who most pushes forward his kingdom. It is the life pushing forward, and up, and out in the trees, which clothes them with beauty and glorifies them. It is the pushing forward into greater discoveries that glorifies natural science and blesses the world. It is the pushing forward of the great missionary spirit into new fields which is to save the world and glorify Christ.

Christian Endeavor has glorified Christ by its forward march. Each private Christian glorifies Christ as he moves forward to a higher life and greater deeds. The glory of Christ our aim, — this lifts one into fellowship with the angels, with Christ, with God. This is in accord with Christ's prayer, "O Father, glorify thou Me with Thine own self, with the Glory which I had with Thee before the world was." "I will that they also whom Thou hast given Me, be with Me where I am, that they may behold My glory which thou hast given Me."

How do it? Listen. You have all heard the story of that common servant girl who was working for a cruel, Christless master. Going to her church one evening the minister exhorted all to live for the glory of Christ. The poor girl was discouraged. She said to herself, "My pastor does not understand it. How can one live for the glory of Christ working for such a wicked master as I have?"

She went to bed feeling that it was no use for her to try, — the minister might do it, but she could not, — and she fell asleep in her tears. The next morning coming down to her work with the same discouraged feeling, the cruel master met her, and holding up a pair of mud-covered shoes, with an oath said : —

"CLEAN THEM QUICK, BETTY."

The girl took them, and with tears rolling down her cheeks she said, "How can I do this for the glory of Christ?" But while she brushed, and brushed, and the tears fell, there came into her mind the greatest thought that ever entered the human soul, "If these were Jesus Christ's shoes, how I would make them shine!" This great thought filled her soul with a new life and lifted her into fellowship with the angels. Whatsoever ye do, do it as unto Christ, and that will glorify Him and move the world forward.

A few years ago there stood in the chapel of the church of which I was pastor an intelligent, modest, sincere, earnest, and splendid Christian girl who had given herself to the foreign missionary work. We had prepared a farewell send-off, and after several speeches of congratulation and good-will, it came her time to respond.

With her natural modesty and the embarrassment of the hour, she only said, "I am going to Turkey to show the Turkish girls what a Christian girl is." She could not have said more in an hour's speech. She went, and just after the horrible mob and massacre at Marsovan, she wrote me, saying, "I took my girls and went into the attic of our house, and with hammer and nails fastened ourselves out of sight till the mob had passed."

As soon as it was safe, she went out and ministered to the needs of the wounded fathers and mothers of her pupils. In doing so she caught disease, and in a few days died. They buried her in the sands of Marsovan. There those fathers and mothers went, and taking the earth from her grave, kissed it. She was an Endeavorer, the superintendent of our Intermediate Society. She went to Turkey to show the Turkish girls what a Christian girl is, and she did it. I had rather be Martha King to-day with her stars in glory than to possess all the wealth of the world.

Friends, that is the whole of it. We are called to go forward and to show the world what a Christian young man is, what a Christian young woman is, what a Christian boy is, what a Christian girl is. Wherever God has placed us, in the pulpit, in the school-room, in the office, in the store, in the shops, on the farm, in the home, anywhere, everywhere, all the time, forward in joys, in sorrows, in health, in sickness, in poverty, in riches, living or dying, *forward*, and show the world what a Christian is.

CHAPTER VI.

Evangelistic Meetings and Picturesqueness.

Endeavorers are not sponges. They do not travel half-way across the continent just to get something for themselves. They like to give as well as get. With this end in view half a dozen daily evangelistic meetings were planned for the Denver Convention.

Four of these were held at noonday: — at the court-house square, and at the Denver and Rio Grande, Colorado and Southern, and Pullman railroad shops. In the evening a gospel wagon went out loaded with Endeavorers (and usually four times as many volunteered as could be taken) to hold meetings at the street-corners.

The following description of one of the meetings held on the court-house steps will serve as a sample of all.

The meeting was in charge of Rev. William Patterson, D.D., pastor of Bethany Presbyterian Church of Philadelphia. He was assisted by Rev. Dr. W. J. Harsha of Denver. With the Christian Endeavorers and the citizens of Denver there was a crowd gathered of about 400 people, when those on the steps struck up the words of "Onward, Christian Soldiers." Mrs. Ray F. Shank then sang a solo, after which Dr. Harsha offered a prayer. F. H. Jacobs then took charge of the singing.

Rev. Dr. Patterson took for his theme the verse of the prophecy, "Thou shalt call His name Jesus, for He shall save the people from their sins." He said in part: —

Religion gives joy and success, and does not — as so many seem to think — take it away from life. Jesus came to save His people, and saved such as the publican and Saul, to leave them as examples of the work which He does. America needs and wants salvation. No nation has so developed, so influenced, so grown, and yet how much the greater would be her influence if salvation prevailed more generally.

Who does He save? Those who will let Him, just as the doctor saves by an operation those that are willing to have him operate. The great Lorenz saved some and many, and earned a fee in one case of $30,000; but Christ saves all free, and He will do so if you will only let Him.

Mr. Jacobs then sang a solo, "A Sinner like me." Mr. Jacobs has a fine voice full of power, and his solo was a very fine rendition. After a prayer by Dr. Patterson the chorus sang "Nearer, my God, to Thee," and the meeting was closed with a benediction by Dr. Harsha. It was a great success, and the crowd of 400 were intensely interested in hearing the great speaker from Wanamaker's church talk in his inimitable way.

At noon the second day Dr. Carson spoke, and several men raised their hands for prayer. Dr. James M. Gray had charge of the third meeting, and one man professed conversion.

At one of the shops the men left their lunches as soon as the singing began. They requested the Endeavorers to come back the next day. More than twenty men in all raised their hands for prayer at these meetings.

An interesting meeting was held in the chapel-car which Mr. Boston Smith had brought to Denver.

One evangelistic meeting not on the programme resulted from a letter to Rev. R. J. Campbell from a woman in a disreputable house asking that workers be sent to Market Street, the slum section of Denver, to hold meetings in behalf of herself and associates.

Dr. Harsha, chairman of the Evangelistic Committee, gladly applied to the police for a permit and protection, and the meeting was held with great interest and encouraging results.

An Endeavor Camp.

An exceedingly picturesque feature of the Convention was a camp of delegates in the North Side of Denver. It was an ideal spot for a summer camp, and the inmates spoke in glowing terms of the exhilarating effects of the atmosphere and scenery.

The Christian Endeavor Museum.

Mr. Merritt B. Holley, of Traverse City, Mich., has spent fourteen years collecting, from all parts of the world, the curios that filled the museum in the Central Christian Church. He is in communication with thirty different countries, and is constantly adding to his collection.

Every curio has a history. The "only whiskey bottle brought to Denver by an Endeavorer" was innocent of color or smell of whiskey, but had a neatly carved cross and scales of justice within it, the work of a life prisoner in the Iowa penitentiary, who committed murder while under the influence of whiskey, but has been converted under the influence of Christian Endeavor.

Mr. Holley's collection of foreign flags from Christian Endeavor lands numbers fifty-two. His collection of Christian Endeavor badges numbers 552, from all parts of the world.

CHAPTER VII.

Under Their Own Vine and Fig Tree.

TWENTY SPIRITED DENOMINATIONAL RALLIES, FRIDAY AFTERNOON.

Christian Endeavor is the best fertilizer of denominational loyalty. It has done more than any other agency to promote fellowship between the young people of denominations, bringing them together from all sections of the land to enjoy love-feasts with those of their own name and faith. Friday afternoon was a high day in twenty churches. Faces brightened at the sight of old friends. Pastors had their hearts warmed by looking once more into the eyes of young people on former charges who had loyally worked shoulder to shoulder with them. Every eye took on a glad lustre, and all lips seemed to be framed in smiles.

REFORMED PRESBYTERIAN RALLY.

Rev. Samuel McNaugher, Ph.D., presiding.

Miss Lizzie Knight of Evans, Cal., read an admirable paper on "Covenanter Youth in Times of Persecution." Rev. Samuel Edgar, of La Junta, Col., delivered a telling address on, "Our Youth and Mission Fields." Rev. J. M. Wylie, of Evans, Cal., spoke on, "What Can Our Young People Do for the Cause of Reform?" Dr. M. M. George read a significant paper on, "The Relation of Endeavor and Sabbath School Work."

Rev. H. B. McMillan of our Indian Mission field gave us "Glimpses of Our Indian Mission Work."

The closing words of consecration were very fitly spoken by Rev. C. McLeod Smith, of Ray, Indiana. They sang the Psalms they love so well. The congregation of Denver gave a reception and banquet. There were delegates present for nearly all sections of the church.

LUTHERAN RALLY.

Rev. M. F. Troxell, D.D., presiding.

The staunch adherents of the greatest of Protestant Reformers enjoyed their best denominational rally, in St. Paul's Lutheran Church. They found a feast spread for both soul and body, for fair hands had decorated the rooms and provided dainty refreshments.

Miss Elizabeth Mester, of Springfield, Ill., read a most apt paper on "The Story of One Society," which proved an outline ideal of what the local society may be.

Rev. Luther P. Ludden, the new western district secretary in the home field for the Lutheran church, was introduced and met with an enthusiastic greeting.

An offering was made at the Rally for the Cleveland Memorial C. E. Church. New officers were elected for the National Lutheran C. E. Union, Rev. P. A. Heilman, of Baltimore,Md., being elected president, Rev. E. P. Schueler, of Quincy, Ill., vice-president, and Rev. C. W. Leitzell, of Johnstown, N.Y., secretary and treasurer.

Rev. Dr. Heilman is the well-known writer of the Endeavorer weekly prayer-meeting topics for the *Lutheran Observer*, and Mr. Schueler is the representative of his denomination on the pastors' advisory board of the Illinois State Endeavor union.

The general secretary of the Luther League of America, Rev. Luther M. Kuhns, was an interested visitor at the Endeavor Convention, and made a very fraternal address to which Rev. Dr. Troxell made fitting response, expressing the hope that all Luther Leagues might join with Endeavor fellowship by taking the same prayer-meeting topics and enrolling as affiliated Endeavor societies.

FRIENDS' RALLY.

Hon. Charles Newlin, presiding.

The "friendly" Friends proved that their nature corresponded to their name. Under their own roof-tree there was so much to tell that no one waited long in silence for the Spirit to move.

Rev. George D. Weeks, pastor of the church, welcomed the visiting delegates. Greetings were brought from different parts of the country.

Rev. Willis Hotchkiss was introduced, and spoke most earnestly of his work in Africa. At the close of the programme a social time was heartily enjoyed by all.

REFORMED EPISCOPAL RALLY.

Bishop Samuel Fallows, D.D., presiding.

Bishop Fallows is a whole rally in himself. Soldier, educator, publicist, divine, lecturer, his name and resourcefulness are a guarantee that any programme will go.

Rev. James M. Gray, D.D., of Boston, was obliged to leave before the close of the meeting, but the thought in his heart for the occasion was that if the Christian Endeavor Society or the Reformed Episcopal Church desired to realize its highest ideal, it must remember that it is as true of either as an organization as it is of the individual Christian, that "he who would save his life shall lose it, and, he who will lose his life for Christ's sake shall find it." Too much subjectiveness had been injurious hitherto in both organizations, and if henceforth they should think less of themselves and more of their witness-bearing for Christ, both would flourish this fruit-bearing.

METHODIST RALLY.

Rev. Herbert E. Foss, D.D., presiding.

Three continental Methodisms — the Methodist Episcopal, the Methodist Episcopal South, and the Canadian Methodist — clasped hands together, at Trinity Methodist Episcopal Church. It was a pleasant family reunion, and a foretaste of what might be if no bar were put in the way of Methodist fellowship with other young people.

Bishop Henry W. Warren, D.D., LL.D., made a most unique and eloquent address of welcome, characteristically vigorous and stirring.

The "Past and Present of Methodism" was Rev. Dr. Reisner's subject, and his address was most happily conceived and enthusiastically received.

Rev. W. F. Wilson, D.D., of Hamilton, Canada, was the representative of Canadian Methodism, and his speech had the ring of sound Canadian conservatism and stability. Dr. Wilson dropped the remark that John Wesley had preached in his grandfather's house.

The next address — a carefully prepared paper — was read by Miss Oswold, of Denver, and was one of the best features of the Rally. In glowing colors she painted the noble women of Methodism from Susanna Wesley, the Mother of Methodism, to Frances E. Willard, its consummate flower, and paid just tribute to the nameless thousands who had helped Methodism to its proud place.

The last speaker was Rev. J. S. Lippincott, D.D., LL.D., of Philadelphia. His theme was "A Family Likeness," and from the law of heredity he drew the lesson that the great leaders around whom the religious bodies had grown up had impressed their personality upon their followers, so divergent bodies of Methodists have the impress of John Wesley's character, beliefs, and methods.

A roll call, by Methodisms and by States, followed, in which many good things were said, and the very successful and stimulating Rally was closed with prayer and benediction by Dr. Wilson.

REFORMED CHURCH IN AMERICA AND SOUTHERN PRESBYTERIAN.

Rev. John H. Elliott, D.D., and Prof. James Lewis Howe, presiding.

Like was drawn to like in this joint rally. The affinity which these two bodies have for each other was discovered by themselves long since, and this brief taste of communion will make them want more.

A delightful spirit of fellowship was manifest throughout, and unusual enthusiasm prevailed. The Southern Presbyterians are quite as conservative as the Dutch Reformed Church, some feel even more so, but for once all prudish restraint and foolish dignity were ruled out, and every one seemed to have a real, genuine good time unhindered by conventionality and unhampered by stiffness.

Rev. L. B. Chamberlain of India spoke on "A Message From the Far Field," Prof. Howe on "Christian Endeavor in the Southland," and Prof. John H. Wycoff, D.D., of India, on "World-Wide Christian Endeavor." Several others made brief but happy and telling speeches, and the hour passed all too soon. Every one gave expression to the conviction that it was a most helpful gathering.

THE BRETHREN RALLY.

Rev. C. F. Yoder, presiding.

"The first, but not the last," was the almost unanimous thought of the Brethren Endeavorers concerning their Rally. They are growing like Illinois corn — so fast you can hear the joints crack.

Reports showed a gratifying growth of Christian Endeavor in this denomination. During the past year there has been a twenty per cent increase in the number of Senior societies, and over one hundred and sixty per cent in the number of Junior societies. Some Brethren societies are giving more to missions than to local work. The greatest number of societies is in the East. The Junior society of Dayton captured the banner given by the city union for the largest society.

The principal address was given by Mr. Samuel Lichty, of Falls City, Neb. Other addresses were given by delegates.

The Rally was enthusiastic, and all present resolved to help make the next one much larger.

THE MENNONITE RALLY.

Rev. N. B. Grubb, D.D., presiding.

Dr. Grubb has had a young people's society in the same church for almost twenty-one years, and a Junior society ten of whose young men have entered the ministry. What a splendid vantage point from which to lead the Endeavorers of his denomination on to fruitage!

Well-prepared papers were presented on "How Christian Endeavor Entered the Mennonite Church, How Received, and What it is Doing," by Rev. C. H. A. van der 'Smissen, Summerfield, Ill.; "Our Denominational Relation to the Christian Endeavor Movement," by Mr. A. L. Halteman, Port Blakely, Washington, A very carefully prepared paper was read by Mr. S. D. Ruth, of Beatrice, Neb. on "Co-operation, a Potent Factor in C. E. Work." This was followed by "A Voice from India," by Missionary Rev. P. A. Penner, of Champa, India.

The concluding paper was prepared and presented by the leader of the Rally, Rev. Dr. Grubb, "Twenty-eight Reasons Why Christian Endeavor should be Welcomed into all Mennonite Churches."

Among those who participated in the meeting were Rev. H. G. Allebach, editor of *The Mennonite*, Berne, Ind.

These papers were followed by more than a score of voluntary expressions and testimony along the line of thought expressed in the papers read. The Rally was the largest ever held by this denomination in connection with any International Convention.

After the large audience had gathered on the awn, a photograph was made, and with a half-hour of social intercourse, the Mennonite Rally at Denver had become history.

CUMBERLAND PRESBYTERIAN RALLY.

Rev. R. Tinnon, presiding.

There was a fine outbreaking of enthusiasm among the young Cumberland Presbyterians. They sniffed the air in expectation of good things, and were not disappointed.

The Rally was surprisingly well attended, representative members being present from no less than sixteen States. Addresses were delivered by Miss Lula Durham, treasurer of the Woman's Board of Missions; Rev. T. Ashburn, Evansville, Ind.; Rev. John Royal Harris, Pittsburg, Pa.; Rev. Ira Landrith, LL.D., editor of *The Cumberland Presbyterian*, Nashville, Tenn.; Rev. W. J. Darby, D.D., Educational Secretary, Evansville, Ind.; State Sunday-school Superintendent H. M. Steidley of Nebraska, and others.

Domestic church expansion was the general theme of the Rally, the topic being naturally suggested by the fact that Denver and Colorado are comprised in the home mission territory of this prosperous denomination, the early union of which with the Presbyterians is one of the pleasing probabilities of the future.

Refreshments were served and a happy social hour was enjoyed at the close of the programme.

REFORMED CHURCH IN THE UNITED STATES RALLY.

Rev. J. H. Bomberger, D.D., presiding.

About three hundred young people of this denomination got together and enjoyed the bracing denominational ozone in the atmosphere that was wafted about in the First Reformed Church.

Rev. D. H. Fouse delivered an address on "The Reformed Church Beyond the Mississippi," mingling words of welcome with words of challenge to Eastern Reformed Endeavorers to assist in spreading the lines of the Reformed Church in the West.

Rev. E. E. Weller and Rev. J. N. Naly of Iowa were among the speakers, and their words were full of inspiration.

Rev. J. H. Bomberger, D.D., of Cleveland, O., spoke on "Reformed Expansion," comparing the geographical distribution of the church to a triangle with its base on the Atlantic seaboard, and urging that they make it a rectangle reaching from the Atlantic to the Pacific, and from Canada to Mexico.

The more formal programme was followed by a very pleasant social gathering, the ladies of the congregation serving a luncheon to the visiting friends.

The Disciples of Christ Rally.

Rev. Charles B. Newnan, D.D., presiding.

Spirited singing, addresses that were messages, splendid enthusiasm, and fellowship most delightful, all combined to make the Denver Rally of the Disciples of Christ most memorable.

Who better could have told them of Endeavor's past, or so splendidly illustrated its youth-giving power, as their own Dr. B. B. Tyler? Bible study found a most eloquent and sturdy champion in State President J. N. Jessup of Arkansas. The Denver Convention watchword, "Forward," found fresh and most helpful illustration as those splendid representatives from China, Dr. Bentley and Miss Effie D. Kellar, urged the claims of the world-wide field.

One of the best suggestions of the afternoon was that of Dr. Bentley, that the Endeavorers specialize in the study of mission fields, one making himself an authority upon China, another upon Japan, another upon India, and so on through the whole round.

Lovingly, earnestly, National Superintendent Waggener, of Kansas City, then turned attention to the two distinctive lines of work which Christian Endeavor among the Disciples of Christ is emphasizing this year, namely, Bible study and Christian missions, especially just now Porto Rican work. No man could better have presented personal work than did that stalwart, earnest Indiana State President, C. S. Medbury, of Angola.

And who could better have read their horoscope and lifted their thought to the splendid future of Endeavor than that good man who, from his watch-tower at the nation's capital, keeps lookout over the whole field? Dr. F. D. Power thrilled all hearts as he told them of the boundless possibilities of Christian Endeavor. And what shall be said of the open parliament, when in thirty minutes they heard more than thirty speeches from almost as many sections of our vast but common country? Dr. H. O. Breeden is past master in the art of conducting such assemblies, and never has he in conducting one had less trouble. One of the best speeches of the parliament was by Rev. W. F. Richardson upon Christian Endeavor's contribution to spiritual life.

The United Presbyterian Rally.

Rev. James D. Rankin, presiding.

It was good to see the large auditorium of the United Presbyterian Church filled. Dr. Rankin made a capital presiding officer, and the stalwart young descendants of the Scotch Covenanters were glad they came.

Rev. W. H. McCreery, the pioneer minister in Colorado Presbytery, gave a brief history of united Presbyterianism in the Rocky Mountain State. Rev. O. A.

Petty spoke on "The Forward Movement in the Church of To-day." Rev. Mr. Lindsey of the A. R. P. Church, Rives, Tenn., spoke of the opportunity afforded by the Forward movement. Rev. George E. Camahan, of Clay Center, Kan., dwelt upon the divine commission as an incentive to this movement. Rev. W. H. McMaster, of Blairsville, Pa., responded as a member of the late General Assembly as to the part missions and moral reform hold as factors in the Forward Movement.

Rev. A. W. Jamison, of Portland, Col., made the closing address by way of commending the movement. This was one of the delightful meetings of the convention. It was a reunion of United Presbyterians and others from all parts of the country, and proved a pleasant social hour to all.

Free Baptist and General Baptist Rally.

Harry S. Meyers, presiding.

The Broadway Baptist Church housed a joint rally presided over by the vivacious and alert general secretary of the Free Baptist Young People. Harmony was the watchword, and it was, indeed, like the ointment that flowed down Aaron's beard.

Rev. R. M. Barrett, Boonville, Ind., gave a short address, setting forth the status of work among the General Baptists, and propounding some of their problems.

Mr. Meyers spoke of the "Needs of More Members, More Societies, and More Work for Missions." The remainder of the time was devoted to informal discussion of the work in the home churches, and help was given by those of experience. The expansion policy was indorsed, and the delegates pledged themselves to a renewed activity in Endeavor work.

Every person present expressed himself as anxious to undertake a larger work. Seven States were represented, and a good time enjoyed.

Protestant Episcopal and Church of England Rally.

Rev. M. A. Johnson, D.D., presiding.

Mother and daughter ecclesiasticisms had a pleasant afternoon together, comparing notes in regard to this, to them, new and hopeful agency for church training.

The Rev. F. J. Horsefield, of Bristol, England, gave an account of the origin and growth of the Church of England union of Christian Endeavor of which he is president, urging the clergy present who had not Christian Endeavor societies to sympathetically consider the advisability of adopting Endeavor in connection with their churches.

Dr. Johnson narrated how he first was led to associate himself with Christian Endeavor work, and said he deeply regretted that hitherto so few of the Protestant Episcopal churches in America had societies at work.

In a spirited speech the Rev. J. Senior, of Lexington, Neb., told of an American bishop who was in deepest sympathy with the movement, and whose wife learned the art of public speaking at a Christian Endeavor society. He gave utterance to many bright, pointed sentences, such as the assertion that "the worst kind of action is inaction," and that hitherto too many of them had been satisfied to convey impressions without seeking to cultivate expression.

He had come to Denver purposely to study the movement, and thought it ought to be considered not critically but appreciatively. He expressed his profound admiration for Dr. Clark and his work.

The Rev. H. R. O'Malley also spoke in eulogistic terms of the aims and methods of Christian Endeavor, and one of the audience told how it had been the means of greatly deepening his spiritual life.

It is to be hoped that the meeting will result in the extension of the movement, and so become, as Dr. Johnson expressed it, a historic gathering.

THE MORAVIAN RALLY.

Allie C. Hege, presiding.

Endeavor work in the Moravian Church had enough enthusiastic exponents to fill the York Street Presbyterian Church, and with their well-known consecration and energy great things may be expected of them in the future.

During the general discussion of topics of special interest, it was gratifying to learn that there were a number of resident Moravians in the Convention City, and a plan was suggested by which it is hoped, not only to bring these into closer churchly fellowship, but to discover others also.

THE AFRICAN M. E. AND AFRICAN M. E. ZION RALLY.

Rev. B. W. Arnett, presiding.

Not only the white but the black Methodisms are beginning to realize that blood is thicker than water, and to edge ardently towards each other. The joint rally held at Shorter A. M. E. chapel, and presided over by a son of the beloved Bishop Arnett, was a good example of this.

R. G. Nelson of Arkansas gave a short talk on Christian Endeavor in his State. Short talks were also made by the Revs. A. A. Burleigh, J. H. Hubbard, and J. T. Smith.

The principal address was delivered by William F. G. Sherman, of Savannah, Ga. His subject was "Christian Endeavor and its Relation to the Negro." He took an optimistic view of the situation, and declared that the future of the negro race lay in the great Christian Endeavor movement. He also spoke of how the white people of the South aided the negro in this movement. Mr. Sherman made an eloquent appeal to the members of his race to do everything possible for Christian Endeavor work.

THE BAPTIST RALLY.

Rev. Clarence A. Barbour, D.D., presiding.

The main auditorium of the First Baptist Church was filled with a joyous, responsive audience of Baptist young people, who sang Baptist songs, spoke along Baptist lines, and gave free rein to the expression of denominational loyalty, not forgetting, however, in their prayers for their own brothers and sisters, to remember the world-wide field.

The interest in the afternoon's programme rather centred about the address of the Rev. Walter H. Brooks of Washington, D. C. He was a black man of the blackest dye, and was so introduced by the presiding clergyman, Clarence A. Barbour, of Rochester, N.Y. And in his remarks Mr. Brooks recurrently touched upon the topic of his racial distinction, and not without well-tempered pride.

"I believe in denominationalism," he said, — at first confining himself to his assigned subject, "Denominational Loyalty," — "at least for the Baptists. But I also believe that there are some issues which require broader platforms. En-

deavor is one of them.   We can all get together in this movement, and I think
we all are together."

The Rev. James H. Franklin, of Cripple Creek, spoke upon the suggestive
subject, "Company No. 1."   The Rev. Stephen A. Northrup of Kansas City was
assigned the subject, "The Pastor's New Guard," and he turned it to the advantage of lauding the work of the Christian Endeavor organization.   In substitu-
tion for the programme space allotted to Dr. Vosburgh of this city, who was
unable to attend the Rally, H. B. Smith, press agent of the committee of 1903,
filled in with a few apt words of welcome in the name of the absent pastor.

A pleasant feature of the Rally programme was the solo singing by Miss
Laura Northrop of Kansas City.   Miss Northrup is a vocalist of wide repute
in the East, and Middle West, where she has done some concert work and given
many recitals.

The Baptist Rally ended with an informal reception in the rooms fitted for
the entertainment of delegates.

THE CHRISTIAN RALLY.

Rev. Horace Mann, presiding.

A quiet company, but one thoroughly enjoying itself, were the representatives of the Christian Church.   Their addresses, papers, parliaments, were all thoughtful and pithy, and the writer, who was present a part of the time, was deeply impressed with the intense practical
spirit of the Endeavorers present.

THE CONGREGATIONAL RALLY.

Rev. E. L. House, D.D., presiding.

Plymouth Congregational Church was overcrowded.   People filled
the aisles and stood on the door-steps.   There were many lodestones
drawing them, chief of which, perhaps, was Rev. R. J. Campbell, of
City Temple, London, though Rev. Harlan P. Beach, Rev. Smith
Baker, Rev. W. H. Brooks, the black orator, and Rev. J. L. Hill were
magnetic enough to fill such a house.

The rally in the church was opened promptly at 2 o'clock by the Rev. E. L.
House, of Portland, Ore., who delivered an address on a "Model Christian Endeavorer."   He was followed by the Rev. H. P. Beach of New York City, who
discussed "The best investment for the Y. P. S. C. E."

One of the best addresses of the afternoon was that given by the Rev. Smith
Baker of Portland, Me., on "The Y. P. S. C. E. esprit du corps."   He argued
that the Congregational Church was not the largest in the work, as well as the
most powerful, simply because its members were too good.   When a church of
their own faith was not available for worship, they would readily join another
church rather than be disbarred from services.

An open parliament was conducted by Dr. J. L. Hill of Salem, Mass., in
which each member of the audience was given just a minute and a half to tell
why he or she was glad to be a Congregationalist.   Then came the address by
Mr. Campbell and the close of the services.

THE METHODIST PROTESTANT AND UNITED BRETHREN RALLY.

Rev. H. F. Shupe and Rev. C. H. Hubbell, presiding.

The representatives of these two denominations who assembled in
Smith's Chapel were on the *qui vive* because of the recent courtship

GOVERNOR PEABODY.

REV. R. J. CAMPBELL.

CONVENTION SPEAKERS.

which is expected to lead to a union of the two denominations. And they were not disappointed. "How to get together" was the key-note of the meeting, and all went as merry as a marriage bell.

Miss Belle Waldo read a bright paper. Rev. John F. Cowan, associate editor of *The Christian Endeavor World*, spoke on the theme, "Fraternize." Rev. J. E. Fout, president of the Ohio union, made an address of "The United Churches and Christian Endeavor." Dr. L. S. Cornell read a paper on "The United Churches and the West." Rev. C. H. Hubbell, Rev. J. L. Hartzell, Rev. H. F. Shupe, and others spoke. Not only were ardent expressions for union rife, favoring the speedy organic union of these two denominations, but a fraternal message was sent to the Congregational rally, which was cordially reciprocated.

THE PRESBYTERIAN RALLY.

Dr. J. W. Cochran, presiding.

Presbyterian rallies are always vigorous, of full volume and attractive, and this one amply sustained the past record. The absence of President George B. Stewart, of Auburn Theological Seminary, who was to have presided, was a distinct note of disappointment. All joined in a prayer expressing sympathy for his recent loss of his wife.

Union of all branches of the Presbyterian Church in America was warmly advocated by the Rev. William Patterson, D.D., of Philadelphia.

Dr. Patterson's subject was "Our Fellowship," and he said that until a plan of consolidation among the various divisions of the Presbyterian Church could be carried into effect it was good to have fellowship among the brethren.

"I believe the time is coming when we are all going to get together," said Dr. Patterson. He declared the tendency of the hour was towards unionism. There was only one Presbyterian body in Canada.

Von Ogden Vogt, the new general secretary of the United Society of Christian Endeavor, spoke eloquently on "Our Secretary," and the Rev. George W. Wright spoke on "Our Foreign Missions." Mr. Wright goes to the Philippines, after a successful pastorate in Chicago. His address was forceful.

Three rapid-fire five-minute talks by foreign missionaries were given by the Rev. A. G. McGraw of Etah, India; Rev. H. C. Velte of Lahore, India, and Rev. Charles E. Bradt of Wichita, Kan., whose church is supporting twenty-five missionaries.

"The Church Side of Home Missions" was discussed by the Rev. James J. Dunlop of Roxbury, Mass. Rev. Sherman H. Doyle, D.D., of Philadelphia, spoke of "The Organization Side of Home Missions," and the Rev. Dr. Robert F. Coyle of Denver on "The Field Side of Home Missions."

Dr. Coyle was given the Chautauqua salute and hearty hand-clapping when he arose.

Rapid-fire five-minute talks by home missionaries followed, the first, by the Rev. A. J. Johnson of the Sioux Indian agency. He said there were Presbyterian Churches in South Dakota filled with Christian Indians. The son of Sitting Bull was a church officer.

Refugio J. Jamello, a Mexican from Walsenburg, Col., spoke in broken English.

Mrs. A. M. Hendee of Central City, Col., spoke from the standpoint of a home missionary's wife.

Dr. John F. Carson, of the Central Presbyterian Church of Brooklyn, conducted the closing three-minute consecration service.

CHAPTER VIII.

Sweet Fellowship.

FRIDAY EVENING, TENT ENDEAVOR.

When the hour for opening arrived a fringe of people ten feet deep surrounded the tent, anxious to catch what they could from within. The audience was estimated at 15,000. There were two interrogation points in every eye — "Shall we be able to hear Mr. Campbell?" "What does the petition mean about which the Denver papers have said so much, asking for the union of all young people's societies?"

Nevertheless curiosity did not fret a bit during the magnificent address of Rev. Clarence A. Barbour, D.D., of Rochester, N.Y., He is a Baptist who is proud of his Baptist faith, and there was pith, point, dignity and classic finish in his address on

THE FELLOWSHIP OF THE DENOMINATIONS, AND HOW IT WILL HASTEN THE COMING OF THE KINGDOM.

"Thy kingdom come!" It is the majestic petition of the prayer which rises like the voice of many waters from this vast throng. "Thy kingdom come!" It is our starting point for the discussion of a theme so comprehensive that the attempt adequately to treat it within the time limit is hopeless.

Matthew's gospel is distinctively the gospel of the kingdom, but in a very true sense the Bible throughout is the book of the Kingdom. If, as one has suggested, the conception of a suffering Redeemer runs as a blood-red cord through the Scripture, it is no less true that the conception of the all-embracing Kingdom and the all-conquering King runs through all the Scripture as a cord of royal purple.

My fundamental proposition is that the Kingdom is of supreme and transcendent importance. The kingdom of God, that divine polity over which Jesus Christ is King of kings and Lord of lords, — that claims preëminent fealty.

The Kingdom is of greater importance than the local church, of greater importance than any communion in any community, of greater importance than any single denomination. With any different conviction the denominations easily become "sects," something cut off in sympathy, as well as in organization and belief, from the rest of the Christian world.

There is real danger that the local church or the denomination be exalted above the Kingdom of God.

Referring to the fact that our Roman Catholic friends say that Protestantism is split up into innumerable little sects, quarrelling among themselves," he said:

That was a mighty service which Bismarck, the Iron Chancellor, did for Germany. He found scores of little German principalities, independent cities, each one making its own laws, acknowledging its own sovereign, having no interdependence with any other German State or city. Bismarck lifted up before the

German people the conception of a united Fatherland, and through that enlargement of horizon has come the power and glory of the German Empire of to-day.

I believe that we are coming to recognize the essential unity of *the* Church, the Church which is co-extensive with the kingdom of God. Many mountains, one globe; many ravines, one mighty earth mass, vastly greater than the wrinkles on her face; many regiments, one army; many denominations, one church; many creeds, one faith; many ways up the hill, one city at the top, where sits the King on His throne. Denominationalism, wisely managed, may be used for mutual provocation to love and good works. Perhaps it is better to be broken up externally, that each denomination may do its own work. But there must be recognition, and that recognition more than a nominal one, of the practical fellowship, the co-operative fellowship of believers.

Referring with pride to his Baptist birth and training, Dr. Barbour drew a picture of a sectarian bigot that was calculated to make small men squirm; but while the latitudinarian laughed at the squirmer, he himself caught it hard through a caricature of " Mr. Face-both-ways," which led to the declaration:

To-day the pendulum has swung to the other extreme. We are in a day when mischievous moral malaria steals subtly into the fibre of strong endeavor. The age is drunk with materialism, the south wind blows softly, and multitudes are enervated by its soothing touch. Some would seem to think that in this day the tower of a lofty Christian life and character and the great splendid structure of the Kingdom of God are going to leap up in the night like Jonah's gourd; that we are going to wake up some fine morning to find the building miraculously finished, without our endeavor, to the turret-stone. Understand me, the heart of the church still beats strong and true, but great masses of nominal Christians are in a lotus-eating atmosphere, listless, idle, unaccomplishing.

"And in the afternoon they came unto a land
In which it seemed always afternoon.
All round the coast the languid air did swoon,
Breathing like one that hath a weary dream.
Full-faced above the valley stood the moon;
And like a downward smoke, the slender.stream
Along the cliff to fall and pause and fall did seem."

No wonder if one in such an atmosphere views with utter indifference those whose names are next his on the muster-roll of the Kingdom.

Dr. Barbour delighted his audience with a succession of terse, polished epigrams: " Federation is fellowship put into practice." " What can the world find to hate in shoals of people whose religion is confined to their tongues?"

Speaking of the good beginning already made in many ways toward realizing fellowship, he said:

Let me suggest two thoughts which may strengthen us in our fellowship. I. *The enemies of Christ and His followers are neither dead nor sleeping.*

Luther said, as a representation of the church in his day, "Who would paint a picture of the present condition of the church, let him paint a young woman in a wilderness, or in some desert place; and round about her let him figure hungry lions, whose eyes are glaring upon her and whose mouths are open to devour her substance and her beauty."

That is the natural condition of the church. When the church in that age, in this age, in any age, is truly alive, and is fulfilling her destiny, she will find about her, as of old, men more cruel than ravenous beasts. Is it true that there is to-day little of the heroic in religion to appeal to men? Alas for us if that be so! The statement comes from some of our theological seminaries that there is some dearth of candidates for the ministry. Why? Why is it that the ministry does not appeal to every stalwart, able, earnest, unselfish Christian man in his college days? It does to some. A part of the product of our seminaries to-day was never surpassed. But why does not the claim of this great vocation press upon *every* such an one, until it is soberly settled one way or the other?

IT IS NOT BECAUSE YOUNG MEN ARE AFRAID.

There was no difficulty in filling up the ranks of the Rough Rider Regiment, though every man knew that he was taking his life in his hands when he volunteered. There was no lack of volunteers for service when the Merrimac was to be sunk at the mouth of Santiago Harbor, though it meant a voyage into the jaws of death. Eight men were needed; you know the response to the call for volunteers. One has put it into verse which ought not to die.

> Eight volunteers! on an errand of death!
>> Eight men! Who speaks?
> Was there a man who in fear held his breath,
>> With fear-paled cheeks?
> From every warship ascended a cheer!
> From every sailor's lips burst the word — "Here!"
> Four thousand heroes their lives volunteer!
>> Eight men! Who speaks?

I will not believe that there is among our young men a lack of courage, a lack of willingness to suffer. Can it be that young men have made up their minds that with the present spirit in the church there is little demand for the heroic in her ministry? They say that a minister makes his church. He does leave his stamp upon the church, but it is no less true that the church makes the minister. And the minister will not go far beyond what the church requires, or at least he will not go far beyond the point to which the church will follow him. If the church of the living God is to any considerable degree honeycombed with indifference, permeated with the dry rot of lethargy, if the heroic element in the church is dying, then the church may hold itself responsible for any diminution in number, and for any lessening of stalwart efficiency in its leadership.

CODDLED MINISTERS.

No man of strength and self-respect is going to submit to being regarded merely as a convenient adjunct to weddings and funerals, as a kind of family pet to be coddled and fed with sweetmeats. If the church wants much that is heroic in her leaders, she must have much that is heroic in herself.

II. *The insistent call for service has not ceased.*

Thank God, history shows that the call has not been in vain. In the sordid stream of the life of this world it is good to think of men and women who have not pleased themselves, but have gone about doing good, great souls who in their stubborn devotion to the truth, in detestation of falsehood and lies, have faced a lying world and the hatred of the base and the storm of weak and cowardly criticism, not holding their lives dear unto themselves, have stood like Savonarola and Luther before kings and priests and were not ashamed. Like Howard, visiting all Europe, "not," as Burke said, "to survey the sumptuousness of palaces and the stateliness of temples, but to survey the mansions of sorrow and take the gauge of despair." Like Lord Shaftsbury, taking up the cause of children in the streets, in the factories, of women in the mines, of little ragged waifs and strays. Like William Lloyd Garrison, living on bread and water, setting himself to the colossal task of proving to twenty millions of his countrymen that they were horribly wrong with regard to the slave trade.

I hear someone say, "We have had no such call as they," but we have. The only call they had, we have, — the call of the need. We might, the humblest of us, be useful. Perhaps very few eyes will be wet for us, and they not for long, while others, with less of opportunity than ourselves, have gone down to the grave amid the benedictions of the poor. Ah, the insistent call for service has not ceased. Can we not strive to rise, to rise unitedly, to rise in ever strengthening fellowship, into such a life as is described by the words spoken of our blessed Lord, — "He went about doing good"?

The great Methodist leader, John Wesley, the bicentenary of whose birth has but just been celebrated throughout the Christian world, nobly said, "I desire a league offensive and defensive with every soldier of Christ." So say we all. Let it be repeated in ever-increasing volume, until the earth shall be full of the knowledge of the Lord, as the waters cover the sea. "*We* desire a league offensive and defensive with every soldier of Christ."

A Topeka minister, a co-laborer with Dr. Charles M. Sheldon, and an expert in prison reform and salvage of prisoners, contributed an interesting feature of the programme, and linked in the world-wide fellowship of Christian Endeavor the "Brother in bonds," the Prison Endeavorer. The speaker was Rev. E. A. Fredenhagen, and his theme

PRISON ENDEAVOR.

Prison Christian Endeavor is one of the series of movements reaching out for the redemption of our brother in bonds. Although the people in the prisons of the United States are 100,000 in number yet prison Christian Endeavor has so far only conquered twenty places for itself, with about 2,000 members. Reports come to us of a great growth under the ten per cent increase. From Utah comes an increase of sixty per cent; from Virginia, one hundred and twenty-eight per cent.

It remains for another State which has high ideals, which does no thing lightly, which arises in its resurrection from dearth and affliction, which dares to put its hand on the saloon and crush it out — it has remained for Kansas to come to the front with one hundred and sixty per cent increase.

The average of a prisoner upon entering a prison of the United States is about the average age of the people in this convention, or less. These prisoners are from your homes, from your villages, from your cities. Go into every county jail and State prison, lay your hands upon those who are dropping below the crime line and prove that Christian Endeavor can prevent crime as well as redeem the prisoners in the prison.

There is no logical connection between penetentiaries and sailors, though they happened to be next-door neighbors on the same programme. Ex-Chaplain Robert E. Steele of the U. S. Navy, now superintendent of the Sailors' Rest, Newport News, Va., is splendidly equipped for presenting that interesting work. His theme was

FLOATING ENDEAVOR AS AN EVANGELISTIC AGENCY.

Floating Christian Endeavor stands for faithful testimony on board ship. Its members are marked men. The little badge worn on the blue uniform speaks constantly to all on board, telling that one at least is not ashamed to own his Master and his Lord.

Floating Christian Endeavor knows no church save the church invisible. Differing from the Society on land, it is the fruit that grows directly from the vine, rather than from the branches. Its point of union is loyalty to Christ. Church organization is impossible afloat. Many most sincere Christian sailors are not members of any church.

It is a sufficient test of sincerity for a man on shipboard to be willing to take the pledge, and wear the pin of the Society. The hypocrite is a fungus which does not long endure the fire of persecution at sea. A Christian sailor is under constant observation. A thousand eyes mark every word, every action. There is nothing to be gained by a false profession of faith in Christ, therefore Christian sailors are usually true stuff. Unite these men, identify them, and you have organized a mighty agency for evangelization.

There should be no associate members in the Floating Society. Like the Spartans at Thermopylæ, none but heroes willing to die at their posts, are fitted for this conflict. The fight is one for life against the darkest forces of hell. Its reward is a Crown and Kingdom. It is not a kindergarten, but a band of Christian warriors, whose war-cry is "The Old Guard never surrenders." In the highest sense, to join the Floating C. E. Society means a public, unqualified profession of faith in Christ. What we need is not quantity but quality — not numbers but sincerity — not endorsement but co-operation.

Rather a society of two members dead in earnest than a hundred half-hearted. Nine boys on the Charleston founded the Nagasaki home. On one of our great war vessels — hero ship of the greatest naval victory in our history — there is a Floating society composed of two only. For over six months no Protestant service had been held for her 600 sailors, when we went aboard one Sunday in May. For six months more these two must stand for Christ alone among their comrades.

It is the speaker's firm belief, based on his experience both in forecastle and ward room, that nothing can work so much good in the navy as the Christian Endeavor Society.

Floating Christian Endeavor has demonstrated its possibilities. For a period equal to four enlistments of three years each, it has won its trophies for Christ afloat. Hundreds of sailors have through it been pointed to the "Lamb of God which taketh away the sins of the world."

In Boston, Portland, Brooklyn, Norfolk, San Diego and Vallejo, its work has flourished. In Nagasaki it established and maintains an institution second to none in existence in real efficiency. Its graduates are to-day preaching and living the gospel in all parts of the world. Three noble heroes, best of all the band, gave their lives on duty's altar, when the Maine was destroyed. It is and has been a living force for righteousness, purity, and temperance.

Missions *to* the sailors have been tried for many years, with meagre results. Now let us build up and strengthen this Mission *of* the sailors to their comrades.

And soon the time will come that wherever flies our flag afloat, the grander banner of the cross will also spread its snow-white folds. And on foreign shores and at home the eager feet of our sailor lads will tread the paths of righteousness and purity, and a mighty anthem of prayer and praise mingle with the ocean's constant music, rising from the fullness of the sea to the great white throne above.

It was at the close of his address that one of the most meaning incidents of the day occurred. He turned to the president of the Convention, Rev. Francis E. Clark, and, taking from his breast a little American flag, presented it to him as president of the United Society. It was the first American flag ever floated in the Philippines and was a gift from the Christian Endeavorers in the United States Navy.

After the battle of Manila, when the Spanish force had surrendered, Admiral Dewey sent a squad of marines under a lieutenant to hoist an American flag over Cavite, the first fortress to fall. Two of these men were Christian Endeavorers. One of them climbed the battlements of the fort and raised the flag. When it was lowered to be replaced by a larger flag, it came into the possession of himself and his comrade. He was killed in a skirmish battle a few months later and the comrade gave the flag to Chaplain Steele to be presented to the Christian Endeavorers, as a sign of their need for the work of the Society in the navy. The flag was received amidst salvos of applause. The audience was then requested to sing "America" and "God Save the King." In doing so it was assisted by Cook's Drum Corps, which occupied a place in the choir.

As the sound of the national anthem died away, President Clark introduced to the audience the noted English divine, the man of all men whom many had been waiting to hear, Rev. Reginald J. Campbell, pastor City Temple, London, England, whose theme was

The Fellowship of the Nations and its Effect on the Coming Kingdom.

Dr. Clark and fellow Christian Endeavorers, I hardly think that you are likely to hear my voice the length and breadth of this great pit, but I must thank you for the way in which you have gratified a visitor from old England who has come a long way to see this Convention.

While you were singing "God Save the King," you brought a lump into my throat, for there is something more than accident that in your country and in mine the same tune is set to our respective anthems. I am ashamed to have to confess I do not know the words of your anthem, or I would have done something else than hum the tune.

Someone cried "Louder." He responded, "Did someone speak to me? Now it is no use for you to do that; I cannot speak a bit louder, and I am sure many will not be able to hear me."

But when he warmed up and the side curtains of the tent had been lifted to place he was distinctly heard all over the vast audience.

When we were coming up in the train together the Connecticut contingent, myself, and my wife, we had a little exercise in singing together, and among other things we sang "God Save the King," and some of the Connecticut people present pretended they did not know it. I did not pretend that I did not know the American anthem, for I assure you, beyond the first line, the rest was new to me. I am learning it and the next time the Christian Endeavor Convention is held in England I hope to start the singing of your national anthem.

My subject for to-night, Endeavorers, was given to me by Dr. Clark. That very fine speech to which we listened to-night with such pleasure, concerning what fellowship should be, from your fellow countrymen, who spoke on the Kingdom, taught me not a little of what that fellowship ought to be.

At the moment when the Master was announced the world was ripe for such a message because political union has been achieved, such as has never been achieved before, the eagles of Rome were soaring over the civilized world. There was administrative union in that imperial city. In that time the Christ you and I know now had not come into existence. There was no "God Save the King" or "Star-Spangled Banner," but at that time the world looked to Rome and Rome ruled the world, and from out of that imperial city there came an imperial idea of the church.

To-night we are all turning our thoughts towards that distant city, towards which the spiritual head of the great principles of Christendom lies dying. None but those who are in sympathy with the Roman Church can realize what it was once in history when the Roman bishop was the master of the political world. A great attempt was made, and I think in some cases, and perhaps for the most part, honestly made, when the bishop of Rome as the vicar of Christ gave law to emperors and kings. The idea of Hildebrand, as Gregory the seventh, has been described as the most magnificent failure in history. You intelligent Americans will not need to be told what it was, who tried to set up a reign of righteousness. The help of God giving law to lawless. He was defeated, and in his dying hours confessed his failure, and Rome went on conquering the world. The kingdom of Christ cometh not by force.

Long centuries after that, another set up the same ideal in a smaller and more beautiful way. Savonarola, the great prophet of Florence, preached the kingdom of God, self-content wherein dwelleth righteousness. They put him to a shameful death, and the great prophet Guenna, whom George Eliot makes him say in the last hour, "When friends forsake me, I think in darkness, I am as nothing, yet the light, Savonarola, I see was the true light." The fair ideal which we want to look at together to-night he could not realize. Why? Not because he drew the sword to do it, but because the people for whom he tried to realize it drew the sword on him. They were not ready for the King.

A friend of mine, who just came back from Florence tells me a great thing. There stands conspicuous a colossal statue of the prophet Savonarola, and upon the base are inscribed the words, "Justice after Four Hundred Years," (*Applause.*) a more magnificent failure than Hildebrand, for the man tried with the love of Christ to bring about the kingdom of God in a political society and failed and died.

A mysterious feeling of sympathy seemed to quiver over his vast audience as he spoke of Savonarola, "the grandest failure of centuries," as he termed him, and it was borne in upon all that Campbell must be a living counterpart of the man who so strangely moved Florence. The idealism, the touch of mysticism, the almost hypnotic power with which he swayed his audience to his will, all showed the man as he was.

That is not all. Our Puritan fathers, to whom the eloquent speaker who preceded me, made reference, tried their hand at this theocracy, too. They had this on their side, at any rate, they were not selfish in their purpose. The moral grandeur of the Puritan has never been equalled in history. Your forefathers and my forefathers were one. I ventured to say to-day, in a smaller assembly, that the indirect effect of Congregationalism was greater than the direct effect on the world. Let me widen the word to include independency, Puritanism on both sides the Atlantic and the covenant of Scotland. My spiritual ancestors, the Puritans, and the Pilgrim Fathers stood together for something. Sometimes they fell out among themselves, but the men who set their feet first upon Plymouth Rock and laid deep and strong the foundations of your commonwealth are not dead, as to their influence on that commonwealth to-day. There is a fellowship of the nations. The Anglo-Saxon race is made possible because the best in our blood is Puritan, and Puritanism is the ideal of the kingdom of God.

I remember when I was at Oxford — I was going to say a great many years ago, but not quite so many as my gray head would seem to indicate —

[Mr. Campbell has been picturesquely referred to as "carrying the silvery crown of sixty on the supple shoulders of thirty." He has a young man's face but an old man's locks.]

I was set to read a certain text-book written by the Frenchman, Bossier. This gentleman tried to trace the origin of civil liberty, and he expected to find it, as all good Frenchmen would, in his own country of France, so he studied very attentively the period of the Revolution. He found he had to cross the Atlantic. He came over here, for he found that the inspiration of the moralists in the Revolution came from this side of the ocean. (*Applause.*) I am afraid you did that too quick.

He found he had to go back, for he found the inspiration of moral grandeur of America came from old England and he ended up in an Independent church-meeting. There it was they made strong men, men who stood for the reign of God in human hearts and rights of the individual to enter into relationship with his Maker without the intervention of prince, or prelate, or priest. Your spiritual ideals in this United States realized, as they are, in this magnificent company, which is made possible by them, have come to you soaked in the blood of British martyrs. You will find, if you go back far enough, things of which you will not be ashamed in the fellowship of nations before this nation was, and may it be the spiritual ideals will be the cause of a closer union between the Old Country and the New Country.

Hung in a conspicuous place near the speaker's platform in the big tent were a Union Jack and the Stars and Stripes, twined about the Christian Endeavor monogram. The eminent London divine who occupies the pulpit made vacant by the death of the famous Spurgeon, repeatedly turned in salute to the intertwined national emblems.

Of the British Empire I was never prouder than I am to-day — and I am not ashamed to say it in the presence of an American audience, for if I were not an Englishman I would soon be an American, you may be sure of that. I feel half naturalized already. I will tell you why.

I bought a crush hat at Wanamaker's, and when I get back I will try whether I can walk down Piccadilly before the Mansion House with it on. They will be surprised, at least, in the metropolis.

I was going to say, "Why should we prate of the comity of our two countries?" We think the two empires can do the biggest things on earth, but we may be mistaken. Some spiritual incentives have come from other races. What about the Moravians? What of the small Swiss people who sent their contingent over here, those heroes who fought against odds in the day of the Reformation, and sent something to England which England sent to you.

To-day I heard a voice from a delegate from Japan raising his testimony in this vast host of Christian Endeavorers and his joint allegiance with us to the Master, Jesus Christ. We are realizing it slowly as the Kingdom comes. It is not one or a few nations but all the nations that must bring their trophies into it. We are not to rest content until the earth is filled with the knowledge of the Lord as the waters cover the deep. Very slowly comes the Kingdom, sometimes it seems we had gone back ages. To-night your warlike spirit came out when Dr. Clark waved his flag in your presence. I saw if there should come a call for volunteers to-morrow the battle spirit would come out again with very slight provocation. Ladies and gentlemen, whether you like it or not, the same thing would be true of old England. (*Laughter.*)

Mr. Campbell delighted his audience with a beautiful picture of a review of the army in South Africa, instinct with a loving loyalty to "a little old woman, a good woman, dying in her palace at Windsor." He quoted Scott's lines, "Breathes there a man," etc., and assured his hearers that when England was gone, and not before, he would emigrate to America.

The Endeavorer motto is "For Christ and Church." Add this to it, "The whole wide world for Jesus." There never was a time when so much was said about Christ as is said to-day, but admiration is not adoration. If any man has not the spirit of Christ he is none of His. One of your earliest poets which in my childhood I learned to love — Longfellow — wrote in the time of your Civil War.

> " I heard the bells on Christmas Day,
>   Their loud familiar carols play,
>   Peace on Earth, good will to men,
>   And in despair I bowed my head.
>   There is no peace on earth, I said,
>   For hate is strong,
>   And mocks the song
>   Of 'Peace on earth, good will to men.'
>   Then pealed the bells more loud and deep,
>   'God is not dead, or yet asleep.
>   The wrong shall fail,
>   And right prevail,
>   With peace on earth, good will to men.' "

But where is the use of talking of human brotherhood unless we realize the divine Saviourhood. I have no patience with a social gospel that is nothing else but social gospel. (*Applause.*) No man can stand in the shadow of the cross without feeling his heart going out in sympathy towards the sufferings of his fellowmen.

You young men are called to big things. There never were bigger problems before men than confront a man in our English-speaking world to-day. You have demons to fight. I heard some of them named from this platform. The demon of lust is not free from your doors. You have a battle with the drink problem, as we have at home. Also the battle for the down-trodden employees who for a bare wage hold on to the far off edge of subsistence.

Some of us don't like to think of these dark corners in our great cities. It is our duty to think of them and go out, and do as the Master would do. You have to break the blank wall of indifference that separates so many of our fellows from the church of Christ. We have to bring them out though it costs something to do it, and you know there is nothing worth having if it don't cost something.

Brace yourself for the conflict, and if America turns to Britain again we may quote a great churchman at home whose message came to this side of the ocean a generation ago. "Be ye as one who never turned his back but marched breast forward. Never doubted clouds would break, never dreamed right worsted, wrong would triumph. Sleeping, rise to fight our battle better. Sleep to awake."

The sentiments of fellowship aroused by this glowing session were not allowed to pass away without the beginning of a movement for their conservation and wide extension. Secretary Vogt presented a petition for the union of all Christian young people in our Endeavor fellowship. Dr. Hamlin the Presbyterian and Dr. Wilson the Methodist spoke in hearty approval of the design. The ten thousand in the audience warmly approved. "Praise God," they sung, "from whom all blessings flow." The petition will be signed by millions this coming year. It will bring before Christendom, as never perhaps in the world's history, the great cause of church union. God grant that in every denomination the petition may be heard and heeded, and our Saviour's prayer be answered, "That they all may be one."

A PLEA FOR THE LARGER FELLOWSHIP OF PROTESTANT CHRISTIANITY THROUGH THE CHRISTIAN ENDEAVOR MOVEMENT, AND A PETITION FROM THE CHRISTIAN PUBLIC.

We, the undersigned, members of churches and Christian Endeavor Societies, and lovers of concord and Christian fellowship, earnestly petition all ecclesiastical governing bodies to allow full and untrammeled liberty to their young people to unite together in the Interdenominational and International Christian Endeavor movement.

This movement, as the history of more than twenty-two years has proved, promotes thorough loyalty to the church and denomination, as well as fraternity between all churches and denominations, and we only ask that in the future the young people may be allowed freely to have both the interdenominational fellowship and the Christian Endeavor name either alone or in connection with their denominational name.

No one can measure the good that has been accomplished in the past by this united movement of millions of youths for good citizenship, pure politics, worldwide missions in home and foreign fields, in prisons and upon the sea; for the unevangelized of our great cities, for promoting confession of Christ and active service among the young people of all churches, and a cordial fraternity with all who love the Master, thus in part fulfilling His dying prayer "that they all may be one." Much has been accomplished, far more can be accomplished, by the constantly increasing hosts in the future, if no ecclesiastical barriers to their fellowship are put in the way.

No other organization has ever done the work of the Young People's Society of Christian Endeavor. No new organization could do it, since the Christian Endeavor Society, for a score of years, has won the affection of the young, and the confidence of the old, and already embraces within its ranks nearly four millions of members in eighty evangelical denominations and more than forty nations.

Not only may the society be an increasingly important link between the denominations but between the Christian forces of all the nations as well; especially the English-speaking nations where it is already so thoroughly established. It brings the younger forces together in their great international conventions; promotes their sympathy for and interest in one another; helps to make war impossible; and a lasting peace, based upon the principles of the Prince of Peace, ever more and more sure.

In missionary lands, where the unity and not the divisions of Christianity should be particularly emphasized, this union of forces is still more important, and any unnecessary separation of forces still more deplorable.

We, therefore, earnestly implore all those who have authority or influence, not only to remove restrictions where any exist, but to promote the reunion of Protestant Christendom the world around, so far as it may be accomplished by the common methods, the united prayers, and the concerted work of the Society of Christian Endeavor.

CHAPTER IX.

The "Development" Meeting.

TENT ENDEAVOR, SATURDAY MORNING.

Percy S. Foster's resonant voice was in. evidence half a block away from the tent. He marshalled the musical hosts with marvellous skill and patience until there was not a laggard, or an Adam's apple that was not vibrating with vocalization.

"I noticed two men and a boy who were not singing that time," he announced at the end of a stanza, during which his eagle eye swept the long rows of seats, as his baton gracefully swept the air. "The chorus would have been much fuller if they had sung. Any one failing to sing this time will be compelled to stand on the seat and render a solo."

Whether it was the terrible threat or no, the volume of jubilant song that arose seemed to stand for the aggregate capacity of all the lungs present.

Dr. James L. Hill, of Salem, proved himself a good toast-master, introducing the speakers with a pat word or two, and lubricating the machinery with his bubbling humor in the form of well-told stories.

The first speaker introduced was Rev. Stephen A. Northrop, D.D., of Kansas City, whose topic was: —

Christ Our Dynamic.

Christian Endeavor puts Christ before all its endeavors, and it was characteristic of our movement that the opening topic should be Christ the Power without which every other resource is useless. Dr. Northrop is a tall, square-shouldered, handsome man, just this side of fifty, with an impressive presence and an easy-running delivery. As he talks he reaches out his long, strong arms and pulls his audience up to him, so to speak.

The word that describes this vital subject has waited nineteen long centuries for an explanation. It is dunamis-dynamic force. It is, however, a word of Christ's own coining. It fell from His burning lips on the eve of Pentecost: "Ye shall receive power." The same keynote was sounded when Paul electrified his Corinthian audience with "Christ, the power of God!" Even before the inauguration day of the Kingdom of Heaven, the great wilderness preacher lifted up his voice, and said, "He shall baptize you . . . with fire!" It was in accord with the Divine economy that Jesus should not only be the Saviour of the world, but the enkindling, dynamic power back of all Christian endeavor, the storage battery, reverently speaking, for on-coming hosts of the redeemed who were to propel His glorious cause to a world-wide supremacy. Within His mighty Personality throbs to-day the energizing potency that is to win this poor, crazy old world God-ward, cross-ward, and heaven-ward.

Christ, therefore, is the motor power to generate and stimulate personal service for the conquest of the world unto Himself, dissipating darkness, scattering light, compelling action, arousing enthusiasm, shattering old forms, creating new methods, awakening dead spirits, and giving new life to sleepy saints. "Not I, but Christ liveth in me," is our motive power, and when it thrills and abides in a Christian Endeavorer, he is a very Boanerges, and the gates of hell cannot prevail against him. Genius, culture, intellect, money and influence, minus this Divine spirit, can never make this sin-cursed world a Paradise. But with almighty God in us — enTHUsiasm — we have exhaustive dynamite sufficient to

BLAST THE KINGDOMS OF DARKNESS.

But take warning, do not reverse the order, "God and I," and make it, "I and God" in this superhuman enterprise. "In the name of the Lord and of Gideon," is the Divine plan. The living Christ within the soul, animating the brain, the hand, the foot, the lips, yea the whole being, will surely Christianize and evangelize the four corners of this earth. From Calvary to the Reformation and from the Reformation till now, this omnipotent power has stirred the hearts of redeemed millions. It was the secret of Paul's masterly achievements. He tells us that "Christ enabled him." The mighty spirit of the Son of God tingled in his veins, and Asia Minor and the Mediterranean Sea trembled beneath the tread of his colossal presence. Without prestige, social or political preferment, he turned the world upside down.

Think of that college of fishermen, poor, illiterate, and timid. Under the influence of one short year's contact, under the impulse of the Christ-power, they go forth charged with enthusiasm, aggressive, untiring, ready for martyrdom. What Christianity needs to-day, what you and I need, what this great host of representative young Christians needs to make them heroes and heroines of the faith, is this Divine life that communicates its own vital energy.

Without this source of power there can be no spiritual awakening.

IT MUST BE INFUSED INTO OUR VERY SOULS.

Suppose yonder is a vast army. Before it is a granite fort which they intend to batter down. We ask them how. They point to a cannon ball. Well, there is no power in that. If all the ranks should hurl it at the enemy, they would make no impression. They reply, "But look at the cannon." But there is no power in that; a little child may play on it. "But look at the powder." There is no force in that. A sparrow can scatter it to the four winds. Yet this powerless powder and powerless ball are put into a powerless cannon, one spark of fire enters it, and then, in the twinkling of an eye, that powder is a flash of lightning, and that ball is a thunderbolt of destruction.

So with our great body of Christian Endeavorers in America, Europe, Asia, Africa, and the islands of the sea. They have human instruments, elegant equipments, open Bibles, long-drawn aisles, cultured hearts, conscience-quickening pledges, inspiring rallies, and all the machinery of twentieth century methods, but, oh for the Divine afflatus and the Christ presence, the dynamics of heaven, the fire of God! Oh for the all-consuming zeal of this Man of Galilee, this God of Calvary! Verily from Bethlehem to Olivet "the zeal of God's house hath eaten Him up!" Yes, and it penetrated the heart of a John and a Peter, a Martha and a Mary.

What a mighty agency for world-wide salvation if this Christian Endeavor host voiced the wish of Brainerd: "Oh, that I were a flaming fire in the hands of God!" or were moved by the sentiment carved on Basil's tomb, "His words were thunder, his life lightning!" The blood-earnestness of a Chalmers, a Judson, a Knox, a Livingstone, and our own Moody should flow into our sluggish veins if we are to take this world for God.

O Thou Christ, give us Thy power, Thy quenchless love, Thy glowing enthusiasm, Thine own dynamic, and the timid will grow bold, and the weak strong, and the stripling with sling and pebbles from the brook shall be mighty as the angel of the Lord.

"This heaven-sent enduement," said Dr. Northrop, "like the rushing wind, is unseen, but potent, nevertheless. The great forces of the world are all invisible, — steam, electricity, gravitation. So with this Christ dynamic. It silently steals over vast assemblies and gives them a spiritual uplift. It fires individual hearts, and puts the live coal of consecration to their lips. Its heavenly flame purges from sin. Listen, do you not hear even now as it moves each heart, enters each soul, and speaks in still small voice: "Whom shall I send, and who will go for us?' Then from quivering tongue there comes the word that reaches the ear of God: 'Here am I, send me.'"

Holy Spirit, Heavenly Dove, hover over us now! Living Christ, quicken us now! Mighty Father, stir us now! Half a soul is a poor drivelling thing, a whole soul is majestic! O, immortal youth of the world, the night cometh. Heaven is dawning! Hell is yawning! In the words of William Lloyd Garrison, let each Endeavorer make solemn compact before high heaven, "I am in earnest — I will not equivocate — I will not excuse — I will not retreat a single inch — I will be heard!"

But how will you be heard, Christian youth? The day of dress-parades and flying banners are over, but the hour of hand-to-hand engagement is at hand. How are you to be heard? In millions of transformed lives which you may lead to Jesus! In the multitude to whom you may tell the story of the "Mighty to save." And how will you do it? In a hundred ways, by letter, by prayer, by face-to-face appeals, by being Aarons and Hurs to your pastor, by the testimony of a goodly life, — in short, by word, by deed, and by song. Let your voice in public and private reveal your personal identity to the Cross.

Dr. Northrop illustrated this point by relating how Patti had once identified herself to a postmaster at Cannes, by using her divine voice in song. He closed with this impassioned outburst: —

Christian Endeavorers, if we are to convince the world of the dynamic power of Jesus Christ, to change human hearts into His own likeness, then we must prove it in life, deed, word, and song. The world will soon discover whether there is music in our soul, and whether the keynote is Calvary.

> "Lord, speak to me, that I may speak
> In living echoes of Thy tone;
> As Thou hast sought, so let me seek
> Thy erring children lost and lone."

To the call for the next number, Amos R. Wells of Boston responded.

"I am going to read you a story," said he, "and see if you can tell what it has to do with my subject — 'Our Resources.'" He told a little tale of misplaced hospitality which was designed to illustrate the theme,

ACTIVE, ASSOCIATE AND HONORARY MEMBERS. HOW TO GET THEM.

I want to tell you the story of Mr. and Mrs. Lonely. It will not seem to have much to do with the subject, but it has everything to do with the subject.

For Mr. and Mrs. Lonely woke up one day to the duties of hospitality. "We have been living for ourselves," they admitted. "People do not call, and we have never had a guest. We ought to have callers. We ought to have guests. What shall we do about it?"

Mr. and Mrs. Lonely viewed the situation.

They were living in a flat. They perceived that if a caller came, his dimensions must not be over two feet, one and three-eighths by seven inches and two-fifths, and he must enter side-wise. So fully awake to the duties of hospitality were Mr. and Mrs. Lonely that they moved at once into the suburbs, where they could afford a cellar and an attic. Still the callers and the guests did not arrive.

"Perhaps," said Mr. and Mrs. Lonely, "our house is not sufficiently attractive." Indeed, it was a bare abode, with little furniture but one rickety table, some chairs, and an organ of which they were very proud because it was the first that Mr. Estey ever made.

So they bought some beautiful pictures, and a lot of flowering plants, and an easy chair, and a bright rug, and a pink piano lamp, with a magenta shade. But still the callers and the guests did not arrive.

To be sure, one caller came, but they did not count him, because he was the minister, and it was his business to come. Why shouldn't a man be counted, even if he is attending to his business? They spoke to the minister about it. "Why do we never have callers and guests?"

The minister was a wise man. He said, "It is because you do not ask them."

So Mr. and Mrs. Lonely began to ask people to come to their house. They asked Col. Cooper, and Mrs. Millionaire, and Professor Ponderous, and Miss Polly Primadonna. Still the callers and the guests did not arrive.

So they consulted the minister again; and he, being a wise man, said, "Perhaps you have asked them only once."

They had asked them only once, so now they asked them many times, and made life miserable for Col. Cooper, and Mrs. Millionaire, and Professor Ponderous, and Miss Polly Primadonna. But the more they asked them the more they stayed away.

Mr. and Mrs. Lonely went to the minister again. "Perhaps," said that wise man, "only one of you has been asking."

That was true, for only Mr. Lonely had asked Col. Cooper and Professor Ponderous, and only Mrs. Lonely had asked Mrs. Millionaire and Miss Polly Primadonna. So now Mr. Lonely asked each of them, and then Mrs. Lonely asked each of them, and then Mr. and Mrs. Lonely went together and asked them in a duet. Still the callers and the guests did not arrive.

Once more they consulted the minister. "Perhaps," said that wise man, "you have been asking only a few people, and not systematically."

That was true, as you know, and at once Mr. and Mrs. Lonely began a systematic canvass for callers and guests. They went up First Avenue and down Second Avenue, and took in all the cross streets. Still the callers and the guests did not arrive.

This time, when they consulted the minister, the wise man gave some especially valuable advice. "Perhaps," he said, "your invitations are general and not specific."

So Mr. and Mrs. Lonely, bent on the duties of hospitality, repeated their canvass. They went up First Avenue and down Second Avenue, and they attended to all the cross streets, and everywhere they said, "Call next Tuesday, at 4:15 P.M. sharp." But still the callers and the guests failed to arrive.

Again they besought their minister to help them out, and that wise man said, "Perhaps you have not been offering them anything to eat."

Well, they certainly had not, so Mr. and Mrs. Lonely once more made their canvass, up First Avenue and down Second Avenue, paying attention to all the cross streets, and at every house they said, "Call next Tuesday at 4:15 P.M. sharp. Cake, ice-cream, strawberries, and lemonade."

They came.

Col. Cooper came, and Jack Nobody. Mrs. Millionaire came, and Sarah Widowsmite. Professor Ponderous came, and Edward Emptyhead. Miss Polly Primadonna came, and Catharine Crow. They came, they ate up the ice-cream, cake, and strawberries, they drank up the lemonade, and they all went promptly away again.

"Why did they all go so promptly?" asked Mr. and Mrs. Lonely. And the wise minister made another wise suggestion, "Perhaps you do not give them anything to do."

Well, they had not been given anything to do, so Mr. and Mrs. Lonely repeated the canvass, up First Avenue and down Second Avenue, doing their duty by the cross streets, and at each house they said, "Call next Tuesday at 4:15 P.M. sharp. Cake, ice-cream, strawberries, and lemonade, followed by something to do."

They came again, so that the Lonely house was crowded. They ate up everything in sight, they drank up everything in sight; but they still stayed on, for the women were curious, and the men wondered what was up.

Mr. and Mrs. Lonely brought out sets of crokinole and dominoes and jackstraws and halma and table croquet and tiddledywinks and ping-pong, and they said, "Here is something to do. Proceed to play." Then the callers tried to play, for they were truly polite, but they did not know how, and the crokinole men got lost, and the halma board got upset, and the ping-pong ball hit Mrs. Millionaire in the eye, so they all went home.

It was then that Mr. and Mrs. Lonely went in genuine distress to their minister.

"How," they wailed, "can we fulfill the duties of hospitality if people will not come, or, when they come, will not stay?"

"There are no duties of hospitality," answered the wise man. "There are privileges of hospitality, there are joys of hospitality, but there are no duties."

"But," said Mr. and Mrs. Lonely, "it would be a privilege and a joy if they liked us. We want them to come because they like us."

"Do you like them?" asked the minister.

It was a searching question.

"No," they answered honestly. "Col. Cooper is proud, and Miss Polly Primadonna is vain, and Mrs. Millionaire is stupid, and Professor Ponderous is oppressive. But we want them to like us."

Then the wise minister led Mr. and Mrs. Lonely, after all their failures, into the true heaven of hospitality. He found a poor cripple, whom they pitied very much. They took him in, they made a lovely home for him; they set him happily to work. Then the minister introduced a lonely stenographer from the country, trying to make her way unaided in the cruel, crowding metropolis. They took her in, and made a happy home for her. As they went on their hearts were enlarged, and their house also seemed enlarged. One inmate was added after another. Cheery songs rang out from garret to cellar. The Estey Organ No. 1 limbered up in every pipe. Happiness and helpfulness proved more attractive than ice-cream and ping-pong. The parlor, every evening, overflowed upon the porch. Mrs. Millionaire began to come, and at last she set the cripple up in business. Professor Ponderous began to come, and learned better than all his books could teach him. Miss Polly Primadonna began to come, and gave the stenographer singing lessons on the Estey organ. Col. Cooper began to come, and at last, being a sensible young man, he married the stenographer. And Mr. and Mrs. Lonely found their names so great a misfit that they seriously thought of applying to the legislature for a change.

That is the story of Mr. and Mrs. Lonely, and I have left only one minute for the application, which is this: —

Don't live in a Christian Endeavor flat. Make room in your society for everybody. Ask them in. Go to them and ask them. Ask all kinds. Ask those that will make active members, and those that will make associate members, and those that will make honorary members. Ask them more than once. Ask them seventy times seven times. Go alone and ask them. Go together and ask them. Ask them in general terms. Ask them for particular occasions. Make things cheery to receive them. Give them something to eat, some genuine food for their souls. Give them something to do, some definite work for themselves and others. First mean it; then ask them as if you meant it. Divide your society into two contesting bands of askers, and see which band can gather the most in. Use all these arts and devices and many more. But remember the story of Mr. and Mrs. Lonely, and into all your asking put the spirit of Christ.

For Christ came to get new members for the Kingdom of heaven His life

Dr. Stephen A. Northrop.   J. H. Bomberger, D.D.   John H. Elliott, D.D.

Dr. F. D. Power.   C. Ogawa.   Henry C. Cloud.

Rev. George F. Kenngett.   Sherman H. Doyle, D.D.   John H. Wyckoff, D.D.

SOME OF THE CONVENTION SPEAKERS.

was one long asking: "Come unto me." And His asking was successful because, first, He gave. Lifted up upon the cross, He is drawing all men to Himself.

O Endeavorers, nail your desires, your time, your strength, upon some cross of sacrifice, if you would draw new members to your societies. For what the world needs, even above method, above system, above activity, and above joy, is the touch of a brother's hand, impelled by the love of our Lord.

Mr. Harry S. Myers is the well-beloved general secretary of Free Baptist young people. He understands the problems of the work from top to toe, and handled in a masterly way the important matter of,

PUSHING YOUNGER MEMBERS TO THE FRONT.

If any good reason ever existed why societies of young people should be formed, that reason to-day demands that young people should be pushed to the front. If a young people's society was ever needed to train us, who have been members for several years, surely the greater number of young people entering the kingdom at the present time calls for a society for the younger young people.

There are at least four adequate reasons why the younger members should be pushed to the front.

First. Our purpose as announced to the churches and the world is to lead young people to Christ and into His church, to develop personal piety, to train them to win their companions to Christ, and to incite them to obey the last command of Christ in evangelizing the whole world. We have neither motive nor desire to swerve from this purpose.

Second. The younger members need to be pushed to the front. Somewhere between five and twenty years ago, some of us were invited, and pushed into the offices of the society. We have received a training for church work. In many instances we are still holding the offices because we have been trained. By this training the society has partially fulfilled its mission to us, and should give the opportunity to these younger members. The young people of from sixteen to twenty are no better fitted for church work than we were when we were pushed into these places, except those who have been favored with the Junior society. They need this special training for the work of the society, and we ought to give it to them.

Third. The church never had so large an opportunity as to-day. The need of real Christian statesmen in making denominational and inter-denominational policies was never so apparent. Every department of church work calls for workers, and every call and every added opportunity emphasizes the need of the church for better trained young people.

Fourth. No pains that we can take are too great to be taken for Christ. Our Master needs and deserves the best that we can do. He needs these younger members. In their lives are spirits, hopes, aspirations that He will use and make beautiful. He needs to have us push these younger members into larger places, that they may work more efficiently with Him.

Likening the Society of Christian Endeavor to a West Point training school, Mr. Myers pointed out four methods of pushing members to the front.

First. We must get them into the society.

Second. We must not speak of the "Senior" society when we mean the Young People's society.

Third. Many of us must refuse to serve as officers and on committees, and push in the younger members, even if they are no more efficient than we were a dozen years ago.

Fourth. We must step aside and take our place in doing the regular work of the church in its various branches.

There was timeliness and point and power about the discussion by
that staunch Endeavor leader of St. Louis, Mr. J. I. McClelland,
who had been assigned for brief discussion,

DEVELOPMENT BY THE QUIET HOUR.

Certainly there are many who realize in their own experiences, as never before, the blessed privilege of "Practising His Presence." Christian Endeavor has
been most unique in its work as an organization. It has ever been resourceful,
blazing its way along many untried paths, and always to the profit of those who
followed in them, but in the "Quiet Hour" a climax has been reached. Other
heights may be attained, but none can surpass it. From this point of vantage
may be realized the fact that much land has been possessed; many valleys of
lowland experiences can be scanned which speak of long travel and weary days
of toil.

We live in exciting times. In the hurry of life, heart and brain are put to
severe tests; the day offers little to quiet the mind, and give proper equipoise to
the life. We must get our bearings before the toil begins — the Master's voice
must be heard before the sounds of earth fall upon us. As the eyelid shuts out
the light, protecting and resting the eye, so the place of prayer may furnish an
ear lid to keep out all distracting sounds.

Mr. Spurgeon has very beautifully expressed this sentiment in the following:
"Standing by the telegraph wires we may often hear the mystic wailing and sigh-
ing of the winds among them, but none know of the messages they bear. So with
the believers' inner life — men may hear the notes of outward sorrow wrung from
us by outward circumstances, but the message of celestial peace, the divine com-
muning with a better land, the swift heart-throbs of heaven-born desire, they
cannot perceive or understand."

Speaking of the opportunity the Quiet Hour furnishes for intro-
spection and retrospection, its reminder of the brevity of life, yet of the
far-reaching consequences of mortal existence, and of the hope it gives
us as we look out upon its possibilities, of saving, uplifting and encouraging weary souls by the way, he said in conclusion:—

Mr. Meyer, I think, has said: "Whatever we are called to do by the grace
of God we will be enabled to do by the power of God." Let us, therefore, act
upon this assurance, and in assuming the covenant of the Quiet Hour, so fittingly
expressed in the following words, "Trusting in the Lord Jesus Christ for strength,
I will make it the rule of my life, to set apart at least fifteen minutes every day,
if possible, in the early morning, for quiet meditation and direct communion
with God," can we not feel that God will call us to many tasks and qualify
us for every service? Let us, therefore, bind ourselves together in this loving
fellowship of "Comrades." I like that name; it speaks of union and communion; it tells of a common need; it also reminds us of warfare, of battles fought
and victories won; it tells us of a leader, and is not "Christ the Captain of our
Salvation"? And shall we not follow where He leads?

Dr. Hill, the wide-awake presiding officer, introduced the next
topic,

DEVELOPMENT BY TESTIMONY,

with a mighty object-lesson. He asked all in the audience to rise if
they could testify from experience to the power of personal testimony
for Christ. It seemed as if all the thousands in the audience rose to
their feet. The speaker was Rev. George W. Wright, who is soon
to prove the power of testimony upon a great field, going as Presby-

terian missionary to the Philippines. He was able to illustrate the power of testimony out of his splendid experience as a gospel worker in Chicago, and he made us all feel that, while our testimony is worthless unless it has a true life back of it, yet our life is almost worthless unless it has a testimony in the forefront of it.

For a number of years I have been trying one day each week to help the young men and young women of Lake Forest College express themselves. I meet a great many who immediately tell me that gesture is altogether foreign to them. "But," I ask, "do you never use your arms at all?" No sooner do they begin speaking than they start to sway back and forth upon the platform. "Now," I say, "you are moving about. Why not organize your movements and have them speak in helpful language?"

So, young friends, I may say to you. It is possible for you to testify. It is simply a matter of determination to organize your speech and direct it to useful ends.

I desire to suggest that the first resources developed are our own. Is it not true that you may read a book and yet not know what is in it until you have told off its contents? Those of you who have most recently been at school understand this. Students have often said to me when failing to make a good recitation, "Why, I knew that before I came over here." But did they? Do we really know anything we cannot express? Do you know your own experience if it be never related? You may think you do. But your confusion comes out in your attempt at speech.

Again, the more one truly testifies, the richer grows the experience. The teacher not only develops certitude concerning his knowledge, but increases also the scope and measure of it.

But a second thought is that our testimony develops another's resources. You meet men occasionally with whom you believe you have little in common until they begin to relate their experiences, when you discover they have many of your own supposedly peculiar conditions of mind, and have thought out the expression of them. When clearly stated by another our own minds come to know themselves. Hence you are to testify, not alone because you know something new, but because you have a common exprience.

Moreover, your testimony not only clarifies another's thought, but develops his testimony as well. Do some of you fail to testify because you think you can do it so poorly? Think of the thousand who hold back for the same reason. Get up and fail, if for nothing else, just to encourage them.

Mr. Wright .told an amusing story of a friend who belonged to a literary club, where every one seemed fearful of reciting. Finally he gave a recitation. Then every one was willing to recite. No one would read a paper or write essays, until he read a paper and wrote an essay. Then every one else was willing. The reason was that no one could do things more wretchedly than he. But no sooner had he announced that he would sing, than all the club got in his way, each tuning up his own voice, otherwise unheard, in order to shut off his attempt at music. But his purpose was accomplished. He had made the dumb to speak.

"Suppose," continued the speaker, "you testify, if for no other reason than to get some one else to talk who is really worth listening to."

But, again, testimony develops the kingdom. Four years ago one of the best young women in our church went to the Christian Endeavor Convention at Detroit, having up to that time never spoken publicly for her Master, although in her heart truly loving Him. The Convention altogether changed her. She gained a victory over herself, and oh, the difference in her life since then. No more does her silence cast reflection on her faith, but her open speech makes it easier for every one else to be a Christian anywhere about her.

There is a mission in Chicago, called the Pacific Garden Mission, where we ministers sometimes go to speak. But I question whether we turn many men to God by our work, for those who come are tramps and drunkards and outcasts. They listen to our message respectfully, but when afterward those who have been redeemed out of lives of shame and sin, such as the most of the audience are living, testify, then the hearers lean forward to catch every sound, wondering whether it would be possible for the grace of God thus to do for them. God forbid that you should have such experience to speak from, but out of that heart which you do possess may the Holy Spirit inspire your open, manly declarations.

The first woman speaker upon the programme, Miss Anna G. Fraser of California, was received with a hearty welcome. Califorina has done magnificent work for the Tenth Legion, and has a right to speak about the development to be gained from generous giving. She spoke on,

DEVELOPMENT THROUGH THE TENTH LEGION.

There is time to speak of just two reasons why the Tenth Legion should appeal to the Endeavorer as a powerful and effective instrument of spiritual power. First, because it is, in so large a measure, a means of solving the ever-present and most important problem of our modern church, that of missions both at home and abroad, and second, because it is the certain test as well as assurance of a deepened spiritual life. I know the subject of church finance has been pushed to one side, I know that it has had to give way to more popular, more spectacular, and, let me say, more easy methods of service. Why talk of money, some say, when we can talk of Christ's grace? Why talk of the need of money when we can talk of the need of Christ's love? Because Christ Himself sits over against the treasury, and has given us this way of using our means for Him, of being co-workers with Him in the extension of His kingdom.

"Vote as you pray," says the ardent political reformer, and "Give as you pray" will surely reform this world for Christ. Christ needs our money that the gospel story may be spread. Nineteen centuries have passed since Christ died, and to-day one-half of the world has never heard even the sound of His name. "We are but playing with missions," says some one, but when Christ's own church awakens to the privilege as well as the responsibility of money gifts, when we give to the evangelization of the world as we give to its education, when we give in some proportion to the way we pray, the mission question will be almost entirely answered. We have heard too much about the size of the widow's mite, and not enough about its proportion — she gave her *all*.

Some would put aside the idea of the tithe as belonging to the Old Testament regime — but the pity of it — that when Abraham could pledge one-tenth of the spoils to the priest of God, when Jacob could take that most sacred pledge, "Then shall the Lord be my God: and this stone, which I have set for a pillar, shall be God's house; and of all that Thou shalt give me I will surely give the tenth unto Thee" — the pity of it that we who have known Christ as a personal Saviour cannot promise what was so freely given by a Jew to whom the promised Messiah was but a future vision.

Miss Fraser went to the very heart of this matter of tithe-paying when she said, "If I want the privilege of sharing in Christ's love, I must take the privilege of sharing in his service."

Sargent, in that great frieze, the Dogma of the Redemption, has told us the story as words fail to do. On the cross is the crucified, dying Lord. On either side, bound to him, types of man and woman, are Adam and Eve. Each holds a cup in his hand and is eagerly catching in it the redeeming love that falls from the outstretched hands of the Christ. That is the lesson for us — if we would stretch out our hands to take of the blessing of His love, and His sacrifice and His redeeming blood, if we would be bound to Him in all the fulness of His spiritual glory, we must be willing to be bound with Him also to the cross of His service and His sacrifice.

All West Virginia honors its State president, Rev. George W. Pollock, who spoke next on the power of our covenant pledge to develop character. It was another step upward in the steady ascent of the morning towards a climax.

DEVELOPMENT BY THE COVENANT PLEDGE.

There are many influences which go to make up character. What a man does repeatedly helps to make him what he is. In other words, habit helps to form character.

The things that we think most about and meditate much upon are a sure index of what we will strive for and, to a degree, eventually become. And, if I mistake not, the purpose of those who formulated the Christian Endeavor pledge was to present to our young people in a visible and tangible form a programme in the hope that an honest effort to carry it out would shape and mould their lives.

The great basal principles of the pledge are worthy of more earnest and prayerful consideration than most of us give to them. And the more we ponder them, the more will we strive to realize in every-day life the fundamental things for which they stand.

If we think much about the strength that is in Jesus Christ and His will concerning us, it will not be long until we find ourselves trusting Him for strength to do whatever He would like to have us do.

One thought, then, upon which I wish to lay special emphasis to-day is the development of Christian Endeavor character by a sustained effort to measure up to the high standard set before us in the pledge. I say *sustained* effort, for that certainly is the suggestion of such expressions in the pledge as, "strive," "every day," "all," "regular," "endeavor," and "my whole life."

"Christian Endeavor," said Mr. Pollock succinctly, "is not a spasm, but a life; not a Sunday practice, but an every-day effort." He showed how the pledge strengthens the will, codifies impulse, and gives to life that steadiness which is power.

The person who takes the pledge conscientiously will often review it and meditate on it, and thus will he be helped and encouraged to grow up to its requirements. "For as he thinketh in his heart — reckoneth within himself — so is he."

Not only does Christian Endeavor character grow by thought, but it develops by obedience as well. This is a second proposition to be emphasized. Right thinking should inevitably lead to right acting. With the Endeavorer, to know should mean to do. Knowledge without obedience will prove a curse instead of a blessing. However, obedience without complete understanding leads to a more correct knowledge. "If any man will do My will he shall know of the doctrine." Phillips Brooks has well put it when he says, "The right thought and the right action make one complete and single man."

Thought and obedience, then, knowing and doing, are two tap-roots of the tree of Christian life that will nourish it and enable it to blossom forth in beauty and fragrance and bear fruit in a happy service "for Christ and the Church." And thus, by this twofold law of development by thought and obedience, are our Endeavorers to be trained "for the cause that needs assistance; for the wrong that needs resistance; for the future in the distance."

Dr. Hill led an open parliament of five minutes, following the address by the Rev. Mr. Pollock, in which all were invited to tell

WHAT PART OF THE COVENANT HAS MOST HELPED YOU?

If any one doubts the loyalty of Endeavorers to the principle of covenants in general and to our Christian Endeavor covenant in particular, he would have doubted no more after hearing the responses. The big tent rang with the testimonies as one after another rose to his feet and told of help he had received from the support given by the pledge. Here are some of the remarks: —

I believe if nine out of ten, ninety-nine out of one hundred children in the public schools will raise up their hands and pledge themselves not to use intoxicating liquor, they will keep it.

If I stand before you a Christian, it is because of the Christian Endeavor pledge. It taught me to pray and read the Bible.

The Christian Endeavor pledge has been the greatest help to me.

The pledge to me is like an anchor to a ship. It keeps me from drifting.

The pledge gives me something to do, and I love it.

I believe very much in the pledge. I would not give very much for a man's Christianity, who wants to take all of God's promises and not give Him anything in return.

Affection is always ready to make pledges.

I stand for the pledge because of its definiteness.

It eaches us to trust, strive, and do.

It helped me to be what the Lord wanted me to be.

The pledge to daily Bible-reading helped me to begin an active Christian life.

The pledge made me a minister of Christ.

When I promise God a few things, He promises me all things.

Like all other open parliaments of the Convention, this could be stopped only with difficulty.

Dr. Hill told the story of Luther's conflict with the devil, whom he conquered by throwing an ink-bottle at him. "Do that," said Dr. Hill wisely, "in all your communities when the devil goes on the warpath: throw an ink-bottle at him." This by way of introduction to Mr. Graff, publication agent of the United Society, who spoke on Resources in Printer's Ink.

Following the open parliament Mrs. W. J. Whiteman rendered "The Messiah." The enormous size of the great canvas auditorium would seem to make the successful performance of a soloist an impossibility, but Mrs. Whiteman accomplished the feat in a most charming manner, singing with apparently the greatest ease, yet sending forth a volume of music that reached every part of the tent.

Dr. A. K. de Blois of Chicago brought to a conclusion this long and practical session by a strong talk on an important question. Would that every pastor in the land could have heard that plea for a loving study of the young people by those in whose care God has placed them!

HOW THE PASTOR CAN DEVELOP HIS ENDEAVORERS.

All development implies an ideal and a movement toward that ideal. As a religious teacher, the minister of Jesus Christ represents the religious ideal. None other is so lofty. It has its perfect expression in the character of Jesus. Paul indicates the goal of all effort: "To me, to live is Christ." To develop the Endeavorer means to set him in the path, and help him on the way, toward the Christ-life and Christly service.

The pastor must bear the brunt of this holy task. He has good material with which to work. The young man in the midst of ʻour modern life is "the heir of all the ages, in the foremost files of time." His are all the conquests and traditions of the past. His are the appliances, the methods, the skill of all the elder generations, in the long upward struggle of civilization. He begins life with an immense equipment. Ten thousand years have toiled and sacrificed in his service.

The Christian youth, the Christian Endeavorer, is yet more highly favored. Besides material and intellectual legacies, he has a spiritual inheritance. He enters a church which has been enfranchised by the heroism of the fathers. No false union of Church and State hinders the play of his free energies. No priest or rubric or confessional stands between his soul and God. To-day no bitter wars of sect, no spirit of devilish persecution, palsy his hand or petrify his zeal, or alienate him from his brother workers in the world's great field. How may the minister of the gospel aid him in fostering a healthy, harmonious and productive life?

The pastor must be something of a psychologist. This is fundamental. To develop his Endeavorers he must know them; to know them he must study them. To him they must be not abstractly a Christian Endeavor Society, but concretely, *the* Christian Endeavorers. He must understand their gifts, their accomplishments, their peculiarities.

A young man said to me the other evening: "I had been in the church to which I belong for six years before my pastor knew me. I met him many times, but he never knew me the next time, until after I had become a deacon." I quote his exact words. Training is impossible on such a basis.

Dr. de Blois showed how suicidal it is for ministers to ignore their young people, or treat them tactlessly, or fail to ponder their characters with "a consecrated shrewdness." "The minister must have not only the power of insight, but also the power of executive control." "He must not only know what needs to be done, and how it should be done, and who can do it, but also he must be able to set them to work." Amen, and amen !

Having found their hearts, the pastor can study, under the most favorable auspices, the personal qualities which distinguish each young life, and differentiate it from its fellows. Thus he learns to know thoroughly the resources, in talent, character, and aptitudes, of his youthful comrades, and having this priceless knowledge he can strengthen and develop these resources. Like the carpenter, he first seeks to know his tools; then he uses them.

We must confess, however, that our training too often fails just here, in its vital beginnings. Almost every pastor is on terms of friendliness, perhaps of real good fellowship, with his Christian Endeavorers. He is interested in their welfare, he prays for their success. He attends their meetings. But there the matter ends. He has not "gripped" them; he has not "got" them; he is not training them. Why? Because he regards them in the mass. He has not studied them as the physician studies each patient, as the lawyer studies the intricacies of every new case.

The problem of the Person is the profoundest of problems. Each Endeavorer, being a Person, is unique. He has no duplicate on earth. He is a microcosm, a world in miniature. To know and know thoroughly each of these persons, who together make up a society, is no light or easy task. Yet the wise pastor will not hesitate. He will make it his most important business to study the drift and bearing of each life. He will remember that he deals with those who are in

a period of transition both intellectually and religiously. It is his high privilege
to train them for spiritual independence, for spiritual maturity. They are not
dumb forces, but human lives, eager, capable, impressionable. Every society is
a collection of related personalities, each of whom has his distinct and tremendous value, his distinct and magnificent outlook for service.

There are two qualities of youth which he should learn to develop. They
are the thirst for achievement and the passion for helpfulness. Youth laughs at
obstacles. Bayard Taylor, in Sicily, alone, without money, without friends,
writes to a former fellow-traveller that he has no idea where his next meal is coming from, but he adds, "I glory in these privations and trials, for I know full well
that in the spirit of youth I will overcome them."

Youth worships ideals. Youth is full of dreams and visions. Youth wel-
comes difficulties. Youth scorns the placid and uneventful life. Youth is armed
with intense energy. Youth is ever ready to "lend a hand." Whatever the
faults of youth, weakness and meanness are not of their number. The pastor
will always find

The Restless Passion for Achievement

a powerful factor in the lives of his Endeavorers. It is newly awakened. It
partakes of the nature of a self-revelation. It is in fellowship with the strong
desire to be of real service in the world, to influence others toward noble ends.
It is interwoven with the high hopes and splendid enthusiasms of an enlarging
life. Here is the great opportunity, for the leader and for those whom he leads.

They have intense ambition; he has wisdom and experience — or he ought
to have. This makes an ideal combination. By thought and prayer, with the
knowledge he already has of them as persons, he should help them one by one
into some form of self-activity. He should show them, by example, precept, and
persuasion, that the highest achievement is the achievement of character, and
that character is only achieved by a self-forgetful service. He should prove to
them that the true spirit of helpfulness reaches out beyond the narrow boundaries of home and church and personal friendships, into the great world-field.
He should inspire them to work for the needy, the discouraged, the lonely. They
are at the period when practical effort is essential to the solidifying of the religious life. They have not emerged from the years which the psychologist calls
"the storm and stress period." The inner life is confused. They need to grow
strong by exercise. But a wise head and a firm hand must direct this exercise,
or it will become churchly rather than evangelistic.

Our motto, "For Christ and the Church," is magnificent. Yet the first two
words are all-inclusive. For Christ first, last, and always must we work. If
we introduce the idea of the church, we should also, in thought at least, add the
idea of human need, which we are to meet in Christ's name. We labor "For
Christ and the Church *and the Man*." Our ultimate aim should not be to win
members for the church, but to win men for God.

Men are More Than Institutions.

Institutions exist for men, not men for them. Train your Endeavorers after
this fashion!

Sometimes we are warned against the evils of over-organization. The danger
exists chiefly in the mind of the zealous critic. The churches in North America
that are over-organized can probably be counted on the fingers of one hand. It
would take a thousand men to count those that are unorganized or ill-organized.
Thoroughness of organization is the watchword to-day in factory, railway, and
bank; with teacher and politician; in matters commercial, social, and philanthropic. In the work of the church, nothing, save the presence of the Holy
Spirit, is so important as the careful and complete organization of forces.

The pastor must always be the master mind in the formation and control of
all organizations. Let him organize the boys and the girls of different ages, the
young men, the young women, the young married people. Let him organize

for open air work, for mission work, for philanthropic effort, for personal work Let him organize for social, physical, æsthetic, and intellectual ends. Let him insist upon conscientious committee work. That word "committee" is a priceless talisman.

FAITHFUL COMMITTEE WORK IS A DYNAMO OF TREMENDOUS POWER.

The pastor who knows how to use it holds the key to the future. His success is certain. Let him have committees and committees and committees, provided they are alive and on fire. And their life and fire will depend largely on the spirit and energy of the pastor himself.

Last in logical order, but not least in importance, the pastor must manifest in all his relations with his young people, a heroic sympathy for all men in every condition of life. He must have something of a heroic strain in his own life and in his way of doing things. And he must make an unceasing appeal to the heroic in others. He must be a hard worker and he must incite others to hard work. Nothing will take such hold of the heart of a youth as to see in his pastor not only a saint, not merely a scholar, but a man who works furiously and who makes other people work the same way. The pastor should be "never idle a moment, but thrifty and thoughtful of others." I just spoke of thrift: it must be joined to a noble thoughtfulness. And so we come once more to the question of heart-fellowship.

Let the pastor banish the word authority, let him lead in chains the word dignity, let him enthrone and crown the divine word sympathy. Sympathy means more than popularity. The eyes of the young people may brighten and sparkle when the minister appears. They may laugh at his wit and cluster about him to hear his stories. They may wonder at his brilliancy and feel proud of his friendship. But the test question is: Will they come to him with their doubts, their trials, their heart-troubles? Do they merely admire, or do they truly love and trust him?

Changing a little the thought of the Abbe Roux, we may say that the minister must be "a shower to the heart burned up with grief, a sun to the face deluged with tears." His training of his Endeavorers should spring from the pure passions of a heart aflame with love and tenderness. If he enter affectionately into their deepest feelings and aspirations, they will enter grandly and loyally into co-operation with his plans and work.

Decrying the prevalence of caste in city churches, Dr. de Blois told how his own Endeavorers in Chicago, though members of a "family church," are not ashamed to sing in street meetings, and one of his young men is chairman of the open-air Evangelistic work for the Endeavorers of Chicago.

Through these three qualities of insight, executive force and heroic sympathy, the pastor may mould mightily the lives of his Endeavorers. But the ideal of all training, the development of Christlike character, must ever be within the sweep of his vision. We are not earth's progeny, but children of heaven's King. We work not for the meat which perisheth, but for the life which endureth. We are builders for eternity. If the chief cornerstone is not firmly set, the storms of this rough age will surely wreck the building. All development must be toward Him, the peerless one, the ever-living Christ. We study the book that we may know Him. We pray that we may learn His will. We worship that we may gain more of His spirit. We give that His gospel may reach the regions beyond. We preach and we listen that we may interpret Him more perfectly.

CHAPTER X.

Sparks From Workers' Anvils.

SATURDAY MORNING, CENTRAL PRESBYTERIAN CHURCH.

Two facts were sufficient to put "ginger," as a Denver paper phrased it, into the conference of State, district, and local union officers. One was that the report of a gain for the year of 2,400 new societies went tingling and thrilling through the audience. The other was that Dr. Clark himself presided, and was in his most inspiring mood.

After Mr. Jacobs had opened with an uplifting song service, and Dr. Clark had appointed Mr. Chase, of Nebraska, as time-keeper, and had made a happy talk upon the importance of the meeting, and prepared the way by his tactful, cheerful way of making every one feel that his is the most important place on the programme, some quick, sharp ten-minute papers followed, the first of which, by Mr. Henry H. Marcusson, president of the Illinois union, was on

CONVENTION PROGRAMMES: WHAT SHOULD THEY CONTAIN?

A Christian Endeavor convention should be distinctively Christian Endeavor. Emphasis should be placed upon that which will make it so. A distinctive feature of a Christian Endeavor convention, therefore, should be that which will place before the delegate most impressively suggestive methods helpful in the routine life of his home society, workers' conference, or round table. Such a conference, at a convention, appeals to an Endeavorer because it throws light upon the problems with which he is incessantly grappling, — methods of work, schemes.

Here are gathered together a host of successful workers. The enthusiastic ones. They bring in array innumerable plans for development of every phase of Christian Endeavor, — hints to officers, plans for business meetings, variety in the conduct of the prayer meetings, an idea for a novel social evening, a suggestion for an instructive missionary meeting, a service of song, how to fill the front seats, etc.; the very best from all sources.

These successful plans, and they are successful because they have been tested and proven such, have not only helped the one who is receiving them as a suggestion, but also the one who has offered them to the conference. The convention has, for the time being, been taken from the convention officers and passed into the hands of the delegates. There is a distinctive value in this. It places a responsibility upon the delegate. It has become his convention. He is necessary to it. The conference places tools in the worker's hands. Without them he cannot work.

By way of practical illustration of the ingredients that Mr. Marcusson, would have the cook stir into every convention programme, he referred to his own coming State convention. If all his bright suggestions could be adopted everywhere, conventions would be as juicy and appetizing as Sunday dinners.

Illinois is looking toward an ideal for her State convention to be held July, 1904, the distinctive features of the program to be about as follows:

Frow eight until nine o'clock every morning, Quiet Hour Service; leader, if possible,· to be as able a man as any who is to speak at the convention. The very best only shall be good enough for this. The Quiet Hour establishes the spiritual temperature of the convention. The same leader shall continue throughout the convention in order that the plan of thought may be consecutive.

From nine until ten every morning, Bible study; leader also to be one of the great men of the convention. The one leader shall continue also throughout the convention, permitting consecutive method. The purpose of the Bible study hour shall be to instruct and suggest a comprehensive, intelligent outline of Bible reading for the Christian Endeavorer's daily reading, thus making the keeping of this part of the pledge a delight rather than a duty perfunctorily performed.

From ten until ten-fifteen, a relaxing intermission for social intercourse, purchase of Christian Endeavor supplies and text-book publications, subscriptions to *Christian Endeavor World*, and other helps so bountifully provided by the United Society and so positively indispensible to a live Christian Endeavorer.

᾽ From ten-fifteen until eleven-thirty, the Workers' Conference. No set speeches. No orations. Just a good old-fashioned Methodist experience meeting — a detailed recital of how we did successful things.

In these three sessions daily the delegate feels a personal responsibility, takes an active part, and receives definite, specific help. These mornings of the convention are his and his for hard work.

The afternoon sessions are to be devoted to addresses upon Christian Endeavor themes, the central thought being based upon the fifteenth chapter of the gospel of John, "I am the vine, ye are the branches." "Without me ye can do nothing."

The evening sessions, as usual, with inspiring song service and enthusiastic addresses, commencing promptly at seven-thirty and closing promptly at nine o'clock.

Workers together, fellowship, mutual exchange of plans and methods for greater variety and deeper consecration in every phase of Christian Endeavor, the distinctive characteristics of the most effective convention program.

The open parliament that followed brought out some pertinent and practical suggestions. Miss Kate H. Haus said, "Let there be ten minutes for change of air at the close of each hour."

It was urged that speakers be secured who are interested and can interest others rather than those whom we hope to interest. Still another suggestion was that there be fewer speeches and more open parliaments; "less platform and more floor."

STATISTICS AND HOW TO GATHER THEM

was the census-bureau topic assigned to Mr. H. N. Lathrop, former president of the Massachusetts Union. Like Disraeli, Mr. Lathrop has learned the art of making statistics as fascinating as fiction. His list of "dont's" is spicy and suggestive.

Don't ask too many questions.
Don't ask unnecessary questions.
Don't ask irrelevant questions.

Don't ask questions in July or August. If you get any answers, they won't come till snow flies.

Don't ask questions from your own Society in January, your local union in February, your district union in March, your county union in April, your State union in May. The United Society will ask them in June. The most faithful secretary in the world would not attempt to answer them all. Secretaries of Christian Endeavor societies are not paid salaries to give their entire time to the work of collecting statistics.

Don't use up all your energy running the machine. The supreme business of a Christian Endeavor society is to gather souls, not to gather statistics. any organization statistics have their place and use, but they must not take too prominent a place.

The keynote of it all must be "Simplicity." Better that no society is asked for statistics oftener than once a year, and then have the questions very few, and get those questions answered. Let the State officers, the district officers, and the local union officers confer and decide on the few vital questions that must be asked, and then boil them down to the fewest possible words. A reply postal card, in my judgment, is the best thing to use, and the number of questions asked should not exceed six. Better if you can condense to three or four.

Mr. Lathrop strongly recommended what business men call the "follow-up" system. If a letter is not answered within a reasonable time, he sends a postal headed "Second Request." If that is unheeded, another postal follows, headed in bold red print, "Third Request." Once, when all these failed, he sent a telegram, and it brought the answer next day.

I am a firm believer in the expansion and development of the district or county union, and that in future years the strongest power in the Christian Endeavor organization, outside of spiritual power in the individual society, must be, not the local union, not the State union, but the district or county union. That is the organization that should gather and keep Christian Endeavor statistics. The field of the local union is too small, the field of the State union is too large, but the district union is just about the right size to do that work and much more that can never be thoroughly or satisfactorily done by either a local union or a State union.

He closed with a warning against manipulating the returns that come in order to get the banner, and explained that there were in the world three kinds of lies: White lies, black lies, and statistics.

But, my dear secretaries, after you do get the statistics, make them count. Search out the weak spots in your district as shown by the returns, and devise ways and means for strengthening them. It may be necessary to put the whole Endeavor strength of a strong, live local union into a section or union in a dead or dying condition. If so, do it, and do it before the patient is dead. Too many weak spots are known by State and district officers through statistics, for months and even years, and nothing is done until some day you learn there is a Christian Endeavor corpse at Jonesville and not enough Christian Endeavor mourners left to give it a decent burial. Why didn't you go in there with your Christian Endeavor vitality and hustle and there would have been no funeral?

This meeting was planned on the principle of getting men who had been doing things to tell how they did them. President John A. Rockwood, of the Oregon Union, who led the splendid campaign that won for his State one of the Extension banners, told about

STATE CAMPAIGNS AND HOW TO CONDUCT THEM.

Endeavor workers all over the country are just getting accustomed to the plan, suggested by the United Society several years ago, of holding the International Convention once in two years, and State conventions in the alternate years. It was the plan of the general officers that during the years when the International Conventions meet, district meetings should be held in the different parts of the States, instead of State conventions. Some States continue to hold State conventions every year in the fall, and when such is the case, they usually hold district meetings in the spring. It is regarding this series of district meetings, called the "State Campaign," that I wish to speak to you to-day.

There are two ways of planning for district conventions: one way is for the district officers to arrange for the meeting in their own district entirely independently. A meeting is planned wholly in reference to the district within itself. there are willing, capable officers, such conventions can be made successful. But the other, and, I believe, the better way, is a systematic plan for holding the district conventions in connection with each other over the entire State. Here, as in everything else, system counts, and the advantages of a systematic plan of holding these meetings are many. Let me name some of the advantages arising from a systematic campaign.

Such a campaign concentrates the attention and efforts of the workers scattered all over the State. A single district meeting creates enthusiasm, but a series of meetings carefully planned in connection with each other will produce more interest proportionately than the same number of conventions schttered through the year which are worked out independently. If the district officers can be made to feel that they are responsible for a certain definite part of a general plan, they will be more likely to perform that duty, than they will if they have to initiate a plan of their own. When these officers are strong and forceful persons, the work will be pushed anyway. But if they are a little inclined to hold back and to need prodding, it is much easier and much more effective to ask them to do a definite part, than it is to ask them to push the work in general.

Make the State funds go as far as you can. Have a series of district meetings, so that the same speakers can be worked in tandem, were some of Mr. Rockwood's pithy suggestions.

A systematic campaign enables the State officers to get in closer touch with the district workers. You all realize how important it is for the officers to know the workers and what they are doing. Everything that tends toward this result ought to be encouraged. A systematic campaign through the State is bound to put the officers in touch with each other, for several reasons. Just the mere arrangement of the meetings involves enough correspondence so that the officers must get acquainted with one another, and must learn in some measure what the others are doing. But more than that, it enables more of the State officers to be present at the district meetings, and actually to get personally aqcuainted with the district workers.

The advantages of a systematic plan of State work in connection with the districts mentioned above, were largely brought out in our experience last winter in Oregon. As you are all aware, our greatly beloved Field Secretary, Rev. C. E. Eberman, and his wife made an extensive trip over the Pacific Coast last winter, and on this trip they gave ten days to Oregon. Their visit was made the basis of our campaign. The itinerary was planned so that they could visit every organized district in the State, and it was so arranged that the district meetings followed one another in such a way that Mr. and Mrs. Eberman could go from one district to another and be present at nearly all the sessions of each convention. Some of the conventions lasted two days; some only one. But at every one of them Mr. and Mrs. Eberman were able to speak at least three times. And it was such a treat to our districts!

On the whole, I believe that the best plan of carrying on a State campaign, especially in the States where the organizations are somewhat weak and un-aggressive, is a series of district meetings arranged in connection with each other by the State officers in such a way that they may be attended by as many of the State officers as possible, and by one or two live, experienced Endeavor workers.

As varied as the rainbow hues were the answers to Dr. Clark's query, "Have you found annual or biennial conventions most helpful?"

Pennsylvania, Massachusetts, Illinois, and most of the larger States, declared for biennial conventions; while Utah, Arkansas, and others felt that annual conventions are a necessity.

OPEN PARLIAMENT: HOW CAN WE EXTEND THE INCREASE CAMPAIGN.

Mr. Frederick W. Chamberlain, president of the Michigan union, "worked the pump-handle," as he put it, for the parliament.

The "pump" worked all right. Officers all over the house gave their ideas. Some found it good to visit, and others to write. In Missouri they emphasized the spiritual features of Christian Endeavor, and that extended the work marvellously. New York, Indiana, and other States believed in working through district organizations.

"The first thing you ought to do is to sit down with a good man of your State, and find out where your Christian Endeavor Societies are," said Treasurer Shaw. "and that will show you where they are not. Then you have located the field, Next send word to societies already organized that there is opportunity to organize new societies near them.

Mr. Shaw further suggested marking a map of the State with red circles for the churches and blue centres for the churches that have Endeavor Societies, and giving copies to district workers, showing just how many Congregational, Baptist, and other churches in their districts have no societies.

STATE FIELD SECRETARIES AND THEIR WORK

was handled by a "Christian Endeavor travelling man," Rev. C. H. Hubbell, field secretary of the Ohio union. Mr. Hubbell has a sententious, snappy style, that, with his genial smile and unconquerable optimism, not only attracts attention to what he says, but compels conviction.

The benefits of field work may be classed under two heads: How it helps the State union, and How it helps the local societies.

Let us consider first how it helps the State union.

It helps materially in securing correct statistics and up-to-date information about the county organizations and the local societies. The secretary is able to learn of changes of corresponding secretaries, new county officers, new societies, etc., because he is upon the ground, and gets the facts at first hand. Being in the field continually, the secretary is able to secure a great deal of this important information, and render it available to the State union.

The field secretary can do good service in popularizing the policy of the State union. Every State union has, or should have, a programme of aggressive work for the year. It is true this programme can be pushed by correspondence, and by the State paper if you have one. But even then, the secretary can supplement this work very effectively. He can explain and emphasize that part of the programme most demanding it.

The field secretary, he declared, is the missing link between the programme and the people. He is a travelling clearing-house of new plans and inspiring news. "Tellaman" beats the telegraph for circulating facts.

Let us consider now how the field work helps the local societies.

The secretary can be a clearing-house of plans and methods, and the clearing-house is peripatetic and not stationary. The clearing-house comes to the farthest society. A plan in *The Christian Endeavor World* is good. A plan in a Christian Endeavor worker is better. And the plan is more apt to be impressed by a person than by a paper. The secretary becomes a Christian Endeavor drummer. He is an advertising agency of admirable and applicable aids, and he delivers the goods on the grounds. These conferences on methods constitute one of the most helpful features of the rallies held by the secretary. In the informality of a workers' conference, he can discover and meet difficulties which a score of addresses might never touch. These conferences may be as varied as the need requires. They cover the whole field. Junior work, committee work, officers' duties, the pastor's place, the relation of the society to the church, the indifferent members, and all the problems of Endeavor, may be freely discussed and their solution suggested. Incidentally there are some sweet surprises. Some of the best methods are not always found in city societies, but in small towns and villages. The secretary is learning as well as leading. Bright bits of news are brought out, good enough to print, and they *are* printed after the secretary has been there.

Mr. Hubbell described some of the best work of the field secretary as leading little, discouraged meetings, where the singing is slow, the spirit is low, and the secretary has to furnish the "go," though he feels as if he would like to go out the door immediately.

The secretary can push the forward movements of Christian Endeavor. He will find many opportunities for saying a good word for the Quiet Hour, the Junior work, the Tenth Legion, the Macedonian Phalanx, Civic Clubs, and all the aggressive movements of Christian Endeavor that make for service. In Ohio a "Forward Slip," giving a chance for individual enrolment in a number of these forward movements, has been used with very good results. The plans suggested by the United Society and adopted by the State union can also be emphasized by the secretary. This affords the secretary an excellent opportunity to exalt motive as well as to explain methods. Every forward movement means a firmer faith, a higher hope, a larger love, and a better life. It develops better and bigger Endeavorers. The secretary is certainly not doing his smallest service when he sets forth the forward movements of our cause.

The secretary can promote the fruitful fellowship for which Christian Endeavor stands. He is the living link between the Endeavorers of the whole State. He brings with him into each rally the greetings and prayers of Endeavorers separated by distance, but united in devotion. He brings Endeavor sympathy and good cheer from city to country, and from country to city.

He can inspire his hearers with the realization of a fellowship that is worldwide. He can define the State union. The State union is not an inner circle of a few officials who are seeking fun or favors or fame. The State union is you and I and the other fellow, banded together in blessed fellowship and fidelity "for Christ and the Church."

The State union — every union worthy the name — is a fellowship where the strong hold forth to the weak the hand of sympathetic service, where all, the large and the small, the strong and the weak, feel the thrill of a common purpose, and stand united by the bond of a common service to God and man.

Mr. Hubbell has succeeded in organizing 335 new Christian Endeavor societies in Ohio within the past year.

To such an ideal of a union, to such a realization of fellowship, to such a fidelity of principle and to such a fruitfulness of Endeavor, it is the rich privilege of the secretary to contribute. And in the vision of that privilege, let him seek to be thankful and faithful.

The secretary has his burdens, but he also has his blessings. It is hard work, but it is happy, helpful work. Best of all, it is God's work for him.

A young Endeavorer once said to me at the close of a meeting, "Well, Mr. Hubbell, I — was — glad to hear you, and I — hope — you'll DO BETTER next time." I hoped so too.

And seriously, as we think of our work, so generous in its privileges and opportunities, I am sure the earnest prayer of every worker is, "I hope I may do better next time."

"I've found my brother!" exclaimed Field Secretary Ward, of Colorado and New Mexico, after listening to Mr. Hubbell's description of a field secretary's work. They were, indeed, twins in experience, barring Mr. Ward's picturesque tour of Colorado in a covered wagon with a camping outfit, which experience Ohio's network of railroads denied the peripatetic Mr. Hubbell. Mr. Ward's theme was

INTER–STATE FIELD SECRETARIES AND THEIR WORK.

Entering upon his office of inter-state field secretaryship, the point of personal contact will continue to be his fundamental characteristic. But in the new capacity four distinctive missions will be his. They can only be indicated.

First of all he will fill the large gap existing between the present orders of field secretaryship. A national representative, with almost a continent to compass, will attempt to reach merely the more important cities, while, because of his human limitations, the scores of villages and smaller towns must remain untouched. On the other hand, the States, except in a comparatively few instances, are not even making the attempt to supply the lack. The State field secretary is yet too new a departure for general acceptance; all have not recognized his essential value; the right man has not in every case been available; more frequently the funds for his support are not in hand, or there is a more serious shortage of faith and courage adequate for the task of securing funds. For various reasons the major portion of Christian Endeavor territory lacks the personal touch.

Until such time as must necessarily elapse before the various unions and particularly the weaker ones can hope independently to assume the responsibility, Mr. Ward advised that every State unable independently to support a field secretary should enter a federation of States with this end in view. Only as many States should enter such a federation as one man can properly cover, and the combined efforts of which, according to their several ability, is necessary to the satisfactory support of the work. Homogeneous character or proximity of location will also enter as determining factors.

In that large gap between the national and State field secretary, he will find his peculiar sphere of fruitful labor.

A second special mission will, in many cases, lie along the line of preparing each State under his general supervision for its own representative. Among the possible varieties, the State field secretary will doubtless continue, other things being equal, to be the most efficient point of personal contact. The rapid influx of population and the increasing demand for special and more thorough work with the individual society, will at an early date, at least in the West, indicate State boundary lines as affording ample territory for one man to handle properly.

Inter-state field secretaries, Mr. Ward thinks, can prepare the way for every State to have its own secretary as soon as it is able financially. Some States perhaps may never be able to support a field secretary alone, and some inter-state field secretaries will always be needed.

A third distinctive mission of the inter-state field secretary will be performed to the federated district by a comparative study of its various parts. Each of these sections will present defects or points of strength peculiar to itself. In one case defects will appear with no explanation for their existence other than that no attention has been given to their correction. As notable instances, could be cited the absence of departments for the furtherance of special lines of work; the clinging to the stereotyped, rather than falling in with the progressive; or the undue emphasis of non-essentials to the neglect of those distinctive aims which have made Christian Endeavor a transforming power of young lives.

Taking one's view-point from the narrower field, the defect might easily be overlooked. But when viewed from the vantage ground of comparison with the larger field and in the light of contrasted excellence, the defect becomes glaring.

On the other hand, the inter-state secretary will be able to introduce from one section to another, approved methods and points of strength which have recommended themselves, not from hearsay as mere theories, but from his personal observation of their practical working. Through enlarged vision and careful experimentation, he will thus become to each portion of his territory a corrective of erroneous tendencies, and for the whole an adept personal conductor of a general school of comparative method.

The perfecting of Christian Endeavor thought and activity in the entire federated district, through a comparative study of its integral parts, will merit his most zealous endeavor.

Not to be overlooked or forgotten in the enumeration of his distinctive functions is the value of the inter-state secretary to the yet wider field of Christian Endeavor. Viewing his district, not so much in its separate parts as in its homogeneous character as a unit; estimating it not so much as federated States as in its relation to other similar federations, each affecting a nation's life and destiny; familiarizing himself with the conditions and studying profoundly the problems which enter vitally into and determine the Christian Endeavor movement as a whole, — standing thus related, the inter-state field secretary becomes a potent factor beyond the narrower boundaries of his immediate field. His findings and his personality become view-points for the world leader. And the same personality becomes the most effective agency for the propagation of a movement world-wide in its scope and bearing.

Along the broader lines of vital personal contact, the inter-state field secretary may render invaluable service.

Mr. Ward believes there is a general noticeable trend toward inter-state field secretaries as the solution of a large present-day problem of the Christian Endeavor movement, and doubtless their appointment will be assured in the not far distant future.

No man knows more about successful press-work than Mr. John R. Clements, of Binghamton, N.Y. He thinks that the religious press has been won already for Christian Endeavor, though there is room for a larger work; but the secular press is only partially enlisted as yet. His subject was,

PRESS SUPERINTENDENTS AND THEIR WORK.

The Church has yet to measure up to an appreciation of the full value of the printing-press as a factor in doing her best, and largest, and most far-reaching work.

We are going to take a lot of things for granted to-day and proceed at once to some definite considerations. As, for instance, we are going to assume that every Christian Endeavorer believes in the use of printer's ink, and puts on it at least the value that the merchant prince gives to it when he spends thousands of dollars for the use of it to advertise his wares; we are going to assume that it does not need any talk of a persuasive character to make every city union and every county union have its press committee; we are going to assume that every State union knows well enough the value of a press committee to make it add one where one does not now exist, and to put larger amounts in its budget for those that are now aggressively advertising Christian Endeavor.

Ideally speaking, the field should be divided as follows: —

I. A press superintendent of the United Society of Christian Endeavor, whose chief duties should be to secure the formation of a press department in every State and Territorial union, and to so post himself as to be able to render any kind of advisory assistance to State unions needing it. In addition to this, to so get in touch with the secular daily, weekly, and monthly publications, as to be able to secure their help and co-operation in "spreading Christian Endeavor."

II. A press superintendent in every State union whose business it will be to secure the formation of a press department in every city and county union, and by oversight, advice, and suggestion aid in the larger development of the work.

III. A press committee in every city union and a press committee as a part of every county organization, these committees to be local in their doings.

But, you ask, "What is there for these three classes of superintendents to do, and what have they to do with?" Let us see.

Mr. Clements is enthusiastic for having Christian Endeavor matter furnished all the large plate-matter syndicates that serve thousands of papers with ready-made matter, and illustrated his point with the case of the managing editor of a large newspaper syndicate whose association served matter to 8,000 publications regularly, and who intimated that but a small percentage of them used Christian Endeavor matter.

If we might press this same line a step farther, it would naturally lead us to an answer to the question about the State superintendent. In helping one county union in a recent campaign of "Every-Society-Visitation" I came in contact with Christian Endeavor and Christian Endeavorers in some very out-of-the-way places. I remember one spot in particular. "Forty miles from anywhere" was a good characterization of it. We were entertained in a home where the little country newspaper, published "over the hills and far away," was the only printed page that came into the house regularly. What that paper told of, the family of seven or eight knew about; what it was silent on, they could scarcely be expected to discuss intelligently. Here was the field for Christian Endeavor. The State superintendent, working through the committee of the county union, could get that country editor to run a column of Christian Endeavor matter in his paper every week. That column could contain a brief exposition of the prayer-meeting topic, some general information, a question box, and a variety of interesting things about the work. That family then (and a multitude of others like it) would know about Christian Endeavor, and who can tell but that the printed lines about "Christ and the Church" might bring the "Light of Life" into some dark soul?

One of the press syndicates of the country has recently been led to link itself to Christian Endeavor along this very line. It supplies its constituency with Christian Endeavor matter at a very nominal sum wherever it is asked for. This leads us naturally to an answer for our question concerning the city and country departments. If the leading paper in every town was properly approached on the subject, in the majority of cases it could be persuaded to use Christian Endeavor plate-matter regularly. The average editor strives to give his readers what they wish most. If he can be assured that Christian Endeavor matter is wanted,

THE PLATFORM DURING THE JUNIOR RALLY IN TENT ENDEAVOR.

he'll undoubtedly make it his business to supply it. In one town I'm acquainted with, a request in the name of the union was all that was needed to get the column inaugurated. In another the Endeavorers held an executive session, and appointed a committee of influential members to wait on the editor; in still another, a series of letters written by prominent Endeavorers requesting the column was all that was required.

There is another line of press department work particularly important for city union committees to look after, and that is the local news item work. I have just had in my hand a full column cut from the leading paper in one town of Ohio. The city union press committee furnishes these items weekly to this paper. They are crisp, breezy paragraphs, that reflect the doings of the various societies of the city, a class of advertising for the cause that has a large local value, and is well worth the effort of consecrated brains and pens.

"Make friends of the newspaper, and the newspaper will make friends for Christian Endeavor," was Mr. Clement's closing motto, and well worthy being emblazoned on the walls of every society room.

Dr. Darby, trustee of the United Society for the Cumberland Presbyterian Church, took occasion to heartily indorse Mr. Clement's injunction to keep in touch with the press. Dr. Darby warmly declared that he had first been introduced to Christian Endeavor through the medium of printers' ink, "and I would that I might be able to pay for that little advertisement tenfold," he cried. Christian Endeavor was in its infancy, but two years old, when Dr. Darby read the press notice, and since that time he has been an ardent and active worker in the society. He also related how, seeing a newspaper item about a church the Endeavorers had built, had suggested a similar work for the Cumberland Presbyterian Endeavorers, and led to the building of two handsome churches.

CHAPTER XI.

The Juniors' Jubilant Afternoon.

TENT ENDEAVOR, SATURDAY AFTERNOON.

The rotund eloquence of oratory gave way for a time to the tender tones of youth. And, if radiantly appreciative face and tear-dimmed eyes are allowed in evidence, there proved to be more moving eloquence in the lute-like utterances of the Juniors than in the ringing baritone and deep bass of world-famed speakers.

The platform was filled with charming childhood. A chorus of 400, an orchestra, reciters, all were Juniors, flanked on right and left by a couple of hundred Junior superintendents and workers whose hearts glowed. Facing these, half-way to the rear of the big tent, in seats reserved, were thousands more of Denver's Juniors in pink and white, who had marched in to music, with sunshine in their faces and banners in their hands. The remaining space of the tent was crowded to the utmost by grown-up people who wanted to see and hear.

The fiddles were soon in harmony and the grand piano was right with them, and —

"Glory, glory, hallelujah!" all had suddenly risen and were pouring out the resounding old hymn in all manner of half-grown tones. But the blend was delightful and the volume of sound was impressive, and how that great audience did applaud at the conclusion of the number!

Twelve little tots now stood in line and recited in concert the parable of the sower, accompanying their words with appropriate gestures.

The next feature was a unique

SPEECH OF WELCOME

by seven little boys and girls. Each of the seven bore a large card, on which was painted one of the letters of the word "Welcome," and they recited a poem

It was a very cheerful, hospitable little poem, with a "Hiawatha" swing to it. At the end of it, the little boy on the right lifted a big pasteboard letter, and said, "W!"

The next said, "E!"

The third, "L!"

Then there came a small hitch.

The little girl who held up "C," let it drop, and there came a ripple of laughter which only helped on the general happiness.

At length, "W-E-L-C-O-M-E" was properly spelled out, and again the big tent vibrated with applause.

"The Story of Christian Endeavor" was told by the Juniors, one for each year since 1881. Each child bore a shield on which was printed the motto of the Society and the year which it represented. The first year, 1881, was a tiny little boy, almost a baby. His chart represented the first year of Christian Endeavor, when the first meeting of any society of Endeavor was held in Portland, Me. The second year was represented by a little girl. The next speaker told of the third year of the work. By this time the Society had gained 2,000 members, and there were fifty-three societies formed. In 1884 there were two or three Junior Endeavor societies, and the first Convention was held, at Lowell, Mass. So the little children told of the progress of the great society during each of the years up to the present. The young fellow who represented 1903 towered up to a height that must have made short men envious.

The programmes distributed through the audience had all the words spoken by the Juniors, so that all knew what they were saying, even if they were not heard; but most of them were heard as distinctly as the adult speakers.

The audience was further aided in understanding the expansion of Endeavor by a map of the world as big as the side of a barn, with C. E. monograms on the countries having Endeavor societies.

This was followed by a surprise for the convention. This was the "mite box" drill and recitation of the children, in which about fifty took part. They represented all of the countries of the globe. The children then divided into two divisions, one representing the English-speaking delegates and the other the foreign tongues. The little Americans and English all had small boxes filled with pennies. The foreign representatives were asked what could be done for them by their American friends. The answer came that money could be given, prayers offered, and missionaries sent into the foreign lands. Then the children emptied the boxes of pennies into a large dish which was placed upon the platform, and requested that the money be sent to the missions in China.

In a banner exercise that followed, crimson banners bearing in white the monograms of the Junior Epworth League, the Junior Christian Endeavor Society, and the Baptist Junior Young People's Union, were brought to the platform and intertwined together, a prophecy, let us hope, of what is actually to come.

When Dr. C. H. Tyndall stepped to the platform, carrying a great black bag, curiosity everywhere was on tiptoe, for he was to give an illustrated address entitled,

Cut Loose,

which he explained by a familiar verse of Scripture, "Let us lay aside every weight and the sin that doth so easily beset."

The bag, he said, had no cat in it. But it proved to have three toy balloons.

I want to illustrate what I wish to say by introducing to you three young friends.

Here is the first. "A balloon," you say. Yes, but it is an unusual kind. We expect balloons to mount upward, but this disappoints us and goes down. So I have named this friend Dick Downward.

He is so like many boys and girls. Do what you will for them, they go down. They get out of their cradle and down from their high chair, and begin to run, but it is on the road that goes downward and not upward. It was so with Dick. He would learn more bad in an hour than you could teach him good in a day. He seemed to take naturally to sin.

Now and again a breath lifts Dick somewhat, but his course is downward. Sometimes he wants to go up, and really tries, but down he goes. His friends try to help him, but they are disappointed. You see, I give him an upward lift with my hand, but down he comes. I try again, as so many fathers do with their boys, and he goes up well for a time, and thinks, "Ah, I am going up finely now." but no sooner said than down he comes.

The trouble is *inside*. Within there is something that sinks him. It is the spirit of evil. So long as that is there, his friends try in vain to help him to go up. That is why he breaks all his resolutions to be good. It is too great a task to go up, when his evil heart is all the time leading him down. Let him once get a new spirit within him, and what a change!

Here is another friend (a second balloon). You are glad to see him, for he goes up. See how he mounts! His name is Titus True-Heart. He is a Christian boy. He has the right spirit. But he has one grave fault. He is timid, and so I have nicknamed him, Titus Timid-Heart. He is so afraid of what the other boys think of him!

He knows Dick Downward, and fears his sneer, and rather likes his approval and his rude, bluff commendation, and so he ties to Dick. (He tied the strings of the balloons together.) He excuses his cowardice by saying to himself that he will help Dick to be a better boy. The boys are friends. How does it work? Is Titus lifting Dick up to a better life? Ah, no! Dick draws Titus down. That is the way it usually is.

Mr. Moody saw a canary in a home in England. Admiring it, the gentleman replied, "Yes; he is beautiful, but he has lost his voice. He used to be a fine singer, but I was in the habit of hanging his cage in the window; the sparrows came around with their incessant chirping; gradually he ceased to sing, and learned to twitter, and now all he can do is to twitter, twitter." We become like those with whom we join ourselves in friendship.

It was so with Titus. He went down with Dick, instead of taking Dick up with him

IT IS ALWAYS EASIER TO GO DOWN THAN UP.

If there were a great hole in the earth under my hand, and I should let go this string, the balloon would fall into it, as a stone would fall. All that kept Dick from such a fall was the restraining hand of God, and his friends. But notwithstanding that, he kept sinking lower and lower, till even Titus began to feel ashamed!of him.

One morning the news spread through the town that Dick Downward had come to his end. It was hinted that he had taken his own life. How sudden was the destruction which came at last! One final touch of sin (touching the balloon, and it explodes), and he is gone!

Every one was shocked, and none more than poor Titus. He was now cut loose from Dick, and began to mount upward. He read his Bible, prayed, took part in the Junior meetings once more, but not long; for his old timid spirit clung to him. For some time it was a mystery to his friends what was keeping him down. Under that handkerchief on the platform rail is the secret sin. I uncover it, and

LO! IT IS A WINE–GLASS.

A friend asked Titus to have a drink, the first one. No, he would not, he had promised his mother that he would not touch it. "Hah, hah, that is a good joke; the boy is afraid of his mother!" That taunt cuts Titus. His bravery is gone, and he is led to the slaughter.

Like so many others, poor Titus was now held fast. Try as best he would, that one sin kept him down. It does not take many sins, one will do it; a secret sin, known only to God, it may be.

Titus had a sister. She is our third friend, and I will introduce her to you. (He drew the third balloon from the bag.) You see, she is as beautiful as Titus. Her name is Hattie Heavenward. That is a beautiful name, and see how she soars aloft. She too has the right spirit, and goes even higher than Titus, but after a time she meets with a weight which checks her upward progress. Here is the secret of it. I remove this covering (handkerchief), and discover a bad book.

She pores over these bad books day and night; in play time and worktime. She neglects her work, her studies, her home, her friends, her prayers, her Bible, her meetings, everything that is good for those bad books. She is really a slave to them, as much as Titus is to the wine-glass. But she is farther up than he, and looks down upon him, and thinks that his sin is perfectly dreadful, and so it is, but she is being kept down by her sin as truly as he is by his.

But one day she saw how sinful it was, and began to pray, and the fire of God's Spirit began to burn brightly in her heart, and then suddenly something happened, — she was freed from the power of bad books. That'holy fire touched the thing that held her down, as this burning match touches the thread holding the balloon down, and in an instant she was free.

She took a sudden start upward, but you notice that she soon became held down by another weight, and for a long time it was not known just what was hindering her. She hardly knew herself. All this time her brother Titus was struggling with his wine habit. Then one day, he, too, made a discovery. It was found in the Endeavor pledge, which he had long known and repeated, but which for the first time he really understood and felt. It was, "Trusting in the Lord Jesus Christ for strength."

That was like one sharp blade of these immense shears, and on that blade those words are printed. And the other thing that Titus discovered was, "I promise Him." That is the other sharp blade, and here are those words. Titus brought these two blades together in his life, and the result was marvellous. Watch. I bring "I promise" (to abstain) down upon "Trust in the Lord Jesus Christ," and it will sever every sin that holds one down. I try it, clip, and away soars Titus, our glad Junior, as free as a bird. He mounts higher and higher. He has laid aside every weight, has cut loose; and that is what every Junior, and every Senior, and every Christian everywhere should do. ("Titus" rose to the top of the tent and escaped through the vent-hole around the pole.)

But look at poor Hattie. She is still held down. I would like to see her mount up too, wouldn't you? There is another weight. I look beneath the covering, and discover that it is a piece of money. Hattie is not miserly, but she loves money for what it will buy. This coin is tied to a hat imported from Paris. She is proud, and likes money, for it gratifies her pride. She looked down with contempt on Titus and his sin of drink, but in her heart was the secret sin of pride, and it was a weight on her soul.

But withal, Hattie Heavenward was truly trying to be a Christian, and like every one who loves God, she won the victory in the end. And here is the instrument that wrought her release, — the Sword of the Spirit (holding up a Bible). We do not always know just what is in it. I find in this one a razor, the sharpest cutting instrument of which I know. It is wonderful how this Word has power to cut one loose from his sins. How it cut Paul loose, and taught him to say: "The word of God is sharper than any two-edged sword." I know of many Christians, many Endeavorers, whom the truth in this book has cut loose from the weights and sins that were holding them down.

Hattie found it so in her case, and I hope you will in yours, if you are tied to any sin, secret or otherwise. I place this razor in the Book, and let you see what it will do to the thread, and what Hattie, our Junior Endeavorer, will do when she is fully cut loose. Clip! Away she mounts, up and up! ("Hattie" disappeared as "Titus" had done.)

May God help us to open our hearts to His Holy Spirit, and then by our trust in the Lord Jesus Christ, and our firm resolve; by the fire of His Spirit in us, and the truth of His Word, let us cut loose from every weight and every sin and we shall mount up with wings as eagles, we shall run and not be weary; we shall walk with Christ, and not faint.

Dr. Tyndall was given an enthusiastic vote of thanks for his superb address.

The story which Dr. W. F. Wilson, the next speaker, told the children, was an interesting one of his own actual experience in Canada.

THE STORY OF OLD GRANNY.

The story I have to tell is not one of Christopher Columbus, Oliver Cromwell, George Washington, or Abraham Lincoln, but about a dear old woman, and we called her for convenience, "Granny."

When I went to Hamilton, in 1900, I found old Granny living on a poor street, in a poor house, on a very warm day. I was told she was the oldest woman in Canada. She was sitting smoking a little old pipe about an inch and a half long. On a table was a dish of milk in which a great many flies had found a milky grave. Sitting at her feet was a little dog.

I said, "It is a very warm day." She answered, "It is." I asked her first if she liked milk, and she said, "Yes." I said, "How often do you get it?" "Every other day," said she; and I asked, "Who brings it?" "Abe," says she. "And who is Abe?" "He's my boy," said she. "How old is he?" "Seventy years of age." "He is the 'old boy.'" I said. "Indeed he is, in more senses than one."

Granny was sitting there in that little room full of the evidence of poverty, and I said to her, "Would you like milk every day, — sweet milk every morning?" She said, "Yes," and I made a report to the branch of the King's Daughters, and as long as Granny lived in that house, every day, at their expense, a pint of fresh, sweet milk was placed at her door.

I said to her one day, "Would you like a visit?" "I would," says she. "Who's coming?" I answered, "Some, nice little girls at my church," and I went to my Junior superintendent, Miss Walton, and I said to her, "Pick out four nice little girls, and send them down to Granny. Have them take a good, big comb with great big teeth, for her hair is matted, and some soap and a nice fresh towel, for her hands are dirty. And have them wash her face and comb her hair, and put a nice cap on her, and sing her a little song, and come away."

They carried out my desires to the letter. The next week I went to see old Granny. I said, "How are you, Granny?" She made no reply to that, but said she, "Those was nice little girls you sent to see me." I said, "Yes." She said, "They combed my hair, after washing my face, and they put this cap on me, and one of them kissed me after they sang to me." And tears came to her eyes as she told me about it In a little while I knew I had Granny's heart for Christ.

"Did you ever belong to any church?" I asked. "No," said she. "Did you ever take the Lord's Supper?" asked I. "No," she answered. "I haven't been in a church for sixty years." "How old are you to-day?" I asked. "I am in my one hundred and sixth year," she said. "Why did those little girls come to see me?" "For Christ's sake; out of our Junior Endeavor society. They have come in His name, sent by Miss Walton, their superintendent, and they are coming again." And she asked, "Will they come?" and I said, "Yes; they will come." And they came again, and sang to her, and it was not long before Granny's heart was won to the church.

To make a long story short, on the first Sabbath in May, in the year 1901, in the presence of a big church I publicly received that dear old body, one hundred and eight years of age, into the church of Jesus Christ, as she sat in a rocking chair, brought by the Juniors, in a carriage provided with money they themselves had gathered. There sat at the end of the railing, one of the little girls, eight years old — a century between them.

There sat an old lady that had seen every president in the United States die, excepting President McKinley. *Every* president! Think of it. She was five years of age when Washington passed away. There sat that old body, and the dear little girl that had helped to win her for Jesus sat at the other end of the railing, and Granny was received into the church of Christ, and that morning she had the sacrament of the Lord's Supper for the first time, at one hundred and eight years.

Last August, the eleventh, I went to see her and said, "Granny, is there anything I can give you?" She said, "No. I only want one thing, and that you cannot give." I stroked her old head, and put her hand in mine, and I said, "If there is anything in reason that one human being can give another, I will give to you."

"The only thing," she said, "I want in this world is my grave. I want to lay down my head — my poor old heart is tired. Jesus alone can give me my grave."

In less than six days, as the sun was kissing the East, on the wings of the morning, the spirit of the dear old mother went up to God. Two days after I took the wrinkled form of clay and put it in the grave. Granny lived a century without Christ, and she has gone to live with him for eternity.

Ye workers discouraged — ye Sunday-school workers discouraged, ye church workers, discouraged, ye pastors in your work, broken-hearted because your words are not obeyed and your desires are not complied with, be not discouraged, keep up a glad heart, and as in the case of Granny, you will win some one that will shine as an undimmed star in your crown forever. Work on, pray on, trust on, and by-and-by the crown that fades not shall be yours.

Dr. Wilson, too, was thanked most expressively.

The afternoon still held a piquant surprise in store. Just before the close Dr. Clark brought forward two little Italian boys in blue overalls and straw hats who had strolled into the tent, explaining that the Juniors of Denver were working for them.

"Have them stand in chairs," sang out some one in the audience, and it was done, their brown eyes looking as big as saucers at the sudden notoriety into which they had been thrust.

Then two Junior girls stood beside them, and they clasped hands, a living symbol of the missionary spirit and fellowship of Christian Endeavor that the audience will not soon forget.

It was a fitting climax of interest to one of the best-planned and best-executed Junior rallies ever held. Much credit is due Miss Williams, of Denver, and her corps of able, devoted assistants for training the children.

JUNIOR HEADQUARTERS.

Would that every Junior worker in the land could have visited that "Idea Gallery" in the First Baptist Church! Walls and tables were crammed with suggestive material, object-lessons, diagrams, printed matter of all kinds, and hundreds of bright ways of illustrating spiritual truth.

One of the most notable advance steps taken during the Convention was the organization of the International Union of State Junior and Intermediate Superintendents. Mrs. Hageman of Indiana is the president, Mr. Logan of Connecticut the secretary, while the executive committee consists of Miss Millikin of Washington, Miss Haus of St. Louis, and Mr. P. A. Doig of Montreal. All hail to this new and important factor in Christian Endeavor progress!

CHAPTER XII.

Patriotism out of Doors.

CITY PARK, SATURDAY AFTERNOON.

Thousands of Endeavorers gathered under the thick branches of a mighty grove in beautiful City Park, on Saturday afternoon. Cook's superb Drum Corps was at its best in its stirring patriotic airs. Bishop Fallows, gallant old colonel of our Civil War, made an ideal leader.

The Rev. Ira Landrith of Tennessee made a short, pointed prayer and then Bishop Fallows told the Endeavorers why they had been thus called together, and his words were often eloquent.

We are here this afternoon to speak of the great country to which we belong and which belongs to us, and I want to say to our English and Canadian friends that if we speak of this country as the very greatest under heaven, it is because we would not make liars of the wisest and most distinguished statesmen and philosophers of your own lands.

It was good Bishop Berkeley who in 1767 prophesied that ours would one day be one of the grandest empires on the globe, and it was he, too, who uttered that grand prophetic phrase, "Westward the star of empire takes its way."

The speaker then talked of Timothy Dwight, the first president of Yale College, and told how after having spent hours on his knees, while chaplain in the Revolutionary army, he had arisen and, with true inspiration thrilling him, written the stirring poem beginning:

> "Columbia, Columbia to glory arise,
> The queen of the world and the child of the skies."

"And he knew absolutely nothing of Colorado," he added, and the great audience under the trees laughed and applauded.

The bishop's address was also full of references to the Civil War and its results. He quoted the saying in Cuba when General Fitzhugh Lee was sent there as military governor,

"Here comes a Yankee ruler," and the poem ending,

> "They say that I'm a Yankee!
> Virginia, can it be
> That history will mention
> The *Yankee*, Fitzhugh Lee?"

"And now," said the bishop, "let us give thanks that the Old Dominion is plumb full of Yankees." "Mostly under ground," good-naturedly commented a Virginian Endeavorer on the platform.

Having paid high tribute to the South and the soldiers of the Confederacy, to President Roosevelt, to the martyred McKinley, to Dewey and to all the khaki boys who fought for the maintenance of American rights and liberties, Bishop Fallows announced with regret that Bishop B. W. Arnett was absent, but that his son, Chaplain B. W. Arnett of the U. S. Army, "a chip of the old block," "if not the block itself," would would take his place.

This young man has both wit and genuine eloquence.

A COLORED CHAPLAIN'S ADVICE.

I am sure I am highly pleased to have a chance to take some part in these patriotic services. I bring my credentials from that matchless statesman and martyr, William McKinley. He said that I had enough of love for America, that he would commission me as a mounted chaplain in the United States army, and to-day I am filled with love, fidelity, and patriotism to the country in which we live.

Our country is filled with striking instances of progress, and side by side we are laboring to sustain the grandest republic upon which God's sun has ever shone. The black man has been in America ever since 1528. The histories tell you that we came here in 1619, but those histories are out of date, and the latest information with regard to the black man is that he came here thirty-six years after Christopher Columbus first caught sight of this glorious land.

Devoting most of his address to the Negro problem, he significantly said, "Christian Endeavor stands for that type of good citizenship that will put a man's religion into his ballot. He will feel that any wrong in any part of this great country is a wrong to him."

There was a time in this country when the most advanced scientists said the white man's brain weighed forty ounces, the baboon's twenty, and the black man was midway between, and his weighed thirty. We have made such an advance since that it is no longer a question of the weight of a man's brain; but in America what we want to know first of all is, what can a man do? If a man is fitted to discharge the duties of an American citizen, we open our arms and welcome all of God's creation into our boundaries and tell them to "Root, hog, or die." There was a time when it was felt we should be a bone of contention in this country, and there has never been so much fun in this country excepting that which has been started up over the black man. We are the fun-makers of America, but we are not only that, we are, under God, becoming the thinkers of America.

To-day before the President's desk there is an instrument called the whisper phone, that is the product of the black man's brain, and President Roosevelt — grand Executive that he is — cannot give an order to any department of this country unless he first speaks through an instrument which is the product of a black man.

We have helped to make this country. Education is now one of the great factors of our progress. *Collier's Weekly*, a few days ago, said the greatest educator alive to-day is Booker T. Washington. God speed the day when right and justice, education, morality, and religion shall be in every home of this great land.

"Yes," added Bishop Fallows, "we'll secure the brown man's rights, and redress the black man's wrongs."

Dr. Northrop of Kansas City was another shining example of ready, full-brained, full-lunged, open-air oratory of the kind that made a restless crowd settle down in quiet until only the chirp of the cricket and the rustle of the leaves competed with the speaker's voice. His address might have been labelled — though it was not —

INDEPENDENCE DAY AFTERMATH.

We have just passed the 4th of July, 1903, the one hundred and twenty-seventh anniversary of our national independence. Seventy-five millions of liberty-loving and peace-living people are to be congratulated. The Almighty hath crowned the year with gladness! He hath strengthened the bars of thy gates; He hath blessed thy children within thee. He maketh peace within thy borders, and filleth thee with the finest of the wheat. He hath not dealt so with any nation!

Patriotism is the word of the hour! Let it go forth on the wings of the press. Let it sing out from heart to heart, from sea to sea. Let joyous youth catch the refrain, and feel the impulse of freedom once again. Let church bells peal forth from valley and hillside in one harmonious chime. Let flags fly, and cannons boom, and skyrockets hiss, and firecrackers burn. Let all the Nation enjoy one glad and glorious holiday on Liberty's jubilee.

It does us good to let these old thrills come once a year. Listen! The clatter of horses' hoofs in Paul Revere's famous ride! The reverberating musketry of Yorktown and Saratoga! Take down the Declaration of Independence; read it once more, and let it stir your inmost soul. Let the names of the heroic signers quicken your sluggish blood. Recall the heroes of Revolutionary fame. Write their memory on your hearts, carve it on your monuments.

Oh, yes; we need this day,

> "Lest we forget,
> Lest we forget!"

The buyers and the sellers, the pushers of this commercial age, the school boy and the school girl, the old as well as the young, we all need to recollect how our forefathers fought for us and left us a glorious heritage. To-day scores of thousands of the boys in blue and the boys in gray sleep in sacrificial graves in every hamlet in the land. In the North they lie under the willow, and in the Southland under the cypress; alike brave, and alike at rest.

Dr. Northrop captured the crowd by his happy reference to the boys, mostly street gamins, that were swarming over the speaker's stand, even giving the orators scant room for gestures. "What is the secret," he asked, "of our patriotism to-day? To find it, you need not stand alone among the heroes who have borne the brunt of the battle, but you must go into the public schools, hear their patriotic songs, and see them salute the flag. America is safe to-day where the boys and girls wave the flag, and hang on the banister to hear the preacher talk." And he snatched a boy's cap, and swung it in the air as he reached his glowing peroration.

Let every patriotic day be a Flag Day. The red, white, and the blue should grace every State house and home, every schoolhouse and church. The folds of our stars and stripes should unroll to every breeze. Old Glory will never have its day, but rather it shall have every day. Wind it around battle-scarred veterans when they sleep their last sleep. Hang it to the halyards, but never at halfmast unless a nation weeps. Wave it from windows. Lift it aloft at the head of processions. Honor it with martial music. It symbolizes sacred memories and lofty principles. "Long may it wave over the land of the free and the home of the brave."

Chaplain Robert E. Steele, who presented the Christian Endeavor Society with the first flag which was hoisted over the Philippine islands by Dewey's forces, spoke on : —

How to Care for the Flag.

I want to take up your time to say a word as to how to treat the American flag. If you have been in a foreign country, a long ways off on the ocean, where the flag never waves, excepting at the masthead of some ship, and then come back, and for the first time in the early morning, as you strain your eyes over the water, you see your flag flying, then it is you know how the sailor loves his flag. Every time we come on deck, we touch our hat in respect, with full salute to the flag. Every morning when it is raised, and every evening when it is lowered, we touch our hat and stand at attention. You should honor it always. Don't leave it up all night. When I looked out this morning to see the Rocky Mountains, the first thing I saw was a flag some one had forgotten, and left out all night. It was at half-mast. Treat it with respect. No army, no navy, flies a flag at night except in an engagement. On all occasions it is lowered at sunset.

Don't let it get torn or tangled. If you see a tear in it, take it down and mend it. Don't let it stand up there tattered and torn, unless the tatters and tears came from honorable warfare.

Again, never let it touch the ground. Don't take it down and throw it on the ground. When it comes from the flagstaff take it in your hands and fold it away carefully.

Never let anybody use the American flag or other national color for a disrespectful purpose. (*Applause.*) I saw once at a great public gathering a flag spread out where the speakers were to stand. An officer present, jumped to his feet as if he had been struck in the face, and dashing up to the stage, took it away. "No man shall stand on the American flag," said he. (*Applause.*)

If you have a flag, and everybody ought to have one in every home in the land, hoist it on proper occasions. Don't leave it at half-mast. It tears the heart of any one who knows anything about it, for it means mourning. First send it up the peak, and then lower it to half-mast.

If you see it tangled, make it your business to get it clear, and then it will fly to the breeze and mean something.

The little flag given to Dr. Clark by Chaplain Steele, — the first flag raised in the Philippines was shown. Men and women crowded around just to touch it, and one old lady stooped quickly down and kissed its sacred folds.

Speaking of the South's acceptance of the verdict of the Civil War, that gallant Southerner, Ira Landrith, took occasion to tell the audience how his declaration of Southern acquiescence in the results of the war was taken, up North, with incredulity.

"You wouldn't dare say such a thing down South," men told him. "On the contrary," said Mr. Landrith, "I have said it on every Southern platform to applauding thousands of men, and it has never been criticised in the slightest. I have no idea that there is an intelligent Southern man or woman who is not as glad as this colored man here that there is no slavery on the American continent."

Another thrilling scene at the close of this outdoor rally was the bringing to the platform of a Denver Jackie, with whom Colonel Fallows stood arm in arm: —

"The army and navy forever,
Three cheers for the Red, White, and Blue!"

CHAPTER XIII.

Jollification.

SATURDAY EVENING RALLIES.

A complimentary dinner was given to the Convention committee by the trustees of the United Society, in the Brown Palace Hotel, at 6 P.M. Saturday.

Dr. Clark thanked the Denver committee for their faultless preparation for the Convention, and the hundred or more trustees present heartily applauded his well-bestowed praise.

In responding, Chairman Sweet told of the perfect harmony and satisfaction the committee had enjoyed in their work, and took the breath of all away at first by announcing that he wished to give notice that a meeting would be called for next Tuesday to invite the Convention to Denver in 1905. That is the dauntless spirit of Denver Endeavorers.

STATE JOLLIFICATIONS.

Saturday evening of Convention week is always given up to State rallies at the Church headquarters. Just as our interdenominationalism does not by any means preclude denominationalism, so our world-wide oneness does not preclude sectional pride and proper clannishness. The State delegations sang their State songs, heard their favorite State speakers, in a lighter vein, usually extolling the glories of their State, and trying to make their Denver hosts open their eyes in wonder over the size of the squashes grown, or the output of gold, or oil, or peanuts, or men.

The assignment of certain State delegations to certain churches for headquarters, and to their vicinity for lodging results always in the formation of many pleasant acquaintances and friendships, so that the State rallies become also on the part of our hosts an opportunity for the climax of their hospitality. In many cases, if not in all, the more formal exercises merged themselves in a family festival, daintily attired maidens distributing refreshments with that beauty and graciousness for which Western girls are justly celebrated.

In some cases these meetings were miniature State Conventions, enough of the officers and Endeavorers being present to transact business. The programmes were carefully prepared, sparkling with wit, warm with good feeling, rich with eloquence. As was inevitable, there was universal felicitation over the year's glad increase in the number of societies in the several States. By special invitation, as always, Dr. Clark and the other United Society officers were kept busy moving from meeting to meeting, and giving at each a word of good cheer. Everywhere they could offer sincere congratulations upon substantial gains, and everywhere they found an earnest determination to go forward, and bring better up to best.

CHAPTER XIV.

The Call of the Church Bells.

SERVICES, SUNDAY MORNING.

Sabbath morning dawned bright and cool, and as the bells rang out their sweet challenge to thousands of listening ears, the streets were lined with badge-wearers hastening to hear their favorite ministers. Indeed some started long before the bells rang, to be sure of a seat in the Central Presbyterian Church, where Rev. R. G. Campbell was to preach.

This church seats 3,000, but 5,000 were crowded into it, the preacher speaking from the organ loft, instead of the pulpit, in order that all might hear. Not being able to have stenographers at every church, we regret that we can give here only extracts from a few of the many edifying and eloquent sermons preached.

Rev. R. G. Campbell, City Temple, London.

The traditional reputed writer of this epistle was known as the "Apostle of Love." The legends built around his name have caused him to be known as the most lovable character. But while the Apostle John has been described as the Apostle of Love, he was not always so.

In my country and here there are many who challenge the statement that God is love and life. We might ignore the grim and dramatic things of life when we speak of love, if such were possible. But only here in Denver within the last few days we have occurrences which bring this grim and dark side of life before us. Two strange facts have occurred only since we came to Denver. One was a murder on Market street; the other, the tragic burning of a young woman. Truly in the midst of life we are in death.

Human sympathy raises an appeal because of these things. Why is it that such agony must be suffered by the innocent. I do not know why one woman was murdered, or why another was burned to death. I do know that out of that furnace of pain caused by the burning of a young woman came all that is good and righteous. Christ leads us through no darker rooms than those which He himself went through. In the presence of pain He shows His love. This I also know, that the love of God is most plainly shown in the tears.

Rev. Stephen A. Northrop, D.D., Kansas City, First Baptist Church.

Speaking on the immortality of great writers, Dr. Northrop said: —

A consecrated Christian who died ages ago has spoken to more than the most devoted Christian of the twentieth century. A dead Paul has declared more

F. H. Jacobs.   Clarence A. Barbour, D.D.   Percy S. Foster.

Austen K. de Blois, Ph.D.   Rev. Harlan P. Beach.   Charles E. Bradt, Ph.D.

Rev. C. H. Tyndall, D.D.   George B. Stewart, D.D.   Rev. Smith Baker, D.D.

SOME OF THE CONVENTION SPEAKERS.

than a living Paul. David thrilled many a heart with his well-tuned harp, but David being dead singeth his spiritual songs that will vibrate in every age and nation. Savonarola is dead, but his words throb in 10,000 temples. A Calvin dead has spoken more than a Calvin living. Bunyan is dead, but his "Pilgrim's Progress" has spoken through 10,000,000 lives, and will ever speak till he stands at the wicket gate of heaven. Jefferson is dead, but bis sermons live in the hearts of the redeemed Burmese. John Howard is dead, but his words live on in a larger philanthropy than he ever dreamed. Wilberforce and Lincoln spoke, and the shackles of millions broke in twain. Thousands of the great and the good, of the base and the ignoble, live through their words, and have passed down the highways of the centuries.

BISHOP FALLOWS, OF CHICAGO, ST. PAUL'S M. E. CHURCH.

Speaking of the new era in which we live, and the unity it is ushering into church life, he said: —

That mother church of England in which my parents and remoter ancestors were born, baptized, confirmed, and married, has changed in her forms and methods since the days of Queen Elizabeth, when nonconformists were subject to banishment and death; when the English inquisition was instituted, and the star chamber positively revelled in religious persecution; a change since the days of King James, when hundreds of conscientious clergymen were silenced, imprisoned, and excommunicated, some of whom our then savage continent roughly received — noble God-fearing men, both Pilgrims and Puritans who helped lay the foundation of the Republic and create the Christian civilization which makes it possible for a general convention of an Episcopal Church to be held alongside a national council of the Congregational Churches.

In those days to have talked of an exchange of pulpits between Methodist and Congregationalist, or between Baptist and Presbyterian, would have been as great an anomaly as to propose that Cardinal Gibbons of Baltimore should preside over an Evangelical Lutheran council in Boston.

The question was solemnly discussed in the past by churchmen across the ocean, whether, for instance, "a pious Congregationalist" was in a better condition than a "pious heathen," like Socrates, or Marcus Aurelius, since both were beyond the apostolic polity.

CHAPTER XV.

Evangelism for Everybody.

AFTERNOON MEETINGS, SUNDAY.

Four great rallies were held Sunday afternoon: for men, for women, for boys and for girls. At each of these the church was crowded to the utmost, and the keenest interest was shown in the addresses. Trinity Methodist Church at which was held

THE MEN'S MEETING,

was crowded long before three o'clock, the hour for services to begin. The aisles were full, and men of all conditions and classes stood side by side packing the rear of the building and even the corridors.

The meeting was under the leadership of Rev. William Patterson, D.D., of Philadelphia. There was a chorus present of nearly one hundred voices, led by Mr. F. H. Jacobs, of Brooklyn.

The first speaker was Rev. C. H. Tyndall, Ph.D., the popular author of "Electricity and Its Similitudes," who has delighted and astonished his readers and hearers with what seems almost like a new revelation so wonderously does he make the forces of nature speak of God's presence and love.

One of the strange things that attracted much attention, was two long wavering poles, placed on either side of the pulpit, just behind the altar and projecting fully twenty feet into the air. With this miniature, but complete apparatus, for wireless telegraphy, Dr. Tyndall illustrated his theme,

WIRELESS TELEGRAPHY AND ITS SPIRITUAL SIMILITUDES.

"If any man hath ears to hear, let him hear." — Mark iv: 22.

Sending messages by electricity without the intervention of wires, is one of the marvels of the marvellous age. For a long time the possibility of it was questioned. Now that the fact of it is demonstrated, the *how* of it is most interesting. This reminds one of the way the fact of God's communication with us men has been doubted and opposed at different times, and that still the *how* of it remains an interesting study.

I have here the apparatus requisite to send messages without wire connection and shall shortly transmit signals through space.

He declared "The spirit of God communicates with the Christian worker just as instantaneously and just as certainly as the bell does when I push this key." Instantly there was a crackling flash from one of the poles, and a bell connected with the other rang out. For a minute the audience gaped in astonishment.

Then Dr. Tyndall explained the phenomenon. It was nothing but a Marconi wireless telegraph apparatus. But he used it to good effect in illustrating and demonstrating the further part of his address.

Our physical and intellectual deficiency which makes us insensible to the electric energy which is all about us, is analogous to our spiritual inability to detect the presence and power of God. Only a fraction of that which He communicates to us are we able to recognize and receive. It is not that He does not speak to us in a myriad of ways, but our capacity is so limited. We are so unlike Him that we seldom see or hear Him. We need the spiritual vision and the divinely quickened ear. Because we hear no voice and perceive no shape, we should not be so illogical as to conclude that therefore God is not now near to us, and does not speak to us. Blessed are we, if we have discovered that the vast unexplored territory which lies just beyond the ken of our natural vision is filled with God, who is waiting to make Himself known to every one who is waiting to have the heart to feel, the eye to see, or the ear to hear.

But these electric oscillations do not stop at our ignorance. They knock at every door and enter unbidden. Many media that are opaque to the light are transparent to them. The earth itself seems to be no bar to these penetrating waves of energy. Wherever they go, they carry, locked within their breast, the music of the spheres, and the beauties of the heaven above and of the earth beneath; and doubtless the time will come when we shall be able to hear their notes of exquisite harmony, and to see the beauties they ever bear on their pinions to our dullard senses in their rapid flight.

The heart of wireless telegraphy is the coherer, or a similar device which, by detecting the etherial waves, becomes our electric eye or ear. That which I hold in my hand is a large coherer. It is a glass, or hard rubber, tube containing nickel fillings, about four per cent of which are silver. Metal filings in a loose state are practically a non-conductor, but an electric wave falling upon them has the mysterious power of converting them into a most sensitive conductor.

As I close the circuit by pressing the key, you notice the signals yonder in the receiving instrument. To every pressure of the key here, there is an immediate response yonder. Each wave falling upon the filings in the little glass tube, converts it into a conductor, but at the same instant, an automatic bell-hammer taps the tube, destroying the conductivity of the filings by sundering them, so that they again lie higgledy-piggledy, waiting for the next wave to transform them once more into a good conductor. And so the makes and breaks of the current through the coherer are read as dots and dashes, forming a message in the Morse code.

In the conversion of the tube of metal filings from a non-conductor to a sensitive conductor, we have a perfect analogy of the transformation which often occurs in the lives of men under invisible divine influence. You might say of them, that they offer complete resistance to the truth of God; they want nothing to do with it. Their spiritual nature is in a chaotic condition; disorder reigns. But the truth which was so resisted is suddenly given access in their lives, and all opposition ceases. The reason for this is clearly apparent to any one versed in the teachings of the Bible. Invisible energy from heaven's battery has come into contact with the soul; disorder has vanished; spiritual continuity with God is established, and resistance has given place to conductivity of the tenderest sort, and it is one also that persists. Such transformations, by the renewing of the mind, are frequent in the spiritual realm, and they are the blessing which we are all entreated to receive.

As the receiver must be electrically in tune with the transmitter before it can respond to the electrical waves, so our heart must be in tune with the Infinite before we can recognize Him, or receive His messages. "The natural man receiveth not the things of the Spirit of God, for they are foolishness unto him; neither can he know them, because they are spiritually discerned; but he that is spiritual discerneth all things." Sin is discord, and throws us out of harmony with God. There is perfect harmany in the Infinite One, and He would produce the same harmony in us by the removal of all discord, or sin, from our lives; and by His own indwelling, He would charm us on to perfect accord with Himself.

Much has been said about the possibility of tapping the wireless messages being transmitted by the Marconi system, and so diminishing their value. But Mr. Marconi has so successfully attuned his instruments that they respond only to the messages intended for them.

As this tuning fork, and the tumbler, and all other objects in the world, have their vibrating note, so have we. The keynote of our soul is that to which we respond. If it be to money, we are covetous, grasping; if to society, we are worldly; if to the sins of the flesh, we are impure; if to God, we are holy. We are coherers like no one else in the world. No one fully understands us, for no one else is like us. There are natures which are more or less attuned to ours, and we feel the response they make to us, while others are repellant. We are like the corrugated half of this bivalve shell. Search the world over, and only this other half produced by the same life, will be found to fit it perfectly. God is our complement, our other half, and He only is able to respond to our every need and indefinable longing, and that He is ever seeking to do.

Our Heavenly Father has found the keynote of our being, and our whole life becomes musical, resonating in secret and beautiful harmony with Himself. He made us to be like the æolian harp of which Frances Ridley Havergal sweetly sings. No human hand could awaken its tender strains; only the breezes upon it when placed in the lifted sash. Oh, that we all might put our soul-harp into the window that looks out upon another world, and "listening, wait the breath of heaven, the Spirit of our God." The joy of heaven is to be in tune with God.

"Oh, may my heart in tune be found,
Like David's harp of solemn sound."

Rev. R. J. Campbell of City Temple, London, next addressed the meeting. He had outlined a short conversational talk of ten minutes, he declared, before he had heard Dr. Tyndall. But then he had decided to change his subject and wanted to talk on psychology. If another man had a right to talk on science at a Sunday afternoon meeting, he couldn't see why his subject wasn't all right. Psychology, he termed the study of the internal man, his mind and soul, as science was the study of the external, its surroundings and conditions. Psychology, he pleasantly assured his hearers, was not so dreadful a word, after all.

A man can no more get away from God than he can get away from his own breath. When we know ourselves, we know God, for God teaches us ourselves.

Our consciousness of ourselves is only a corner of our personality. He illustrated this by referring to the fact that ladies were rigidly excluded from the meeting. I don't see how the programme committee dared to do it. " I saw some turned away, and said it is a shame.

"American ladies are the most charming creatures in the world, except the ladies of my own land."

But Mr. Campbell assured the audience that in spite of the rule and the ushers, one lady had got in. It was a young girl who had accompanied him.

"And there she is," said he, "hiding behind that bit of woodwork, and she's going to stay here."

She is too young yet to realize what a power she is going to have by and by over the hearts of men. She, like all the rest of us, is living in a corner of herself. Only as God teaches us does our consciousness of ourselves enlarge.

"I must come back to my little maid," said Mr. Campbell presently. "Jesus Christ set up such a little child as a model in the kingdom of heaven. Yet how hard it is for us to understand the childlike qualities, meekness, for instance!"

He facetiously alluded to Mark Twain's remark at the Queen's diamond jubilee that he had found Englishmen mentioned in the Bible, because it said the meek should inherit the earth, and they had got nearly all of it.

The laugh that followed, and the neat turn made in alluding to our action in the Spanish-American war, proved that, if Mr. Campbell is mystical, as his critics and analysts are saying, and if he does reel off Tennyson by the yard, he is also a humorist and satirist.

"But I have already gone over my time," said Mr. Campbell in the midst of an eloquent outburst.

"Go on! Go on!" shouted the audience.

"Ah, yes," was the retort, "that's just your American courtesy. I've no doubt you want to say, 'Hold your tongue, and sit down.'"

But he did not sit down until he had pressed home in a masterful way the thought that God was speaking to the men of that audience.

When Mr. Jacobs's voice died away in the last note of his singularly sweet and heart-thrilling solo, there were many hearts stirred to responsiveness to the still small voice as they had not been for years.

Taken all together, it was a wonderfully and blessedly impressive and heart-warming meeting.

THE WOMEN'S MEETING.

The scene at Central Christian Church Sunday afternoon at the women's meeting was one which perhaps has never been duplicated in Denver. Every inch of space was taken in the auditorium up-stairs long before the meeting hour, and then people were lined up all along the sidewalk and out into the street.

It was finally decided to hold an overflow meeting in the basement, and the doors were thrown open. The crowds poured in, and crowded in, and pushed in, and still there wasn't room. Women had to sit on the steps outside, and even the low stone wall surrounding the yard nearest the church was utilized for seats. Here women sat in the hot sun and waited simply on the hope that some one would come out of the church and leave a vacancy.

The young lady ushers estimated that at least two hundred men were refused admission.

Mrs. James L. Hill of Salem, Mass., presided up-stairs, and Mrs. Francis E. Clark took the meeting down-stairs. Then the speakers appeared before each audience in turn, the time of their transit being filled in with music.

The programme was an interesting one, and embraced the general topic

How to Serve.

Mrs. R. J. Campbell, the gracious wife of the distinguished English divine, though unwilling to make an address, consented to assist in the opening exercises by reading her favorite psalm. After she was introduced and before she began to read,

"Bless the Lord, O my soul, and all that is within me bless His holy name," she said. "This is the first time in my life that I have ever faced an audience. I have never before spoken a single word in public. You see I had to come to America to learn Endeavor."

The general theme, "How May We Best Serve?" was discussed by women from Florida, California, China, Japan, Australia, and Massachusetts, and suggestions were made of service for Christ and the church, in temperance, missionary, evangelistic, and Junior work, and in bringing out the latent abilities of young girls.

"Now I'll bring you an Australian breeze," said Miss Miller from Melbourne. She turned to the lady presiding, and said, "Let me take the watch. I'll hold it. "There," said she, "two minutes have gone," and again, "Seven minutes are up."

On going down to the overflow meeting to repeat her address (as all the addresses were given in both places), Miss Rebel Withers, of Florida, with native modesty suggested that to enlarge the participation there be a praise service; but voices from the audience said:—

"Please repeat what you said up-stairs." Her story of her work among girls was so inspirational that about forty young women from the audience came to her after the meeting to talk with her about their beginnings in the Christian life, and some of them expressed a desire to correspond with her.

Miss Anna G. Fraser, an enthusiastic young woman from Santa Monica, Cal., told of the work the Christian Endeavorers of that State were doing to drive intemperance out of the State.

She described the "Coffee Club Associations," which are endeavoring to place a coffee "saloon" wherever a liquor saloon exists. With her young enthusiasm she had much to say about the church people of California who are not doing what they should in prohibition work, and said that the young people were doing what in football would be called "running around the end" in an effort to capture the demon rum.

Two very delightful solos were sung, one by Miss Laura Northrop of Kansas City, and the other by Mrs. Ray Shank of Denver.

A missionary spirit was given to the gathering by the presence of several returned missionaries, who wove their foreign banners in with the other drapery and gave their talks attired in foreign clothes. Miss Hartwell was one of the speakers, and she told about the work in China. Miss A. E. Garvin from Osaka, Japan, made an interesting talk.

In the upper room, by an almost unanimous vote, the women who were present pledged one another that, on returning home, each one in her own individual way would do what she could in service for Christ and the church.

BOYS' MEETING.

Dr. James L. Hill held the reins in a masterful way in the boys' meeting, in the Central Presbyterian Church.

"Want to tell you about a funny thing I noticed the other day," Dr. Hill began without any preliminaries. "The doctor was called to see a sick man, and he leaned over him and asked to see his tongue. Just as if his tongue was sick! It seems that, when a man is sick inside, it does show itself on his tongue." Then Dr. Hill went on to say how when a *boy* is sick inside, when anything goes wrong with his soul, it is sure to show itself on his tongue. "Show me your tongue! Smut on it. You're sick. Sick all over. I can tell just what kind of boy you are by looking at your tongue."

The boys were fascinated with Dr. Hill's account of his visit to the Palo Alto stock-farm, and the colt kindergarten there, and miniature track, where the colts are trained, and he applied the whole in a crafty way to the need of training the human colts sitting wide-eyed before him. Before he got through, Dr. Hill preached a most effective temperance sermon, and got his lively congregation to agree heartily to the total-abstinence stand.

If any speaker during the whole Christian Endeavor Convention was thoroughly enjoyed by his hearers, that person was Judge Ben B. Lindsey of the Denver juvenile court, who addressed the boys' meeting at the Central Presbyterian Church Sunday afternoon. Judge Lindsey's constant contact with youngsters of all sizes and conditions has given him an extensive vocabulary of just such words and phrases as boys alone understand, and which appealed as nothing else could have, to his young hearers. He spoke just as one boy would speak to another, calling them "kids" and using the slang terms that are the delight of every youngster's heart. There was not a boy present, no matter how young, that did not fully comprehend everything he said.

The judge emphasized the fact that it was the first step toward evil-doing as children that finally places men in penitentiaries and sends murderers to the gallows. The youthful conscience must be taught to recognize the exact line where right leaves off and wrong begins: He said:—

I judge that most of you youngsters are between ten and sixteen years old. Now, let me tell you that you have reached the most important part of your lives. Between the ages of ten and sixteen you are brought face to face with the big job of learning what is right and what is wrong — where your nose leaves off and the other fellow's nose begins. If you get a good start now you won't need another boost to keep you right — you'll more than likely grow up to be manly, honorable men, fellows your parents and your country will be proud of.

But if you get a bad start now you'll find it the hardest thing in the world to break off your bad ways and turn around in your tracks later in life. More kids form their bad habits from trifling things — from mere fun that is carried too far. They at first don't know they're doing a thing wrong, but the habit to do these things grows as they grow, and by the time they're men they're pretty apt to turn out bad all over if they don't see where they are drifting and turn around.

Why, I had a bunch of kids up in my court the other day for throwing rocks at a poor, old crazy man who was trying to work and earn a living. They had been having a lovely time. They couldn't see why the old fellow wasn't having a lovely time, too. It was just lots of fun to shy rocks at him. And, don't you know, those young rascals couldn't see where they had been doing a thing wrong.

They couldn't see where their own noses left off and the old man's began. They thought because he was crazy they had a perfect right to have a good time with him. Most kids shy rocks at cats — and they have lots of fun doing it. Some kids kill cats, too. But these urchins thought it was lots more fun to shag rocks at the old man.

" I've got the word right, haven't I? " inquired the judge.
" Sure thing," exclaimed the boys in a chorus.

Thought I hadn't got mixed, replied the judge. Now just let me tell you something: I have far more respect for the kid who shags a human being than I have for the kid who shags a cat or any sort of dumb animal. A person can turn around and smack the kid back, but the cat can't do a thing but suffer.

A few weeks ago I had a little colored fellow in court for stealing. I asked him what he stole the stuff for?

"Deed, judge, I never stole it — I only swiped it," he wailed.

And that's just the point — if you don't learn the difference between "stealing" and "swiping" now, as well as the difference between fun and cruelty to dumb animals, you're likely to be sorry for it when you become men. Find out what is right and what is wrong, and stick to the right. You'll be men who are a credit to yourselves and country if you do that.

Mr. Horsefield also knows just how to talk to boys.

He told a most effective story about a patient little boy whose leg was pinned under a car in an English railway accident. At last a great, strong fellow came along, worked like a giant, and sawed and pried till he got him out.

As the lad, his leg broken badly, lay upon the track, he felt in his pockets till he found among the rubbish there a ha'penny (a cent), and feebly held it up. "It's all I have," he said; "but I want you to take it, for you deserve it." The man did take it, and valued it always, and gave the boy much more than a cent in return, because the grateful boy had given him his all. The application to Jesus was beautifully made — how He has saved us, and how He wants the ha'-penny of our lives, though they are worth very little in themselves.

Dr. Elliott caught the attention of the boys by telling of a dog whose collar, when the curious pushed aside the long hair, was found to contain the words, "I'm Bill Jones's dog; whose dog are you?"

The speaker declared: I am the boys' dog, for there is nothing else I like so much as the boys, — except, perhaps, the girls!

Let me tell you about a poor boy sent from New York out into the country. They put before him a bowl of creamy milk. "What's that?" asked the boy. "That's milk." "Naw; that isn't milk; milk's blue, and that's yellow." Dr. Elliott's talk was a straight-out description of the "foursquare boy," who, like Jesus, grows in body, and wisdom, and favor with God and man.

Rev. C. H. Bandy, of India, has been for years a tower of strength to our Christian Endeavor cause in that great empire. He brought the meeting to a glorious climax.

He explained just what it means to be a Christian, and he asked all the boys to rise that were ready to give their lives to Christ and count themselves Christians from that time on. Some forty boys rose, in a splendid, manly way, and without a particle of urging. When the older persons present were called upon for just such a determination, at once four or five of them took their stand with the boys. It was the most beautiful and profitable scene of the entire Convention, and richly worth all that the entire Convention cost.

GIRLS' MEETING.

No one who visited the First Baptist Church could fail to be impressed with the fact that Christian Endeavor, whatever it means to the older people, means a very great deal to the young girls. They were there at the church in hundreds.

The meeting was opened by devotional exercises, led by Miss Williams, the Colorado Junior superintendent, who earnestly impressed the warning, "Remember thy Creator in the days of thy youth."

Miss Kate Haus, of St. Louis, followed with an interesting chalk-talk based on Rev. iv: 1–7, impressing the truth that Christ must have the throne of our heart, our pledge must be unbroken, our strength, brains, sacrifice, and swiftness be used in soul-winning.

Miss Teachout of Cleveland, O., sang a beautiful solo.

Miss Eakin, of Siam, gave an instructive and pleasing address in behalf of Siamese girls, telling how much Christ is doing for Siam, and begging for our prayers and help.

She told of the boys and girls of that far away land; of some of their strange customs, and of how unfortunate they were when compared to the boys and girls of free America. Interesting episodes of child life in Siam were related, and a story told of one little boy who died soon after he was converted to the Christian belief. His mother was a heathen, and it is usually the case when a child dies in Siam for the mother to make the air hideous with her lamentations. Upon this occasion, however, the little boy, although very ill, had been very happy in the thought of dying, and his mother could not but contrast his experience with others. When at last his little body was laid away in the tomb, and the mother had not shed a tear during all the time, one of the missionaries asked her if she did not feel the death of her little boy. "Oh, yes," she replied, "I feel it, but how can I weep when I know he is so happy?" The recital of this little pathetic tale brought tears to the eyes of many in the audience.

Miss Gibbons, of Tacoma, Wash., spoke enthusiastically on the topic, "Only a Girl," proving the wonderful power that God has placed in a girl's hand, and entreating that it be used for God and for soul-saving.

The meeting was one of the most enthusiastic and helpful of the Convention.

CHAPTER XVI.

The Triumphant Eleven.

SUNDAY EVENING.

The famous Denver "Eleven," were not a foot-ball team, but the eleven Sunday evening meetings that packed eleven of Denver's prominent churches as full as city ordinances would permit them to be filled.

THE EVANGELISTIC RALLY

was held in the First Baptist Church, and by the time the services began the building was crowded to its utmost capacity.

The meeting was in charge of Dr. James M. Gray, of Boston. Rev. W. H. Brooks of Washington, one of our honored colored trustees, spoke first, presenting the gospel invitation in a beautifully simple and impressive way.

He was followed by Mr. Campbell who spoke for the third time that day, in an address that showed the power of the man as did nothing else in all his many contributions to the Convention. It was an expository sermon, and was wholly extemporaneous, taking up points that had just been suggested by Dr. Brooks.

One strong element in Mr. Campbell's magical control of men's hearts is his fearless originality in Scripture interpretation.

He took a view of the dying thief on the cross and of Mary of Magdalene such as probably no one else in his audience entertained, and he made it seem not only possible, but in many ways beautifully probable, and in any event wonderfully suggestive. The "thief" had been trying by revolt to procure for his people freedom from Roman tyranny. Christ had proclaimed a spiritual Kingdom, not to be won by the sword. "You are right, Master," says the discouraged revolutionist, "and I was wrong. I am dying, but they will not kill You. Soon you will break Your bands, descend from the cross, and set up Your kingdom. Remember me, when You come into it."

Mary the Magdalene, Mr. Campbell pictured as Mary of Bethany, the fallen daughter of Simon the Pharisee, returned home because Jesus had gone there and in the faint hope of pardon from her stern father. But the father only says, "What kind of prophet is this, not to know what sort of woman our Mary is?"

"Repentance," the preacher taught, "is just rising up and going home, with or without the feeling of remorse. *It is the climax of a state of mind in which God seeks man before man seeks God.* Never say that lost innocence cannot be regained. Is there anything the gospel of Christ cannot do? Now come; let us break through prejudice. Theoretically we say, No; practically we say, Yes. My feeling is that there is no moral task too great for Christ. Innocence comes back when holiness comes, for "innocent" means not unstained, but unhurt.

Mr. Campbell's address had evidently greatly impressed his audience, and Dr. Gray seized the opportunity to call for decisions for Christ, whose loving sympathy had been so powerfully pictured. The vast majority of those present were Christians, but one conversion at least was made known as the result of the gathering — a result over which the angels in heaven rejoiced.

THE TEMPERANCE RALLY.

The crowds poured into the People's Tabernacle until even the window casings were crowded. The seats of the chorus were taken and even the ladies' and gentlemen's rest rooms held all that could shove into their confines.

That women were absolutely responsible for even the moderate drinking that is going on in our country was the declaration of Rev. Ira Landrith of Nashville, Tenn. He spoke on "The Liquor Problem as Related to the Individual," and insisted that if the women of Denver really wanted drinking to stop they could stop it by to-morrow night and so effectively that not a saloon would be open in the city.

"Ostracize the drinker," he said, "it doesn't make any difference whether he only takes one drink a month, whether he is a moderate drinker or gets drunk every night." Treat him just the same."

In closing his address Mr. Landrith gave his one counsel to the moderate drinker — "Quit." Then he quoted the couplet with which somebody has described President Roosevelt,

"When he sees a thing is true,
He goes to work and puts it through."

Calling upon all who would unite in it, he repeated a revised version of the couplet, and almost the entire audience arose and joined in saying with vigor and earnestness: —

"When I see a thing is true,
I'll go to work and put it through."

Rev. W. F. Wilson of Ontario, who discussed "The drink problem as related to the Nation," declared,

The ravages of rum are the curse of every nation. The saloon everywhere is a curse; in London, Paris, Berlin, Glasgow, Boston, Washington, Toronto, and Denver, it is the same. The United States stands fifteenth on the list of nations in regard to the amount of alcoholic drinks consumed, yet her drink bill last year was $1,500,000,000; so we see that the prosperity of even this great and growing nation is imperilled. The saloon is the Gibraltar of greed, the Jericho of lust and crime, the slaughter-house of character and health, the sewer-pipe of misery and despair. What power rules this Republic and our Dominion, — the forces of the decalogue or the demijohn? the church or the saloon? This traffic is doomed; you can no more regulate it than you can cholera and smallpox; it must be stamped out.

THE MISSIONARY RALLIES.

Missionary rallies were held at Trinity Methodist and Central Presbyterian Churches, and the capacity of both church auditoriums was taxed. Music was given especial prominence at both meetings. The speaking was divided among five missionaries at each place of rally, and the time limit set upon the remarks of each was ten minutes.

At the Central Presbyterian Church, the Rev. E. E. Chivers, a Baptist field secretary for home missions, related instances of "heathenism" existing in the States and urged more home missionary work.

He recently made the entire trip by wagon through the Big Horn basin of Wyoming, and it took him eleven days. He preached at every available schoolhouse and farm, and was at no time closer than fifteen miles to the railroad. He had a true taste of frontier life, driving through swollen streams and over uninhabited country. There are more than 1,000 people scattered about through this basin who were reached with preaching. He was accompanied by a missionary worker and an evangelistic singer. There is a great field for missionary work among these people, and he went himself to look the ground over.

Rev. W. P. Bentley spoke for China, his theme being

God With Us.

"God with us" is the known or silent motto of every valiant soldier of the cross.

Take China, for example. As a result of their ages of experience, the Chinese are familiar with the fundamental conceptions of the Christian religion. They have a religious vocabulary. Their ideas of God, sin, punishment, forgiveness, mercy, sanctity, righteousness and eternal life, have to be corrected and elevated, but not created. They have also developed lofty social and ethical codes. Indeed so thorough has been their schooling, that it is not so much doctrines they need, as a new *life*. It is Christ they need. They need new convictions, new impulses, new motives.

God has also been educating the Christian church to a sense of its responsibilities in the case. First the dawn of modern missions. Then nearly a century of experimental training in mission work. The rise of Young Men's Christian Association, Christian Endeavor, and kindred movements; the growth of the spirit of Christian union; the growing sense of the needs of the pagan nations, and the consequent responsibilities.

Mr. Ogawa, the delegate from Japan, dressed in cool, Oriental costume, spoke the closing words of this inspiring meeting.

At Trinity Church, mission stations in Japan, Siam, India and Africa were represented respectively by Miss A. E. Garvin, Miss Eakin, the Rev. John H. Wyckoff and Rev. Willis R. Hotchkiss. Dr. Wyckoff said: —

The great problem that confronts the missionary in India is how to rescue the Hindoo from the baneful effects of false philosophy. The essence of that philosophy is contained in the brief formula which translated, reads: "God is one, no second." On first hearing these words some of you might think the Hindoo was as Orthooox as he ought to be, but do not so easily be deceived. These words in the mouth of a Hindoo do not mean all you think. When he asserts God is one, there is no second, he means indeed that there is but one God, but one in such a sense that there is not only no second God, but no other existence in the Universe except God. Brahminism teaches there is but one supreme being in the world, and all men from highest to lowest are but manifestations of that being, all life, men, birds, trees, fishes, all is God. All my thoughts are thoughts of this one supreme mind. All my acts are the acts of this one universal will. There are two practical effects of this theosophy. All worship is the worship of God, and the Brahmin has multiplied the number of his Gods, and now they number 330,000,000. In India, nearly everything you see has become an object of worship, and is defended on this principle that everything is a manifestation of God. India is the most idolatrous country on the face of the earth. Wherever you go you may see idols on the wayside. On every hillside, under every green tree, idols painted with the most hideous countenances, for the Brahmin teach the people God is angry with his votaries and can only be appeased by their offerings. I said India was the most idolatrous country on the face of the earth. I do not hesitate to say India is the most immoral country on the face of the earth, due directly to this pernicious doctrine. There is more true morality in this single city of Denver with less than 200,000 people than there is among the whole 40,000,000 of Hindoos in South India. I do not hesitate to go further and say that there is more true manhood, and womanhood within the walls of this tent at this moment, than there is amongst the millions of Hindoos in that great land of South India.

Now Christian Endeavor is helping us to solve this great problem of India's conversion, and it is doing it in three ways. First, by cultivating among the young people of this land a missionary spirit. Second, Christian Endeavor is helping to solve the problem of India's conversion by actually sending missionaries to the heathen, and supporting native workers upon the field. I believe we will be astonished to learn what a large factor Christian Endeavor has become in the solution of the problem of the world's evangelization. We have now in India 600 Christian Endeavor Societies. Through these Christian Endeavor Societies thousands of heathens every year are hearing the glorious tidings of salvation.

Rev. Willis R. Hotchkiss said in behalf of Africa:—

A little boy was making mud-pies by the roadside. A good lady coming along said to him, "My little man, wouldn't you like to be an angel in heaven?" "No," replied the little fellow, "want to be an angel here in the mud!"

There was an good deal of philosophy in the little fellow's reply as related to the work of Christ in the world. What the great world of heathendom wants is not angels in heaven, but men and women with the spirit of heaven down here on earth.

Christian Endeavor was born into the world to help bring this vast human need and the Divine supply together. Some of the principles underlying this movement fit very closely into the problems that confront us in the Dark Continent.

Christian Endeavor stands for the idea of the priesthood of believers. It believes in harnessing the whole body of Christians to the work of the church. This means in Africa a self-supporting, self-propagating native church.

Yonder on the shores of the great Victoria Nyanza we are a little force of seven missionary Endeavorers in a tribe numbering a million people. But what are we among so many! Seven against a million! One against a hundred and forty-two thousand! Can we compass the need? Nay! But we can train a force of native workers, who, in God's hand will do the work much more quickly and effectively than we could do it ourselves.

Another principle of Christian Endeavor which vitally affects our work in Africa is that of Christian citizenship. No lazy man can be a good citizen. God has left no place in His economy for the professional tramp. "Six days shalt thou labor" is as binding upon men as "thou shalt rest on the seventh day."

Africa is in the midst of a great transition, The mighty forces of civilization and progress are at work. The long silence of her forests and plains is broken by the screech of the locomotive, and the throb of the propeller is felt in her rivers and lakes, while the tides of commercial activity rise higher and higher. Unless the African is trained in habits of industry to meet these changes, he will go down as the American Indian has gone down, before the advance of civilization.

THE SABBATH OBSERVANCE RALLY.

Two very able papers were delivered in the Central Christian Church. Rev. Luther P. Ludden, D.D., Western district secretary of the Lutheran Board of Home Missions, had for his theme,

SABBATH OBSERVANCE — A DAY OF WORSHIP.

I do not believe that the church is declining. Its outlook was never better. More people worship to-day than ever in the world's history, but still there is a great host that do not regard the Sabbath as a day for worship. As each generation passes away, God's work has been found to advance. Years ago the great, work of Sabbath worship swung out this way. In the days of the Puritans, this gave the rigidity to worship that to many was very oppressive, and under its sternness the church suffered, and there was a turning away from it, and when the reaction set in, the pendulum swung away to the other extreme, and an attempt was made to force the continental Sunday upon our American people, and then came the trying time of the church. It needed the mighty force of the united church to prevent the pendulum from remaining away over to the one side.

It is beginning to swing about right, and the Christian world is coming to see the Sabbath as a day of sacred worship. We can keep it so if the great multitude of Christian Endeavor workers will simply put their shoulders to the wheel and crowd forward in the steady way they know so well how to do, and the sacredness of the Sabbath, as a day of worship, will be manifested, and the church will cease to grow in conformity to the world, and will develop gradually along the lines God marks out. This true worship on the Sabbath will bring back greater study of the Bible, new forms of religious activity, and larger accessions to the church, while everywhere will be seen manifestations of the filling with the Holy Spirit.

The pendulum for sacred Sabbath worship is swinging just about right now. The possibilities of the age are crowding the work of sacred worship upon us, and shall we, with our great Christian Endeavor numbering millions, step into the gates that are opening into the wide, wide world? All that seems necessary is for us to hitch our hopes to the great triumphant chariot of Jehovah, and go forth and possess what lies just a little ways beyond.

Rev. Alexander Esler, Toronto, Canada, proved himself a popular and helpful speaker in his address,

THE SABBATH — A NATIONAL NECESSITY.

To yon seventh story office I may go either by the fire-escape, the stairway, or the elevator. It is profitable for me to take the elevator — not absolutely necessary. I may climb up the stairs — I'll be a fool if I do, but men can and often do elect to be fools. But suppose there is no stairway and only the elevator; then to reach yon office it is absolutely necessary to take the elevator. Can we declare so emphatically as that, that the Sabbath is necessary for the preservation of our best national ideals and securing the prosperity of the people? Cannot the best national ideals be preserved, and the prosperity of the people be secured if we had no Sabbath? Crafts answers the question, "No nation can reach its high ideal without it." Rev. George T. Washburn, in a letter from India, says, "There is not a non-Sabbath keeping nation that is not abjectly poor." The only assurance a nation has of continued prosperity is in the health, character, virtue, intelligence, moral, religious and spiritual welfare of its people. The Sabbath is necessary for the development in the individual citizen, and is necessary to the prosperity of the nation.

First. The Sabbath is necessary for the best health of men. In Europe where there are many Jews who strictly observe the Hebrew Sabbath, and Gentiles who do not observe Sunday, the physical difference is more and more marked. The average life of the Jew in those lands is ten years longer than that of his Christian neighbors in the same country.

Second. The Sabbath is necessary for man's mental development. The great majority of men are engaged in manual toil — they come home at night tired — physically exhausted — they are not in condition for thought. If a man works seven days in the week he is incapacitated for study; those of us who have tried it have found how difficult it is to work and study, though we had the Sabbath to rest; how hopeless would our task have been had we had no Sabbath. We might have remained hewers of wood and drawers of water, and never have been good for anything else than to be kicked about by idlers who bossed us. Thank God for Sabbath liberty — to have one day in seven as a free man, fifty-two days in the year all my own in which no man can boss me.

Third. It is necessary also for the moral and religious welfare of the individual and the nation. During six days of the week spent in worldly things the judgment is liable to become twisted, and needs to be made straight. Sabbath gives the time to come away from the influences of all metallic and other attractions, and get the moral sense righted, and if a man has not the time for getting straight he will get very crooked in course of time.

Fourth. The Sabbath is necessary to develop man's social and spiritual life. Fathers, even with the Sabbath, have not too much time with their families; but what would they do if they had to work seven days in the week? I tell you it would break up the home. In Sabbathless countries free divorces or crimes against the marriage law or both are alarmingly common.

The Sabbath wipes out class distinctions. The working man washes, changes his clothes, goes to church the peer of his master — yes, any man, if he have an honest heart. In church the rich learn humility, and the poor self-respect. Without the Sabbath we can have but a nation of slaves — with the Sabbath a nation of free men.

THE HOUSEHOLD ENDEAVOR RALLY.

One of the new ideas which has recently been promulgated in Christian Endeavor work was the topic for the service at the Plymouth Congregational Church. This is "Christian Endeavor in the Home," which is an attempt to extend the principles underlying the Christian Endeavor Society into the actual home life, not only by the young people, but also by their parents.

Dr. Francis E. Clark opened the discussion with an address on "Household Christian Endeavor," in which he pleaded for the keeping up of the family altar.

For years Christian Endeavor has stood for religion in the home as well as in the church; for family prayers as well as for prayer-meeting prayers; for household piety, as well as for civic righteousness and missionary zeal.

Let us enlarge our boundaries until Christian Endeavor principles of outspoken devotion affect all the households in the land so far as we can reach them. Why should not children have part at the family altar, as well as the father or grandfather? Why not make daily prayers interesting and profitable to all by giving all a part in them?

The young people's prayer meeting has been rejuvenated in this way; why not the family meeting for prayer be viewed in the same way?

At least once a week give a chance, not only for the father but for the mother, if she will, and for all the boys and girls, to have part in reading the Word and in prayer. The children's prayers may be very simple and short, indeed, they should be, but they are as effectual, I believe, as those of the gray-haired saint, and heard as soon by the Creator in His dwelling place.

Such weekly family prayer services are already held in many homes, and most delightful services they are, as I can testify from actual experience and observation. One of my friends (Mr. Stinson of Mississippi who speaks from this platform this evening) makes a distinction between family prayers and household prayers. He conducts family prayers himself every morning, and *household* prayers, in which all, down to the lisping four year old, have part, every evening. Why may not every family have such a blessed service at least once a week? It will cement family affection, lead the hearts of all to the great Father, accustom even infant lips to prayer before others; prepare the children for prayer and service in their society and the church, and bring to all the unutterable blessings of outspoken devotion to the Elder Brother, in that most sacred spot in all the world — the home circle.

Dr. Clark was followed by Mrs. John A. Stinson, Columbus, Miss., who could tell of a practical test of the home Endeavor ideas.

I feel grateful to the committee that I have been assigned a subject so near my heart, and one so important in the great cause of Christian Endeavor. Lack of time will prevent my discussing at length every feature of this important subject, and I shall begin by saying Christian Endeavor should begin in the home, and I believe if the homes which are every day being begun by our Endeavorers, will begin as real Endeavor homes, homes founded on prayer and the precepts of God's word, that with every Endeavor home there will be a family altar where night and morning the incense of prayer will rise to the throne of God, I believe that His love will be the oil in the lamp on that altar and that it will light the house with the beauteous rays of God's eternal love, blessing not only the present but generations yet unborn.

Mr. Stinson makes a distinction between family devotions and household devotions.

He has family prayers every evening led by himself, but every morning he has household prayers for family and servants, in which, as in an Endeavor meeting, each one takes a part "aside from singing."

All the servants in the South are negroes, and Mr. Stinson testified that household devotions had exercised a softening effect on the most uncertain-tempered servant of his household, who, as he was leaving for Denver, called out cheerily, "Good-by, Mr. Stinson; I hope you done goin' talk good to dem peoples up dar."

The question is often asked why so many ungodly children come from so-called Christian homes? I answer thus: The absence of a family altar and the neglecting of the daily reading of the word of God. Thus have they unconsciously erected selfish human standards, created wrong ideals, and can you expect a child reared under such circumstances to be other than ungodly? Now I ask you the simple question, how many bad men and women do you know who came from homes where consecrated fathers and mothers, each day, led them to a family altar and poured forth their souls in prayer that God might ever shield their young lives from temptation? or, better still, give them strength to overcome it, and let each succeeding day witness a strengthening of character in the lives of their children. Few children from such homes have ever brought reproach on the name of their God, or remorse to the loving hearts of their parents. Ah, true as the needle to the pole, so true are they who have been taught the great principles of right thought in the tender years of childhood, that they might practice them in the more mature years of young manhood and womanhood.

'Sampson was blind," were the opening words of Dr. William Patterson's address,

SCENE IN TENT ENDEAVOR.

But he was long-headed. He knew that if he could remove the pillars of the house it would fall; and so he got the boy to lead him to the pillars of the Philistine palace, and pulled them down.

What those pillars were to the palace, prayer and the Bible are to the nation.

"You can't do much with the old sinners," he said. "They are like the blackthorn sticks that grow in my native country; some people get as twisted as corkscrews." "But you take the boys and girls when they are young, and you can grow them straight."

Dr. Patterson roundly scored the fashionable club as an enemy of the home. Some fathers hardly know their own children when they see them. He had heard of a father, who, for a wonder, one night stayed at home and cared for the children. When his wife returned, he told her that he had a good deal of trouble in getting the fourth son to bed. She reminded him that he was father of but three boys, and examination showed that he had put one of Jones's boys to bed as his own.

No meeting in the entire Convention went to the roots of things more directly than this one, and it must provoke wholesome thought and wise action.

WEAVING OUR OWN DESTINY.

The following address was delivered by Rev. E. L. House, D.D., Portland, Ore., Sunday evening, at Boulevard Congregational Church.

"My days are swifter than a weaver's shuttle." — Job vii: 6.

It is not my purpose to use the text in the exact sense meant by Job when he alluded to the swiftness of his days, but to convey to you another picture which must have been in his mind when he spoke the words of our text. Job must have seen weavers at work somewhere, or else he would not have thought out the comparison he made in the text.

According to Greek tradition, the idea of weaving was gathered from the web of a spider. At first, simple interlacings of shreds of bark, plants, vegetable stalks were used; later fibres, such as flax, hemp, cotton, and silk were used, and finally wool and hair were utilized. Such in a word is the history of weaving.

But now before a man can begin to weave he must have given unto him that which is called the "warp." This consists of threads of yarn extending from end to end the whole length of the web. It is mounted on the loom for weaving, and into it the "weft" is thrown by means of a shuttle. With this "warp" as a foundation and the "weft" at hand awaiting man's bidding, one can weave a beautiful pattern which merits the applause of all who see it. In the spiritual world

ALL MEN ARE WEAVERS.

God has not only given to us this great world as the loom, but has also provided the "warp" and "weft," we need in our natural endowments. And of what does our "warp" and "weft" consist? There is the human brain, a wonderful piece of mechanism, whose power no man fully knows. What wonderful things it hath wrought! "Who can stand in St. Peter's, at Rome, and listen to the deep toned organ reverberating from arch to arch, with a chorus of human voices alike pathetic and triumphant in their hymns of praise, without feeling the divine harmony in architecture, poetry, and song?" And yet, man, so small in stature, conceived and perfected that vast cathedral, with its magnificent dome, strung every key in that grand organ to answer to a master's touch, and trained every voice in that great choir to melody — to perfect time and tune — a combination in grandeur surpassing, far, the seven wonders of the world.

Then there is that wonderful gift of memory. Memory is to the thinker what vaults and their contents are to the banker. It is life's battle, on whose walls are hung the flags that tell of the struggles through which we have marched. It is the heart's mausoleum, in which are treasured the loves that made golden the days that have dropped into sunset. With it we can gaze back into the past, revisit our old home, and the familiar places of our boyhood; we can recall the faces of mother, father, brother, sister, child, and friends. To open the window of this chamber may mean to flood the soul with sunshine, or shadow it with the sullen frown of the storm cloud. The soul increases in knowledge and culture, because as it passes through life's rich fields, memory plucks the ripe treasure on either hand. Hence

A Man's Memory is His Entire Capital.

It is his great reservoir, the great storehouse from which he draws his supplies. "Memory is a library holding wisdom for to-morrow's emergencies; it is a granary holding bread for to-morrow's hunger; it is an arsenal holding weapons for to-morrow's battle; it is a medicine chest holding balms for to-morrow's hurts." Through memory man strikes a larger radius of power and intelligence every day he lives.

Then again what a wonderful help to man his senses are. A man is like a vast union depot with lines running out through his senses into all the world. Great train loads of power and influence are brought over the lines to make him strong, and ready for divine service. Without the senses man would be a dungeon, but now he is a palace beautiful. How the palace has been adorned through the eyes and ears! How it has been supplied through the sense of taste! How it has been refreshed by the sense of smell! How it has been protected by the sense of touch! Through these avenues of man's being, great blessings have come. How vividly Helen Keller, deaf, dumb, and blind, illustrates in her wonderfully developed life, the value of one of these senses, the sense of touch.

I wish I had time to tell you about the imagination, the reason, the will of man, but I can only allude to them. The imagination is the noblest faculty of the mind. By it we leap beyond the bounds of the human and dwell with the saints of light. By it we transcend the earth, escape the limitation of space and create new worlds of beauty. Reason is a bond-slave to the imagination. "Reason collects facts, imagination constructs these facts into new art products. Reason collects sounds; imagination turns them into symphonies. Reason collects ideas of right and wrong; imagination turns them into ethical systems." Both are great factors to a man's greatness.

The Will is the Executive Force.

of man. It cannot be overthrown, cannot be compelled to abdicate and give up its throne and sceptre. No weapons can batter down its walls. No science can bore through its defences and search out its secrets. It is the power in man that enables him to say "no" to God, and make good the defiance. It is the engine in man that furnishes the power for him to go on with his plans, and executes them, in spite of adverse winds.

Oh, the wonderful power of man! With his wonderful gifts he has conquered the sea and the storm, and all nature. He has harnessed the lightning and flashed his words under oceans, over mountains, across valleys, until the world sits at his feet and tells him her trials, battles, successes and victories. And is this all? No! Man has caught the sunbeam and made it draw his picture; he has opened rocks and made their atoms give up their laws, and tell him the story of the past; he has made the telescope, and through it read God's handiwork, and glory in the worlds above.

Man has Seized the Wilderness.

and cleared it into the city; he entered the desert and it became a garden; he turned the forked trees into ships and houses; chiselled huge stones into temples and cathedrals; wrought papyrus leaves into books, iron and wood and brass into music, and wool and cotton into clothing. Surely the "warp" of man is equal to all the demands that the old world shall make upon him.

But let us now notice the important part the shuttles play in the weaving. They are filled with different fibres and colors. If all our fabrics were of one color and quality, we should soon grow tired of them. But when we see the different shades and qualities, we find something new and pleasing for our apparel and for the furnishings of our homes.

Our Heavenly Father delights in variety, for He has written this law over all His works. The earth is in no sense like a desk full of drawers of the same geometrical arrangement. It resembles rather a mansion, no two rooms of which are alike. An ever varying pattern is seen in the world of nature. Here is a mountain, over there, a valley, a prairie, here an ocean, over there, a river, a lake; here a chasm, over there, a cataract, and so it goes bringing added interest to the sons of men as they journey over, and inspect their wonderful home.

And God does not cast us in the same mould. For there are no two human faces alike, no two human voices alike, no two human minds alike, and

No Two Human Souls Alike.

We have a color, an individuality, all our own. Our life represents a shuttle and it is God's desire that we shall bring just what he has given us, and weave it in His great plan for the race of men. Diversified as are the talents and spheres of men, each has a design to fill up, an end to reach, something to do — a life to live, whose grandeur is to be measured, not by the flash and the noise it makes, so much as by the simple fidelity with which it accepts and uses its trusts.

"God hates uniformity. The imminent activity of God, i.e., that activity which is expended upon and within His own essehce, we can not scrutinize. That remains His own eternal secret. But whenever and whatever activity proceeds from God an extra, it is always complex and infinitely variegated. 'There is one glory of the sun, and another glory of the moon, and another glory of the stars, for one star differeth from another star in glory.' Whatever glimpses are afforded us in the Book of the Life of heavenly intelligences, they all show us an endless variety; archangels and angels, seraphim and cherubim, thrones and principalities and powers — all reflecting some distinct ray of the divine power and perfection, and all moving in their own appointed orbits of celestial praise and occupation. The cosmos tells us an endless story of change and variety, but its every radius runs to one common center — God."

"Not all birds sing the same song; not all trees yield the same fruit; not all mines give forth the same precious metals; not all fields wave with the same harvests. The law is individuality, variety."

The Great Thing is Faithfulness.

whether a man is on a farm or vessel, in store or mill, in law or medicine, in teaching or preaching, in writing or editing, so that it can be said he is inrceasing the world's good." The humblest life is not meaningless, purposeless. In its place and true intent it is the interpretation of God's design. The clear apprehension of this fact kindles the spirit of one's mission and becomes a source of all mastering strength. Let a man feel that he is needed, that he has a work to do, that he is in his appointed place and engaged upon his allotted task, and he cannot be weak and wavering, easily discouraged or driven from his undertaking.

Again notice, that the weaver has his pattern given him. Before him has been placed a design which he is instructed to reproduce in his weaving. His value as a workman depends as to how near he is capable of reproducing that which his pattern calls for in design and color. In our spiritual weaving we find a pattern. It is Christ, the Son of God. After passing through thirty years of trial, subjected all the while to the severest trial and ordeal that Roman hate and Jewish prejudice could invent; after being watched and criticized at all times and places — on the streets, in the synagogue, in the homes of the Scribes and Pharisees, they utterly failed to find any just accusation against him. And at

last when betrayed, arrested, and hurried by cruel hands before the court, and
into the presence of those who sought his life, and were thirsting for his blood;
even here, with bribed and perjured witnesses all around Him, no charge of guilt
could be sustained. Pilate was compelled to say:

"I Find No Fault at All."

And this same person who stands faultless before the world, before angels, before God, the Father, is our Saviour, our King, our great Exemplar, and the divine Model, after which we may well fashion our lives.

Our value as men depends as to how near we can come to this divine pattern,
and the truths He has spoken. He has laid the foundations of our Christianity.
It is His work. If we commit ourselves to it, we shall make no mistake.

A few years ago the first iron railroad bridge was built in Pennsylvania. The
building of the bridge was of great interest to railroad men, for it the builder
should do what he claimed for his new invention, it would revolutionize bridge
building. The day of proving his claims came. A large number of men were
present to watch the inspection and see the testing. Three large engines were
there to be driven onto the bridge to test its strength. When the engineers saw
the small iron girders which were to sustain the weight of their engines, they said
the bridge would not hold them, and refused to run their engines upon it. In
vain, the builder protested, telling them that he had tested every piece of iron
before it came from his factory, and that he knew the bridge would hold the engines. What was he to do? It seemed as if the testing would be a failure. He
could not run the engines upon the bridge himself, for he knew nothing about
the running of engines. At last a thought came to him, and he began at once
to put it into execution.

Going down to the side of the river, he jumped into a little boat and rowed
away. What was he going to do? In a few moments the wondering spectators
understood. The builder rowed out into the middle of the stream, up to the
middle of the river under the bridge and anchoring his boat directly under the
centre of it, folded his arms and with a voice full of intensity said: "Ride on with
your engines; I put my life under this bridge that it shall hold."

When the engineers saw that the man was willing to put his life under the
bridge they said, "It will hold," and they rode on with their engines, and it stood
the test, and there it is to-day.

Now God the Father, Christ the Son, and the Holy Spirit, built this bridge
of truth.

Christ's Life is under It.

We need not fear to test its strength and efficacy. Millions have passed
over it to the better land, and to-day millions are crossing to the land of light
and eternal joy. Christ is our pattern; look at His life, test His truth, and you
shall find the Holy Spirit directing you to that which is highest and best in life,
and your weaving will take upon itself the color and beauty of the Master's
life.

And now the strength of the whole fabric depends on the quality of each
thread. If there be one thread of inferior quality, the beauty of the fabric is
marred. How often we see some beautiful piece of texture damaged by some
little thing, and the result is that the piece of goods is sold below cost. How
many lives are marred by some little thing, and yet a little thing may turn the
current of a human life. A cannon is but a short tube, but its direction at the
moment of its discharge governs the whole flight of the ball. A clay mould is a
fragile thing; but the molten metal poured into it may retain the shape so given
ages after the mould has crumbled to dust. The plate prepared by a photographer
may be exposed to the light only a second, but the impression there caught may
be retained for many years. Little things affect the quality of our lives more
than we know.

What We Need To-day is Quality.

We are sometimes told that the Church of God has not the moral influence to-day that it had in the days of our forefathers. What is the trouble, if this be true? Is it because we have not as much intelligence, as much wealth, as many adherents? No! for we have more of these than at any other time in the history of the church.

Ole Bull and John Ericsson were born in the Old Country, about the same time. They grew up together, and early in their young manhood, emigrated to the United States. Each became famous, one as a great violinist, the other as a great mechanical engineer. After awhile their lives were separated and they saw nothing of each other for a number of years.

One day they met on the streets of New York, and after they had exchanged greetings, Ole Bull said:

"John, have you heard me play lately?"

"No!" said John Ericsson.

"Come up to the Academy of Music and hear me play to-night," said Ole Bull.

"I can't very well," was the reply. "I would like to for old friendship's sake, but I am very busy, and to tell you the truth, Ole, I haven't any love of music in my soul." And he did not go to hear his friend play.

One day a few weeks after, Ole Bull went down to John Ericsson's shop, and called for him. "He is out in the shop," said his bookkeeper. Out into the shop went Ole Bull, and he soon located John talking with one of his workmen. Just as soon as he was disengaged Ole Bull stepped up to him, and shaking him by the hand said, "John, something is the matter with my violin, and I have brought it down for you to see it."

And they talked about the tones and the half tones, and John Ericsson became interested in the mechanical part of the violin. After a few moments, Ole Bull said, "John, I'll tell you what I mean by a tone and a half tone," and putting the violin up to his shoulder, he began to slowly draw his bow across the instrument.

Suddenly the air was vibrating with sweet, melodious music that stirred the very depths of one's being. All the men hearing, looked up, and seeing the author of it, began to leave their benches, and soon were about the great musician,

Enraptured with His Wonderful Music.

Faster, and faster, went his bow, more wonderful was the music, until it seemed as if there was a great orchestra present and many instruments were lending their skill to make harmony that would cause even the angels to listen. The men were swayed in their emotions, now crying, now showing dilated eyes, and vision faces.

Suddenly in the midst of one of his wonderful harmonies, he stopped short, and there stood John Ericsson, his face all lighted up, tears were running down his cheeks, and his whole being was stirred to its very depths, and as soon as he missed the tones that had brougdt a new world into his being, he cried with great intensity of feeling:

"Play on! play on, Ole; I have found out what I lack in my life; play on!"

And then once more the great wizard of the violin took up his instrument, and played until it did seem as if the angels of God possessed it, and down in the depths of his nature, John Ericsson found that there was something that had been lacking in his life.

And is there not something lacking in our church life, although many seem to be unconscious of it? And what is this lack? A lack of quality. A lack of the Holy Spirit. Would God, we would listen to Him, and let Him touch our hearts with heaven's melody! Then would come power that should enable us to meet all the requirements of the times, and to follow in the footsteps of our Lord Jesus Christ.

Again, going back a little, you remember that I intimated that each flight of the shuttle leaves a contribution behind it. And so does each life. What influence will we leave in this world after we have gone through it? "None," answer a hundred voices; "we are not one of the immortals." "Fifty years after we are out of this world it will be as though we never inhabited it." "You are wrong in saying that.

A Man Leaves More than a Gap.

and a memory behind him at death.

"He leaves words and deeds and forces and tendencies, and the thousand and one influences which represent power; and these remain, not for one year or two, but for all time. In many instances this is admitted and observed. The author, the composer, the inventor, and all such cannot die. And so is it with the lesser men, they live in others, only in lesser degree." One immortality you will take with you at death; another you will leave behind. It shall stand above your grave when the mound is fashioned and the mourners depart, and shake itself as a strong man rejoicing in his strength, and go forth as one of the forces of the world. It will be impersonal; it will bear no name; it will show no face; and yet, it will be you, your worse self unchecked, unrestrained by the good that was once mated with it, and that kept it within bounds. The young vulture having once broken its chain returns no more, but sails away on wings that grow and darken as they sail guided only in its cruel flights by the license of its coarse instincts.

So is it with sin. Once out of our reach, it is forever beyond our control; we cannot check it; we cannot limit it even. Like a freed vulture we know not where it will fly; we know not on what innocent thing it will pounce, what it shall mangle, or what other sins like unto itself it shall beget.

Then again have you ever noticed that the weaver is sometimes interrupted in his weaving by the breaking of a thread, and this causes annoyance and disappointment. In our life weaving we are often interrupted by providences which we cannot control. We are compelled to weave in the dark threads when we would prefer to weave in the light.

Why Are We Called upon to Suffer in this World?

I cannot answer the question as I would like to, and as you wish to have me. I know that we sometimes bring about our own suffering by our sins and actions. I also know that suffering is corrective, and educational, and that it brings men and women nearer to God. But as to why God sometimes hedges up the path of the just and not the guilty; why he takes my child and leaves yours, I am not able to tell. But one thing I do know, and that is, that God is never so strong and helpful, never so near and so precious to his people, as in hours of need and trial. "Places of suffering are rare spots for seeing things."

When children gather to see the magic lantern, the figures may be flung upon the sheet and yet be invisible, because the room is full of light. Darken the room, and instantly the circle of light is filled with brilliant color. God our Father has often to turn down the lights of our life, because he wants to show us mercy, or to fit us for some great work. Whenever you get into difficulties or perplexing circumstances, be on the watch.

It was when suffering that Bunyan saw his wonderful allegory, and Paul met the Lord. It was when he was blind that Milton wrote "Paradise Lost" and "Regained"; it was when her heart was crushed, but clinging to God that Jenny Lind thrilled the world with her music; it was when exiled and alone that John the Beloved Disciple looked through heaven's open door, and gave to us his wonderful revelation.

"The Night is the Time to See the Stars."

Then again, we as weavers, are seeing our work from the wrong side. When I was a little boy I remember seeing my grandmother at work weaving on an old-fashioned loom. As I gazed upon her work I could see nothing but a tangled mass of ends. There was no beauty, no design there.

Noticing this I said, "Grandma, why don't you weave a beautiful rug of roses and all the pretty colors, such as Aunt Mary has in her rugs?" She at once understood my trouble and said, "Sonny, you just get down and look up under the rug." I did as she told me, and I saw it all at a glance. I had been looking at her work from the wrong side. The roses, the colors, the design were all there.

And so we as Christians are looking at our work from the wrong side, the world side. No wonder that we get discouraged, for our work often seems to be confusion, there is no beauty in it as far as we can see. But if God should draw back the veil and allow us to see things in heaven's light, how amazed we would be at the revelation. For we should see that nothing that is noble and true is ever lost. The kind word spoken, the hearty hand shake, the "God bless you," the giving of means to help some unfortunate one, all these have changed the current of many a human life, and they have become redeemed souls because we simply touched their life by a kind deed.

We Christians often make the serious mistake of being consecrated unto results instead of being consecrated unto God. How much good we are doing, we will not know until we see it in the other life. Our direct influence upon souls around about us is of a kind which we cannot measure now. Some respond to suggestions at once; but many a hard nature does not respond easily, and yet the work is none the less real.

"The seed does not always come up when you sow it. Some seeds do not grow the same season that they are planted.

Some Seeds Need to Be Cracked.

by the winter's cold and frost.

"Some seeds lie in the ground two or more years before they come up. There are those who read these words, who can testify, that God blessed to them the labor of some parent, some pastor, some teacher, some friend, long after the benefactor had gone. Somewhere, at some time, all good work will avail. If we are consecrated unto God, He will take care of results. No work done for God, however small, is lost."

And if, the Christian sees his work from the wrong side, so also does the sinner. Sinner, if you could only see the awfulness of sin as the angels see it, you would forsake evil in all its forms as the one thing to be dreaded in life. I wish it were possible for us to see what it cost the Master in the Garden of Gethsemane the night He wrestled there for the world's redemption. And if the angels could speak to us about Calvary what a story they would tell us of the awfulness of sin. My brother, we must bring our sins to Calvary or else we shall feel the terrible condemnation of its Christ. "O friends, there is a vast difference between the morning of sin, that is its beginning, and the evening of sin, that is its ending. The first is exhilaration, the second is despair. There are men among us to-day who must repent or, go down. The wrong must be put down. Right cannot stand still. Light shall slay the darkness. Why set ourselves against it? We cannot resist the supreme purpose, except to our destruction.

How sin has cursed us. It has thrown up a barrier between ourselves and God. It hath unstrung our harp, and filled the air with discordant music; it hath dug every grave in the bosom of the earth; but for sin we should not have known the name of widow or orphan, tear and sigh, sorrow and death; but for sin, our hearts had been untorn by a pang, and our joy pure as the ecstacies of heaven." God help us to

See Sin Not from the World's Side.

but from the light of heaven and revelation.

And now lastly, as the weaver's work is inspected, so must ours be. It is said that in our mills to-day, after a piece of goods has been placed upon the market, if a flaw is discovered the superintendent can tell who did the work by looking at it. He keeps a record of all the work done by those who are in his employ. Our work must be inspected.

Living in such a world as this, and having such endowments, we ought to make good use of our time, and of our talents, and ought not to be ashamed of any inspection God may make concerning us. The time is coming when we shall stand in the presence of God face to face with our own lives. What will be our feelings as we come into the Judge's presence?

Here is a court-room! There on the platform sits the judge. Through yonder door comes a man, hesitatingly, tremblingly, his face and every movement show fear. He takes his seat and fixes his eyes upon the floor, or he looks around with a haunted look. Hardly has he seated himself, before the door opens again and there comes up the aisle, a young boy, his face radiant, his form erect, his step, elastic. There is no look of fear in those eyes. He walks rapidly along in the presence of the people, comes upon the platform, beside the judge and whispers into his ear. The judge replies;

The Boy With a Look of Happiness Kisses the Judge.

and walks rapidly out of the room. What makes the difference in the relationship of these two persons to the judge?

One is a criminal, and the man is his judge who is to pronounce sentence upon him for wrongdoing; the other is a son and that man is a loving father; he has been a true son, therefore he has no fear. When we stand before God what shall He be to us? We can answer the question by observing what our weaving has been. God help us from this hour to be better weavers, to weave the good and true, the light rather than the dark, that we may be worthy of our time, and talents.

"Let us learn a useful lesson — no braver lesson can be —
From the ways of the tapestry weavers the other side of the sea.
Above their heads the pattern hangs; they study it with care,
And as to and fro the shuttle leaps, their eyes are fastened there.
They tell us this curious thing beside the patient, plodding weaver,
He works on the wrong side evermore, but works for the right side ever.
It is only when the weaving stops, and the web is loosed and turned,
That he sees his real hand-work, that his marvellous skill is learned.
Ah! the sight of the delicate beauty — it pays him for all his cost,
No rarer, daintier work than his was ever done by the frost.
Then the master bringeth him golden hire, and giveth him praise as well.
And how happy the heart of the weaver is, no tongue but his own can tell.
The years of man are the looms of God, let down from the place of the sun,
Wherein we are weaving, till the mystic web is done —
Weaving blindly, but weaving surely, each for himself, his fate.
We may not see how the bright side looks, we can only weave and wait.
But looking above at the Pattern, no weaver hath need to fear,
Only let him look clear into heaven. the Perfect Pattern is there.
If he keeps the face of the Saviour forever and always in sight,
His toil shall be sweeter than honey, and his weaving sure to be right.
And when his task is ended, and the web is turned and shown;
He shall hear the voice of the Master: it shall say to him, "Well done.'
And the white winged angels of heaven, to bear him hence, shall come down,
And God shall give for his hire — not golden coin but a crown."

The Endeavorer's Vision.

The following sermon was given Sunday evening at Asbury M.E. Church, by Rev. Herbert E. Foss, D.D., of Philadelphia : —

More than twenty-seven centuries ago one of God's prophets said to those who sat at his feet. "Your young men shall see visions," and every generation since has had its vision seeing young men and women.

Every noble life, every splendid deed, every great achievement, has been vision born.

The young people's movement has doubtless been an evolution, but its primordial germ was surely a vision in a far seeing and divinely touched soul.

The young people's movement was a vision of fellowship.

I do not mean the fellowship that means merely social amenities, good times, the enlargement of acquaintances, although if nothing other than the wide social contact of millions of young men and women under inspiring and safe auspices instead of under the dangerous and often absolutely pernicious direction of the world had been accomplished, the movement would be worth all it has cost in time and strength and money.

But by fellowship I mean organization, co-operation, combination.

The movement had its birth in a time of organization and combination, and the spirit of co-operation has steadily increased until it is scarcely an exaggeration to say that some form of organization and combination puts the cost mark on the swaddling clothes in which we are wrapped when we come into the world, and upon the shroud in which we go out of it.

We hear a great deal of trusts and combines in these days and many would like to see them eliminated from our economic life, but they have come to stay simply because the enterprises and undertakings of this great century are too stupendous to be factored by one man or a single company.

The most we can do and the best is to so control them that they shall be our servants and not our masters.

Then, too, there is a combination of evil forces.

The saloon, the bawdy house, low amusements, vile literature, and Sabbath desecration, combine against all that is good and pure. Each of these pernicious forces preserves its own autonomy; but for purposes of protection ·and imperialism all stand together. Strike one and you are faced by the whole unholy brood.

Too much in the past the Kingdom of God has been fighting, regiment by regiment, the Kingdom of darkness in its entirety. To-day we have millions of young people — the very flower of our familes, the chivalry of the church, the light horse of the army of Jesus Christ, entering with all the ardor of youth every moral battle, and nowhere can there be found so hopeful a rallying point as where these embattled millions stand ready for united action.

Fellowship Multiplies Power.

There were always large numbers of young men in the world, but their power did not begin to be realized until organizations like the Young Men's Christian Association showed the power of fellowship.

The power of womanhood was sadly underestimated until the Woman's Christian Temperance Union began to close saloons, drag unworthy judges from the bench, defeat impure Congressmen and turn from the doors of our National legislature men whose beliefs and lives were fundamentally opposed to our constitution.

The multiplication of power which resides in fellowship may be seen in the splendid work that is being done to bring the world to Jesus Christ by the missionary organizations of women in the home and foreign field alike.

There were always a good many children in our churches and we loved them and called them sweet names and made pets of them, but it was only when we organized them and loaded them with responsibility, and gave them plenty to do that their full power became apparent.

The possession of power is the measure of obligation, and hence the fellowship of the young men and women of the church of God, multiplying power and imposing obligation has driven them to the altar of consecration, and all this has im easurably deepened the spiritual life of our young Christians.

The Young People's Movement was a Vision of Usefulness.

When Dr. Clark first caught the vision he did not say to himself, "What good times these young people might have if they were only banded together, or what a spectacle these marching millions would make!" I am sure he said rather

"What waste of power is here! What latent energy! What undeveloped possibilities!"

He who thinks of the Young People's Society as a centre of good times, the arranger of straw-rides and candy-pulls, the getter up of sociables for the sake of sociables, has greatly mistaken the spirit of the movement.

The motto of the Endeavor Society is, "For Christ and the Church." The motto of the Epworth League is, "Look Up, Lift Up." If the Young Men's Christian Association has a motto it is "To God, for Man." The words that flash from the badge of every King's Daughter is "In His Name." At the heart of every kindred organization of youth you will find some suggestion of usefulness.

Fads pass; fakes come and go; that which is merely ornamental is relegated to the shelf, but the demand for service, for usefulness is widespread and universal. Our young Christians have seen grand visions of usefulness, and are magnificently working them out.

A young woman in a New England city had received a medical education, and entering into practice, had achieved a very flattering position in the most aristocratic section of the city. All at once she went across the city to the most neglected and sin-cursed portion of the great town and spent years of her splendidly-equipped life among the lowliest of the low and the worst of the bad. Why? She had seen a vision of usefulness which drew her to a wonderfully, beautiful ministry to her fallen sisters.

Frances Willard turned aside from one of the finest educational opportunities a woman ever had to accept the presidency of the Chicago Woman's Christian Temperance Union, in spite of the advice and protests of her friends. She could not have foreseen the throne to which that pathway was to lead her, but she did catch a vision of the possibilities of the world's united womanhood, and saw a field of hard work and sacrifice but of usefulness, and turned that away.

Do you say that these lives are exceptional, and that you are but ordinary? Do you complain that pulpit and platform are always holding before you lives and achievements so great that you cannot hope to equal or very closely imitate them?

The man with the artist's soul traverses continents and crosses oceans that he may sit for months or years before a masterpiece with never a hope of painting its equal; but he'd rather paint a thousand miles below a masterpiece than on a level with a daub.

So, young friends, he who hangs up before you

MASTERPIECES IN FLESH AND BLOOD.

is your best instructor and inspirer.

But there are plenty of homely visions of usefulness.

The world is full of young people who are not entering the doors of the church. Go out and invite them to come in. Go twice or thrice, and if need be, show them the way to the church where a sitting and a welcome await them.

In the midweek meeting of the church you have the amplest opportunity for useful service.

What are you doing Sunday evening, after the young people's meeting has closed? Are you hunting around for some religious entertainment, for the latest ecclesiastical fad, for the show service of the town, or are you standing by your pastor and your church and your duty? Here are fields of usefulness so simple that the humblest one of all the brotherhood of Christ can find a place that he can fill, and work that will tell for the Master.

Pleasure, fortune, fame, are often but transitory things. Usefulness is immortal. Do you sigh to do something that will last; to cut your name where the centuries will not wear it away? Do something humanity needs and God wants done. The most imperishable thing is a human soul. Build yourself then into the souls of men and you have won a blessed immortality of service.

The Young People's Movement was a Vision of Conquest.

Constansine saw, or thought he saw, in the sky, a cross and around it the words " By this sign conquer."

Whatever weight may be attached to the vision of Constantine we have come to know that, standing before individual sin or organized iniquity our only hope of victory is the cross of the son of God.

We were organized for victory. We follow a matchless leader. We are thrilled with the traditions of victory. We believe we are predestined to conquer, and so we are if we are true to the vision God has given us, but if we are untrue to it we shall be victims instead of victors.

Our vision of conquest is of a business life which, laid on the Golden Rule, the Sermon on the Mount and the Decalogue, will coincide to the outermost edges of these great rules of human living.

Such business as we cannot do and be loyal to these high principles shall be left undone. If we cannot win great fortunes and shape our lives by God's commands, we will be content with less. We will not barter principle for property.

Our vision of conquest is of a white life for two. We believe in equal wages for the same work. We believe in equal punishment for the same crimes. We believe in the same social treatment for the same social sins. The rake is as bad as the harlot. Young women who, with gathered skirts, pass carefully by a fallen woman only to accept the fellowship of the man who is responsible for her fall, encourage men in sin. Let our Christian young women teach young men that the only pathway to a good woman's heart lies over the hills of truth, and across the plains of sweet and virtuous living.

Let no social sins be tolerated or condoned because the social sinner happens to be of good family, or to possess a fortune and a fine address.

Our vision of conquest is of a race of men in public life who will be as conscientious in the spending of the people's money as in the spending of their own; who will care for the child of his poorest constituent, in legislation or administration, as for his own precious children; who will stand between the humblest home in the community and the enemies that threaten its peace and prosperity as if he were fighting for his own.

Do you say that this is a great undertaking — nothing less than the conquest of the world? Well, when did youth ever falter before a great undertaking?

Every Great War has been Fought Through by an Army of Boys.

Most great achievements have been wrought out by the hand and heart of youth. God seems to use even their inexperienced fearlessness and their hot blooded and uncalculating ardor.

In united Christian youth I see the world's greatest promise of victory.

God has given us great visions. Shall we be true or false to them? We sometimes hold the cross before the closing eyes of the dying. We would better lay it on the heart of the living until its spirit is absorbed and reproduced.

It is not larger numbers that we need, though we will welcome increasing thousands to our ranks. It is not more machinery to buzz and whirr, though we believe in proper organization. Our pressing need is not for more or larger conventions, though our gatherings are fountains of inspiration from which flow streams of fruitful influence to every acre of our heritage. What we most need is a deeper consecration, a broader outlook, a vitalizing enduement of the Holy Ghost. While we tarry at Jerusalem may the power come!

CHAPTER XVII.

Two Important Conferences.

FIRST UNIVERSALIST AND PLYMOUTH CONGREGATIONAL CHURCHES, MONDAY MORNING.

"How can one possibly take in all the meetings in which he is especially interested?" asked a breathless but despairing delegate, scanning the morning's appetizing menu.

"By everlasting hustling," replied a young man without abating one of his long strides towards the first of two important conferences programmed for that morning.

FLOATING ENDEAVOR.

Although still in its childhood, the Floating Christian Endeavor bids fair to become a potent factor in the work, and it was for the purpose of discussing practicable means for extending the work on land and shipboard that a score of the Floating Endeavorers met with Mr. John Makins, late superintendent of the Christian Endeavor Seaman's Home, Nagasaki, Japan, as leader, who said,

I believe there is no movement that is so practical, and that can do so much good for the sailor as Floating Endeavor.

Societies of two or three or a dozen Christian men on a man-of-war go into the bos'n's locker, or the fighting top, and hold their little meetings.

Such a meeting on a British man-of-war, the captain of which was a Christian, was held in a gun-room. A fireman led. The men made some wonderful prayers. While the captain was gone to detain a launch that was going ashore, that I might go in it, the meeting came to a close. The men crossed arms, clasped hands, and were singing "God be with you till we meet again."

The captain returning, broke into the circle, and clasped two of the men by the hand, and sang with them. It was a wonderful demonstration of the way Christian Endeavor fosters fellowship on shipboard, in spite of the strict discipline of navies.

He introduced as the first speaker Ex-Chaplain Robert E. Steele, superintendent of the Seaman's Rest, Newport News, Va., who was for several years chaplain in the navy, but gave up his position that he might promote the Floating Endeavor work. He had a special plea to make.

It is most essential that we have better general organization.

I would have a Floating Society in every port, and one on every ship where there are as many as two Christian men. I would have all the societies and men enrolled, and a copy of this list kept constantly revised furnished the workers in every port.

We need a system of correspondence by which some Endeavorer ashore shall "adopt" each Floating Endeavorer and keep in touch with him by frequent correspondence.

At the close of his remarks Chaplain Steele submitted suggestions to the World's union for putting Floating work in better shape, all of which were unanimously adopted.

A telegram of greeting was received from Miss Antoinette P. Jones, of Falmouth, Mass., who has done so much to foster Floating Endeavor.

Chaplain Edmonson, of Denver, who served in the United States Navy for several years, spoke upon some of the essentials toward promoting the work among the sailors.

"We need men, men, men; not puny, political favorites, to teach the gospel of Christ to our sailors," he concluded.

Conspicuous among those present and attired in the blue togs of the United States Navy was James Williams, of Denver, a youthful member of the Floating Christian Endeavor, and but recently from the United States ship Alert   He was accorded hearty applause upon entering.   ·

The establishment of homes for the sailors while on land, was urged by Miss Minnie A. Gibbons, who has been sucessfully conducting the work of the Floating Endeavor at Tacoma.

The sailors come ashore thinking no one cares what they do, and because they be not known they care not what they do, and you know what happens. What we need are homes for these men at different ports, where they may be kindly entertained and kept from the toils of land sharpers, for whom they fall easy prey.

The meaty and stimulating conference was closed by Miss Lulu Phillips, of Virginia.

FLOATING ENDEAVOR AND THE STEREOPTICON.

In this connection should be mentioned the delightfully interesting illustrated lecture on Floating Endeavor, given on Friday night by Mr. Makins.

The entire evening was spent in going around the world with the Endeavor Jackies. They were shown afloat and ashore. Many interior views of The Christian Endeavor Seaman's Home were exhibited. During the past four years this home was ministered to thousands of United States soldiers and sailors passing between the United States and the Philippines. Uniformed men in a Japanese port are given a hospitable reception. $20,000 dollars of the sailors' money has been kept in the safe of the Home in one year.

The audience was particularly pleased with a fine picture showing, in her own home, which has been an altar of devotion to the welfare of the boys in our navy and merchant marine, Miss Antoinette P. Jones, Falmouth, Mass., the "sister" of every sailor afloat. To Miss Jones's faithful, self-sacrificing labors, as much as to any other one person, are due the 103 Floating Endeavor Societies now enrolled, and the deep interest felt everywhere in the work.

PRISON ENDEAVOR.

The young man with the long stride saved time by sharpening his pencil as he stepped off the few blocks intervening between the last conference, and that in which great-hearted, tender-hearted men and women discussed various phases of Prison Endeavor, led by William Shaw.   Miss Edna Berger of Santa Fé, attractively described

EDUCATIONAL CLASSES.

If you distribute literature, do not think that the only suitable papers are the church periodicals; in most places they are not appreciated half so much as illustrated magazines of the better class. *The Christian Herald*, with its wealth of pictures, *The Union Gospel News*, and *The Christian Endeavor World*, are all good. The "boys" of our society enjoy, strange as it may seem, the Sunday-school papers for the primary classes. The reason for this is due to the fact that they have easy words which the men are able to read. If possible, a library in the jail is of great benefit to the men. The late Mr. Moody presented the entire set of books published by his Institute in Chicago to our "boys" and we have also many of the standard authors.

Even in county jails are often found men who are anxious to know how to read, and although their term may be short, it may be your opportunity to show your interest in their welfare, and your teaching may be the wedge to open their hearts to better things. Ignorance and crime go hand. in hand. Our jails are occupied by a large percentage of illiterate men, the percentage in the New Mexico Penitentiary is large, the percentage of those who wish to learn the elements of the three R's is also great. The Mexicans and the foreigners are especially anxious to learn the English language, and in teaching them we have gained friends for our society, and members that could have been approached in no other way. Many Catholics are loyal to the society and all it stands for, whose prejudice has been broken down through this channel.

In the educational work, those who are younger in the Christian life and feel that they are not able to do the cell work, may here employ their talents. Patience in teaching, deliberate consideration of the time and labor the class work involves, and a willingness to be faithful in the work are the requirements for such workers. Circumspection and personal dignity and love for God's creatures are also necessary for successful prison teachers.

She told of one of the New Mexico Prison Endeavorers who is doing evangelistic work in the West, and another who is working in the McAuley mission, New York.

James Hiler, incarcerated for seven years in the New Mexico Penitentiary, was unable to read, used his Bible in learning to spell, was led to Christ, became a personal worker among his mates, was immersed with the rites of the Baptist Church in company with two other prisoners. He gave up the idea of getting even with the man who had broken up his family, and when discharged returned to his old home preaching the gospel at night while working for wages in the mining and lumber camps during the day; has interested people in jail work in the county seats by taking Christian people to hold services in the jails. He is now a self-supporting missionary highly spoken of by the New Mexico Superintendent of Baptist missions.

Miss Lola V. Murphy, Iowa's State superintendent of prison Endeavor work, gave a number of concrete examples of how it pays to give a boy another chance who has fallen through law-breaking.

GIVE THE BOYS A CHANCE.

One young man I met in prison said to me: "I never had any raising, Miss Murphy, I just grew up on the streets. If I'd understood religion, I couldn't have held out so long." At that time he was an Endeavorer, and seemed to grasp the principles of the Christian religion quite well.

A paroled young man wrote me, "Do pray for me and write often. I sometimes think there is nothing between me and destruction but these messages from my Christian friends." A few months later he was happily converted, is now married to a Christian woman, has established the family altar in his home, and earns a salary of eighty dollars a month and expenses.

Another wrote, "God alone knows where I would now be had it not been for that blessed army of His — the Christian Endeavorers."

One boy of whose reclamation she told had been helped by an Endeavorer who she said was in the audience, and who, though nameless, was roundly cheered.

Give the released man a place to go, and something to do.

A young man once under arrest for vagrancy has recently written Mayor "Golden Rule" Jones of Toledo, that he is now a useful member of society, and earning a salary of $2,000 a year, and that he owes his success to the kindness and encouragement then given him by Mayor Jones, who released him with fatherly advice.

An Iowa Endeavorer who is an up-to-date good Samaritan took an ex-convict into his home one night, then paid his bill at a near by hotel, slipped $20 into his pocket, and gave him letters of introduction to friends in the city where he found employment.

I visited with that young man as I came through Omaha and he is soberly and industriously trying to redeem the past.

It pays, it pays, to give the boy a chance! Iowa now has a *home* for paroled and discharged men where they may remain until suitable employment can be found.

No one knows more of the practical details of Prison Endeavor than Mr. Robert J. Jessup of Salt Lake City, who read a most valuable paper on the same general theme.

HOW TO EXTEND PRISON WORK.

If there was any organized effort in the prison field, up to twelve years ago, it was in the Salvation Army. But when Christian Endeavor entered the lists by showing its colors in the Wisconsin State prison, that special line of work became part and parcel of Christian Endeavor, until now, with twenty prison societies in existence, prison Christian Endeavor has become a factor of such importance, as to call, it seems to me, for a special department with a secretary and a regularly detailed staff of organizers.

An experience of over four years in evangelical prison work has convinced me that here is a vineyard, the wonderful riches of whose returns have barely begun to be appreciated by Christian people. The inauguration of the work has been attended by difficulties.

One Western prison was referred to by Mr. Jessup, in which the Endeavorers gained entrance only after years of opposition from the officials and Roman Catholics. Now it is a flourishing society, and contains many Catholics.

I do not know of one instance of failure in prison work where the society was once established. Of course there has been, and will be opposition from prison officials who do not understand the real nature of the scheme. But if argument will not move them, influence with the executive of the State will, for when a governor indicates his wishes to a prison warden, those wishes are apt to be respected.

The suggestion of a general secretary for a prison department and a corps of organizers comes independently from several different sources, which makes one naturally think there must be something in it. Brother J. E. Wood of Santa Fé, thought of the idea some time ago; it occurred also to Rev. P. A. Simpkin of Salt Lake City; also, to Secretary J. C. Schuckers of the Utah State Prison Christian Endeavor Society, as well as to myself, and I believe others. Brother Wood suggested dividing the country into districts, with an organizer for each district.

But in speaking of organizing, I would like to say that there has been and always will be one great source of help, and that is the W. C. T. U. Both at Santa Fé and at Salt Lake, the prison soil was ploughed and turned over and made ready for the Christian Endeavor sower by the local W. C. T. U. and in the reaping of the harvest let these Godly women and the Christian Endeavorers rejoice together in what God hath wrought.

Several forms of prison pledge were given by Mr. Jessup and others, and suggestions as to special prison prayer-meeting topics. One other thought emphasized by Mr. Jessup received unanimous approval, and is in close harmony with the principles of Christian Endeavor — local autonomy rather than centralized management. He said: —

I believe that in every prison town the active management of the prison work should be left to the local Christian Endeavor union, or societies, with a prison committee to be chosen by the State convention, the State executive committee having a supervisory interest. There should be five persons on the committee, the president of the local union, where there is one, to be chairman ex-officio. Each member of the committee should have one Sunday, for the direction of whose meeting, he or she ought to be responsible, and preside at the prison meeting for the visitors.

A good organist is a necessity, and good singers most desirable. I have found it works best to allow the prison society to conduct the meeting itself, with its own leader, until the members are through with their part of the service. Then the meeting can be turned over to the visiting Endeavorers, who may speak and introduce singers or instrumental performers, to enliven the hour.

The prison committee ought to be in close touch with the officers of the prison society, and some of the latter ought to be seen or communicated with every week relative to the work. A great deal depends on securing officers whom the other prisoners will look up to and respect; and for that reason I would advocate the approval of elections by the warden before the officers elected assume their duties. The election of men for whom the other prisoners could have no respect would wreck a prison society in short order.

A most valuable contribution was the address of Judge Ben B. Lindsey, of the Denver Juvenile Court, whose experience with the kindergarten of criminals enabled him to speak golden words on

How to Save the Boys

If we would do the very best we can in the reformation of a wayward boy, we must recognize his natural, legitimate, and excusable delinquencies. This may sound paradoxical, because you may ask, if natural and excusable or legitimate how can they be delinquencies. They are such only from the standpoint of the law, not from that of the child. Right here is the beauty of the juvenile court idea. It is a forum where the harsh standards of the criminal law meet the case from the standpoint of the child. The result is justice is more nearly meted out.

The end of all law is justice. It never was and never will be just to judge a child by the same rules as an adult. A certain act may be defined by the law to be a crime. In an adult it may be. In a child it is more often mischief, fun, love of adventure, etc., — instincts as natural as hunger, or love of the open air and sunshine. A child, especially a boy (for they outnumber the girls twenty to one, as juvenile offenders), will satisfy their desires unlawfully just in proportion as there may be in its brief life a lack of those things which tend to make it obedient and law abiding; for instance, lack of control or direction of excessive energies, as in the case often of boys under ordinarily good influences and home training, or what is more often, lack of proper home influences, discipline or environments.

In dealing with a boy you cannot expect to find a man's head on his shoulders. Neither can you put it there in a month or a year. If you would succeed you must recognize his natural state. You must also know his life, parents, home, history, habits. In other words, know your boy, which you cannot do unless you know these things. Then must come patience, tact, and firmness that commands and does not repell.

Judge Lindsey said that in Colorado and six other States that have juvenile courts an officer who should incarcerate a boy under sixteen in a common jail would be liable to change places with the boy.

Since we started the Denver Juvenile Court nearly three years ago, I have had to deal with considerably over one thousand boys, including voluntary and involuntary probationers. I might cite a few cases as illustrative of some methods we have employed in extremely difficult cases. In doing this I do not mean to say such methods have been unattended by any failures. There are some, generally accountable for, for reasons I cannot attempt to discuss here, but such failures are trivial in number compared with those we may account successful. It will be observed in the cases cited, I have acted in the dual capacity of judge and probation officer. The judge of a court, because of his position, has a power and influence over a boy, when properly exerted, which his personality, or that of another, alone might otherwise not command. It is a great help, therefore, when the judge of the court can come frequently in personal touch and contact with the boys.

I like boys, and have many friends and companions among good boys, many never in court. Some of the manliest, best boys I ever knew have been to the juvenile court for admitted violations of the law. I have been a frequent companion and in constant personal contact and touch with the worst boys the police have had to contend with. I count this as the chief factor in the successful handling of these very difficult cases. Lack of time and other duties may often prevent this service entirely with some judges and exact it exclusively from probation officers. It has, much to my regret, limited my own experiences.

He told how he has a letter in his desk from one of the worst boy burglars in Denver, who had been arrested repeatedly for crime. The police protested against his parole, but the boy is now a trusty, prosperous young employee whose employer vouches fully for him.

I now recall eight boys who were expelled from school, and for various misdemeanors brought to the juvenile court. How often around my table evenings, and after my adjournment, with a busy civil docket, have I met these boys! How often have I slapped them on the shoulder, looked into their eyes and told them they would succeed. Quietly I induced other district schools to accept five of them. They are all now, after at least nine months' trial, splendid boys. I don't think I ever gave one of them a cross word.

The Judge likes to tell the story of little "Morris," a newspaper vendor, who applied to the juvenile court to protect his "rights."

He came to the bench with the following complaint: "You see, Judge, its dis way: dere's a new cop down to de Mining Exchange where I sells papers. I always hopped de cars 'till dis fly cop comes round. Now he stops me, and I'se losin' fifty cents a day."

"Well, Morris," I responded, "what can I do?" He quickly replied, "yer can give me one of dese here injunctions against him."

The boy got the injunction. As to the effect, he afterwards reported to me:

"Oh, it worked all right; he liked to dropped dead when he saw it. He's tryin' to get on de good side of me now, 'cause he tinks er got a pull wid de court, but I don't tink I'll let him in." At this time, over two years since we got Morris, he owns a horse and wagon and is in business for himself, giving every prospect of a useful man.

There were plenty of meat and practical helpfulness in the address of Rev. Frank Emory Lyon, of the Central Howard Association, Chicago, on

How Endeavorers May Help Ex-Prisoners.

The problem of the prisoner will always be primarily a religious and moral one, but it will perhaps never be wholly so. The most important factor in the man's reformation will be to instill in him a definite religious purpose, but in the working out of that purpose it is well for us as Christian Endeavorers to remember that that religious purpose, to be effectual, must be applied to the practical affairs and temptations of life. That purpose alone will not absolve us from keeping him away, if possible, from temptations to drink, for example.

The problem of the prisoner is largely a temperance one, and we should see that a man is not tempted beyond that he is able to bear.

The question is also in a great degree an industrial problem, since the first thing a man needs when he comes out of prison is a chance to earn an honest living. The man who is without work, without friends, without money, and without anything to eat is quite as helpless as the child upon the street corner, if not more so, for we all know the child needs help, but we are apt to think a man can help himself.

Mr. Lyon quoted a prison warden who said that the efforts of a warden or chaplain to help a prisoner for ten years may all be counteracted in ten days after he gets out.

Do not give him money; probably that he may spend to his own hurt, but see that he has friends and see that he has work. Manufacturers are generally quite willing to employ one of these men occasionally, and you may find an opening for him, if it is necessary to get him employment at once.

It is a still more difficult thing for these men to secure employment and to keep it, if it becomes known that they are ex-prisoners. Hence the need of some agency as a mediator between the employer and the worker to get the right work and send the man to it. It is usually best for the employer to know the man's history, but not best for the fellow-workman or the community at large to know it. For this reason each Endeavor Society should designate one of its social committee to look after any cases of this kind, and give special attention to securing friends for the man who is being helped, without the other members of the society knowing of his history.

Sympathy is just as necessary as employment. Mr. Lyon suggested that Endeavorers write letters to prisoners about to be released. Speaking of the methods of the Central Howard Association, he said:

Do not hold him off at arm's length and say, "There is an ex-convict. Watch him and see how quick he will fall," and then say, — "I told you so." But rather we put about him our arms of sympathy and discriminating helpfulness, and by our mental attitude toward him, re-inspire confidence in himself, and help him to become what we desire him to be and what he, in his best moments, desires to be. In this way, I am glad to say, we have had the most gratifying results in helping the men. Fully ninety per cent of all we have helped during the last several years have responded to our efforts and been permanently helped.

The unification and advancement of Prison Endeavor, in the hands of Mr. E. A. Fredenhagen, of Topeka, proved prolific of suggestions. Mr. Fredenhagen is founder and general superintendent of Societies for the Friendless, and a prison evangelist of large experience.

HOW CHRISTAIN ENDEAVOR IN THE PRISONS CAN BE UNIFIED AND ADVANCED.

There are now twenty Christian Endeavor Societies in the prisons of the United States, with a total membership of 2000. As the prison population of the United States is over 100,000, this is only two per cent. The estimated number of criminals outside of the prisons is estimated at 150,000 more, or 250,000 in all, making the number in the Prison Endeavor Societies less than one per cent of the whole. Under the ten per cent increase movement many have been added. The largest gains are reported by the society in the Virginia State Penitentiary, of 128 per cent, and by the one in Kansas Industrial Reformatory, of 160 per cent increase. The gain in the Kansas Society was made through re-organizing it as a Prison League of Christian Endeavor, by the Superintendent of the Society for the Friendless, who, with one of his assistants, has given it personal care.

Agreeing with the experience of others that a special prison pledge is needed, Mr. Fredenhagen submitted the following form: —

MEMBER'S PLEDGE.

PRISON SOCIETIES OF CHRISTIAN ENDEAVOR.

First. I will accept Jesus as my Lord and Savior.

Second. I will try to learn and do His will by forming the habit of praying and carefully reading my Bible daily, and by thinking, speaking, and acting as I believe He would in my place.

Third. I will obey the prison rules, will treat the officers with respect, and, so far as possible, will conduct myself without offense toward my fellow-prisoners.

Fourth. When able to do so, and not prevented by my duties to the prison, I will attend all the meetings of the League.

Fifth. I will wear the official button of the league, and will endeavor to make it both the means of helping others and an honor to the cause of my Master.

Sixth. On leaving the prison I will enter some honest employment and become an upright and helpful member of society.

Mr. Fredenhagen would also have the model Constitution amended to meet prison needs, and special uniform topics, as suggested by Mr. Jessup and Mr. Shaw.

A fourth step toward unifying Prison Endeavor is correspondence between Prison Societies.

This bring us to the question,

How Christian Endeavor in the Prisons can be advanced.

1. In the list of "topics" issued by the United Society, at least one topic yearly should be upon Prison Christian Endeavor. This might be stated thus: Prison Sunday — Missionary Work for and among Prisoners; Prison Christian Endeavor. (I would suggest that this occupy the last Sunday in October, the day chosen by the National Prison Congress.)

2. The second step for advancing Christian Endeavor in the prisons is Jail and Prison Evangelism.

This evangelism should not be confined to prisons only, but should extend to every county jail and city lock-up. Here is a mission for the local Christian Endeavor Society. Wherever a jail has been found with inmates, there have also been found a few workers upon whom our Lord has laid the burden of the prisoner's soul. These, as a rule, are wise, mature, and loving; therefore, efficient. These should be organized into committees to have charge of the spiritual work in the jails. Christian Endeavor should lead in this, but should include all whom our Lord has so called.

When a prisoner is first arrested, the remorse of wrong-doing is strong upon him, and this is the time to bring him to Jesus Christ. If he shall go to the larger prison he can enter at once into the Christian Endeavor Society there and maintain his relations to Christ throughout his prison residence. This will guard him from the temptations which association with hardened criminals always furnish to the first offender. Even though he shall be old in crime, if he be won to Christ in the smaller jail, he may grow in grace in the prison. Given a complete chain from the evangelism in the jail, through the League in the prison and the Prisoner's Aid Society after release, it is possible to overrtake a man in his first law-breaking, win him to Christ, and hold him until he shall attain honorable self-support and upright living after he leaves the prison.

3. The third step for advancing Prison Christian Endeavor is the development of a literature and hymnology adapted to the prisoners.

There are few, of any hymns, adapted to the prison life. Searching through the old hymnals one finds, now and then, an isolated stanza which might meet modern prison conditions, but they are few. In general, all hymns which nourish the Christian in the church, in a measure help the prisoner, but a special line is needed, written to meet the spiritual needs of the prisoner. If any to whom our Lord has given the gift of hymnology shall hear this, I hope they will respond. The following verses, written on the League mottoes of Mrs. Maud Ballington Booth and the Societies of the Friendless, are submitted as crude indications of one type of hymns which would be useful in prison evangelization: —

(*No tune selected.*)

> "Look up and hope. Your dungeon's pall
> Reveals a temple at your call.
> Its narrow walls cannot withstand
> The touch of Christ's expanding hand.
> If from your sin He sets you free,
> You shall His holy temple be."

> "Upward with Christ; 'tis Jesus who is calling,
> My loving Savior seeks to save my soul;
> Sweetly his message in my heart is falling,
> ' Come unto me, and I will make thee whole.'
> Jesus, I hear thee, Jesus, I come,
> Cleanse my heart, take my hand, lead me, —
> Yes, lead me safely home."

A committee of five was appointed to take into consideration the various suggestions made, and to prepare prison prayer-meeting topics for 1904, to be printed by the United Society.

A BIRD'S-EYE VIEW OF THE "WHITE CITY."

CHAPTER XVIII.

Missions Blaze Out.

TENT ENDEAVOR, MONDAY MORNING.

While these intensely interesting and practical sessions were in progress, the young man not only wore blunt the point of his neatly sharpened pencil, but he lost a splendid missionary session which even seven-league strides could not have saved for him without the sacrifice of the other. But what magic could not enable him to do, this report does, — to be in two places at once. The Rev. Teunis S. Hamlin, D.D., of Washington, D.C., presided. He is a courtly, square-shouldered man, with the face of a supreme judge. Probably he has more supreme judges and senators and cabinet officers in his congregation than any minister in the land.

Much vim was put into the song service, which was conducted by the thunder-throated baritone, F. H. Jacobs.

HOME PROBLEMS.

Chairman Hamlin introduced the Rev. Sherman H. Doyle of Philadelphia, who stands six feet high and more — is smooth shaven and reminds one of a Roman Senator. He is the author of one of the most valuable recent books on missions, "Presbyterian Home Missions." Dr. Doyle dealt largely in facts.

OUR HOME PROBLEM.

The population of the United States in 1900 was 76,303,387; of this number 10,460,085 were foreign born, and 15,687,322 were the children of foreign born parents. Thus, on an average, every third person you meet in the United States is either foreign born or the child of foreign born parents. If the immigrants to our shores were fewer in number, the problem of missions among them would be comparatively small, but how appalling it becomes in the light of the fact that they comprise practically one-third of our vast population.

One might begin to cherish a hope that Europe had "leaked" paupers and peasants about as long as she could; but no! Dr. Doyle said that almost a million are coming this year, and these mostly from Italy, Asia, and Southern Europe.

Think of it, 312,275 immigrants from Italy, Hungary, and Russia as against 77,935 from England, Ireland, Scotland, Germany, France, and Greece! Four times as many from the undesirable as from the desirable nations. How serious the problem involved from this standpoint or this phase of the subject.

The segregation of the scum of Europe in our cities is another grave problem. Look at this!

The school census of Chicago for 1899 showed a total population of 1,851,588. In this aggregate *twenty-five different nationalities were represented, and the Americans numerically stood second on the list.* There were 490,592 Germans, and but 488,683 Americans.

In Philadelphia, the most American of all our great cities, it is possible in one section of our city to walk ten squares and to hear nine different languages. Most of our large cities have their "little Germany," "little Italy," "little Scandinavia," and "Chinatown." The shop signs and newspapers are in foreign languages, and American is spoken only by the children who attend the public schools. The people live in crowded quarters, surrounded by squalor and confusion. The Sabbath is desecrated, children are neglected, criminals are educated, and vile and immorality abound, and much of the social and political degradation in our cities is made possible by the presence of these large numbers of foreigners in their midst. Next to the cities the chief centres of segregation are the industrial and mining sections of the East and the agricultural regions of the West and Northwest. Here they live as they have lived at home and in the industrial and mining regions are largely the cause of frequent industrial discontent and strife.

Showing the inferior quality of many of these immigrants, intellectually, morally, spiritually, Dr. Doyle concludes: —

Our foreign problem at home is thus seen to be a very great one. We must lift them up or they will drag us down. We must Americanize and Christianize them or they will Europeanize and un-Christianize us. In this work the church must bear a prominent part. It is her golden opportunity. The church used to pray, "Lord, open the doors of heathen lands," God has not only answered this prayer, but has brought the unevangelized in large numbers to our shores. Christianity, patriotism, personal interest all demand their Christianization. Much already is being done. Christian denominations, Christian Endeavor Societies, the American Sunday School Union; local churches in large numbers are reaching out a helping hand to "the stranger within our gates." And the gospel can save them. One of the elders in my church is a carpet manufacturer; in visiting his business place one day he introduced me to a young man, an Italian, converted in the Presbyterian Evangelist Tabernacle. On his carpet loom he kept a copy of the New Testament, so great was his desire to learn the word of God which had brought to him salvation. And what God has done for one he can do for millions. "The gospel is the power of God unto salvation." Will we give it to the millions of foreigners in our home field?

THE MORMON QUESTION.

A very earnest speaker, nervous and full of the eloquence of facts, came next — the Rev. T. C. Smith, D.D., of Denver. His topic was "The Morman menace," and he made a deep impression on his hearers.

"The question with me this morning," he began, "is not what I shall say, but what I shall leave out. There is so much to say on this subject, and so little time in which to say it."

In the first place I want you to sharply discriminate between the Mormon people who are honest, sincere, and confiding, — as largely so, perhaps, as any people you may find, — and the system to which unfortunately they have become victims. I wish we could also discriminate betweeen the masses of the people and those who rule them, for by long experience in two generations they have become exceedingly skilful in their peculiar form.

Defining the Book of Mormon as a plagarism, not from the old Bible but from King James's translation of the Bible, he went on to say: —

Doctrinal Mormonism is an attempt to draft the Mormon's patriarchial age and priesthood that never existed into barbarism, cruelty, and animalism. It uses Christian terms almost exclusively, but in every instance these have been corrupted, and they do not mean what Christian people mean when they use the same terms. They believe in God, and their God is a being of body and bones. Our God, the only God with whom we have to do, in their theology is the Michael-Adam, who came to this earth with one of his wives that he might people it and rule it with his many wives. "Now, what we are," they say, "God once was What God now is, we may become."

To this extravagant doctrine must be added the revolting blood-atonement teaching of Brigham Young that has incited to the mountain Meadow Massacre and untold murders.

As an organization Mormonism is a secular, semi-religious body. They sing — but they have substituted the dance for the prayer meeting, and Morman theology has taken the place of devotion, and you will find they have no real book of devotion published by them.

It is as absurd to say the American church as an organization is not a political factor as that Tammany is not. No man can be elected to a State office in Utah to-day without the consent of the dominent church. Senator Smoot, who is one of the Representatives in the highest legislative body of our nation, had a clear way to the Senate, not because he is peculiarly, particularly a man of influence among them — he has never held an office, he has never managed a campaign, as far as I know he has never sounded the political keynote of a campaign — but he was the church candidate, and no man dared to stand in his way. No opposition.

Last October, in the great conference held in the Tabernacle, Senator Smoot said he had received a letter from Bennett Rich, one of their missionaries, and he had offered him a place in his house and would use his influence for him. Did such an offer ever come to any other missionary? It was a bid for patronage.

In answer to the query, Is Mormonism a menace to this country? the speaker called it a "firebrand from the beginning," and closed with this cutting arraignment of the immoral octopus: —

Mormonism is un-American in that it isolates its people, holds them together, and in their colonies and throughout Utah there is an air of alienation, a foreign atmosphere all around you. It lays an arbitrary tax upon its people. It administers a vast income of a million dollars every year without any accountability. It is anti-American in that it is decreed to set up or establish an arbitrary priesthood government in the midst of an American State. In the Republic the people are the authority — in Utah the Prophet and his apostles are the authority. It means war upon Christian marriage, and to-day the great crime of Mormonism is not that once bigamy was incorporated into it, but that to-day the president of the church and a majority of the presidents associated with him are living in open, flagrant violation of their pledge they gave to the general government, and of the statute law of their own State. That is the crime of Mormonism to-day, that it defies law and public opinion, and will not brook interference with their own peculiar institutions.

At the conclusion of Mr. Smith's address a petition against seating Smoot was circulated, and copies of a leaflet were distributed showing how Mormonism is false .

It was a courageous and confident man who took in hands a knotty
and stubborn proposition when Rev. Chas. E. Bradt, Ph.D.. of Wichita, Kan., proposed to tell

How to Get a Church to Give.

The church is rich and growing richer. During the past fifty years, the people
of the United States have created and accumulated fifty thousand million dollars.
They are now amassing wealth at the rate of $7,000,000 a day. This wealth is
God's entrusted to man, and great sums of it are in the hands of God's own people
Yet the Kingdom of God is suffering for want of funds. Why is this? It is because God's people, that are called by His name, do not believe in and obey the
great commission; and this is true because the preachers and leaders of the people
do not set it before them as a command to be literally obeyed. But until they
do, the vast sums of money needed to extend the Kingdom of God will not be
forthcoming. It is not to be wondered at that people, even professing Christian
people, should not give their money more largely than they do, under the circumstances: there is no adequate demand for large self denial giving unless the
work outlined by Christ in the great commission is set before the church.

After showing conclusively that there is no urgent call for large
Christian benevolence in behalf of colleges or church-building, — there
are church sittings in the land for 45,000,000, — Dr. Bradt proceeded
to show that, nevertheless, the tithing principle of the Bible holds
good, and there is one large demand for Christian giving.

But there is an occasion.
Let us hear Jesus Christ say, "Go into all the world and preach the gospel
to every creature." Let us hear Jesus Christ say, looking out upon a starving
world, starving for the Bread of heaven and the bread of earth, "Give ye them
to eat!" Then we will realize there is a demand for colleges, schools, seminaries, preachers, teachers, physicians, churches, hospitals, and benevolent institutions which tax our largest resources. For there are a thousand million people
who are far away from the Kingdom, and there is only one Christian worker for
each 50,000 of them; and they can almost be said to have as yet, no churches,
nor schools, nor colleges, nor preachers, nor teachers, nor physicians, nor hospitals; and we of this land and country must prepare these men and women and
means, and send them forth, equipped in mind and heart and pocket-book to
furnish all of these things for a starving and dying world.

Illustrating his subject by the quick response of this nation to the
cry of the 2,000,000 in Cuba against political despotism, Dr. Bradt
made an eloquent appeal for the millions under spiritual despotism
and cited practical instances of what may be done.

Seven years ago the First Presbyterian Church of Wichita, Kansas, was in
dire distress of debt. It had an old church building which ten years before had
been considered too disreputable to be used any longer as a church house. It
had about 800 members, almost every one of whom had come out of the boom
practically bankrupt. It had a debt of $18,000 resting against its old dilapi-
dated property which probably could not have been sold for $1800. It had a
floating indebtedness which had been rising higher and higher each year until
of itself it threatened to submerge the church.
Thus affairs were rapidly getting worse. And when neither sun nor stars
shone upon them for many days, and no small tempest lay on them, almost all
hope that they should ever be saved as a church was taken away. Some even
advocated that the church should be abandoned and allowed to go to pieces.

Then there stood up one in their midst and said: "Now I exhort you to be of good cheer, for there shall be no loss of the life of the church, not even of the old building. For there stood by me this night an angel of God whose I am and whom I serve, saying thou and this people must stand before princes and preach the gospel unto the uttermost ends of the earth, and lo I am with you. Wherefore brethren, be of good cheer, for I believe God that it shall be even so as it hath been spoken unto me."

And while he yet spoke, calling attention to the latest and greatest command of Christ to preach the gospel unto every creature, linked with that best and blest promise of Christ to be with those who should go for Him on this Mission of mercy, the money began to flow in from unseen and unknown sources to send the glorious gospel to the ends of the earth. The miracle of the meal was literally wrought over again. During the past seven years $15,000 has come in, practically unsolicited, to preach the gospel to the heathen. Another $15,000 has come in the same way and time to preach the gospel in our home land. More than $40,000 has come in the same way and time to liquidate our indebtedness and to support our local work.

The secret of it all is found in the fact that the church had heard Jesus Christ say, "Go ye into all the world and preach the gospel unto every creature, and lo I am with you alway even unto the end of the world." If that church under those dire and distressing circumstances of poverty and debt could and would respond when the great commission of Christ was thus set ringing in her ears, there is no church in this land of ours but will do the same.

The superb singing of "Some Sweet Day" by Mrs. W. J. Whiteman now thrilled the audience, after which Henry C. Cloud, the bright young Indian from Winnebago, Neb., addressed the Convention on

What Christian Endeavor Has Done for the Indian.

The Indian is invariably on the frontier, in contact with the rougher element of mankind. He does not come in touch with the better portion of our civilization. Exemplary Christianity is at a premium or wholly wanting, and little is known of those principles which have made us a great nation.

Our Indian agents, too often, are like a father that permits his children to do as they please, "They make themselves vile, and he restrains them not " For political reasons the Indian agent yields to the demands of unscrupulous white men; he puts no restraint upon the heathen dances and feasts of the Indian; he does not enforce lawful marriage among the Indians; he does not rebuke their excessive drunkenness. As a consequence the domestic life of the Indian is demoralized; the Indian's sense of chastity has been destroyed and childhood often knows no father. The Indian's sense of honor and honesty has been outraged, and he might well cry out in despair, "What is truth!" The Indian's farms and pastures and water supplies draw the covetous eye of unprincipled white men and it becomes a question of privilege where "Poor Lo" shall pitch his tent. Such conditions and influences breed intemperance and vice and death, and some tribes, at least, are weakening under this awful pressure and are fast fading away.

As to what Christian Endeavor has done for the Indian, we know only partial results. Frederick L. Moore, an Alaskan Indian, a bright young man, has recently closed a life of marked, faithful, devoted, loving service to his Lord and Master. Edward Marsden is a well-known Christian Endeavor worker and a recognized leader among his people at Saxman. The first Indian Christian Endeavor Convention of Alaska was held last fall at Wrangle, and more than one hundred Indian delegates were present.

The Presbyterian Church reports twenty-one Christian Endeavor Societies in connection with its Indian work, and possibly the whole number of societies among the Indians would not exceed fifty.

The Christian Endeavor Society at the Santee Mission among the Dakotas was started fourteen years ago. Thirteen members have since become missionary teachers; others have been leaders in Sabbath-school and Christian Endeavor work; others have taken up independent lines of prayer meeting work.

Speaking appreciatively of what Christian Endeavor with its pledge of daily prayer, Bible-reading and testimony has done to develop the Indian, Mr. Cloud concluded: —

There is yet a large field for Christian Endeavor to occupy among the Indians — large in the sense of the Indian's deep need.

Indian education is generally recognized as a failure. The government schools educate, but do not Christianize, and among the Indians the fact is established emphatically that education is not civilization. The Indian's school has failed in opening to him God's Word, and failed in revealing the true cause of his helplessness.

May the Christian Endeavor, as a united society, take hold of this particular field and train the Indian lads and lassies into stability of character and purpose, so that they can assume the responsibilities of leading a people into the light.

Three spirited, experienced, and Spirit-fired speakers presented the foreign missionary problems of the church in relation to Christian Endeavor. The first was Rev. W. P. Bentley, who spoke of

CHINA AS A MISSION FIELD.

China is a great mission field because it is a great country, inhabited by a great people, which have produced great and noble institutions throughout a long and honorable history.

China is a great mission field because it is a country of great material wealth, of vast industrial potentiality, and of unmeasured moral, ethical, and religious possibilities.

China is a great mission field because it will require great efforts to win her to Christ.

China is a great mission field because she will be the seat of a great Christian community, great in numbers, character, and power.

China is a *responsive* mission field. After years of bigoted resistance, every Province in the Empire is now open to the heralds of the cross. Hunan, the last province to open her doors, is already calling for preachers and teachers. Religious liberty has fought a winning fight, and a royal decree of toleration grants the privilege to all of entering the Christian church, and guarantees them protection. Hospitals now receive not only the grateful praise of healed patients, but the enconiums and money contributions of viceroys, governors, and other officials. Christian schools, which formerly enticed students with free board and tuition, and perhaps a gratuity, are now turning away hundreds of applicants for lack of room. And the government has ordered that the temples of the country be gradually transformed into public schools.

Illustrating China's responsiveness by the rapid development of Christian Endeavor and Young Men's Christian Association work, and the splendid native ministry furnishing so many heroes of the cross, he continued: —

China is a *needy* mission field. And this is not because she has not an actually large number of workers, but because her problems are so immense that the present force is relatively inadequate. The three thousand laborers need to be doubled speedily if they are to meet the pressing needs of the case. There is need for preachers. Millions have never heard the name of Christ. More than a thousand walled cities await in despair the advent of a deliverer. And even established work is hindered for lack of laborers.

There is need for teachers. Nearly all the colleges are undermanned. It seems impossible to awaken the church to the educational crisis in China. It is an unexampled opportunity for the church. So vital is this need that a special appeal has been sent out by the Educational Association of China. "The modern educational system of China is now practically in the control of Christians who are representatives of various missionary societies. This brings practically under the control of the Christian church one-fourth of the youth of the whole human family. By perfecting and strengthening this arm of the service, we increase the probability that the future governmental educational system of China will be largely influenced and moulded by such superior examples."

He poetically likened China to "a child crying in the night," out of the bottom of some deep pit, and picturing her helplessness and vascillation closed with this burning appeal: —

She needs help *now* — to-morrow she will have chosen, she cannot wait. Russia and France and Germany will not let her wait. Commerce will not let her wait She moves with other world events — and she is not prepared. Yes. Her people will be there to-morrow. But, we shall forever have lost the opportunity to create for them a Christian environment.

It is to-day that her people who hunger for righteousness should be fed, that yearning souls should be satisfied, and all the deeper longings of a gifted and noble people should be met.

To-day, if we will, we may give her a school system, a Christian code of laws, a pure literature, and a religion. To-day, to-day, to-day.

Know ye not the day of your visitation?

"India" was the theme of the Rev. John H. Wyckoff. He is a large, kindly-faced man, who began by telling of the "pantheistic theosophy of India," as he termed the Brahmin religion.

The Gibralter of Hinduism.

. The essence of Brahmin philosophy is contained in this formula: "God is one; there is no second." On first hearing that formula some Christians might think the Hindus as orthodox on the subject of God's unity as they ought to be; but let us not be so easily deceived. Those words in the mouth of a Brahmin do not mean what you think. When he asserts that God is one, " no second," he means indeed that God is one, but one in such a sense that there is not only no second God, but no other existence in the universe except God. But you say to the Brahmin — "If I am God how is it that I do not realize that fact, but am conscious of existing independent of Him?" His reply is, that your failure to realize your oneness with God is due to two causes — viz: " maya," and "karma." And what is " maya," and what is "karma?" Sanscrit words that are on the lips of every Hindu. "Maya" means illusion or ignorance, and is the word used to express the conditions under which the Divine spirit comes when enveloped by matter. God and man are really one, says the Brahmin, but owing to "maya" does not realize that fact; get rid of maya, and he will at once realize his identity. But now you say, if this illusion is caused by the soul's union with matter, how is it that I do not get rid of it at death, when the soul leaves the body. To this the Brahmin has a ready reply, viz: that it is not simply "maya" that fetters the soul, but also "karma."

And what is "karma"? The word means literally "deeds," but may be more properly translated by our word "fate." The Brahmin teaches that all the conditions of our present life — our joys and our sorrows, poverty and health, sickness and death, indeed, all that we are, do, and suffer, are the result of deeds done in a former state of existence; and that the soul must after death be born again to reap the fruits of the deeds of the present life, and that these births must continue until they reach the astonishing number of eighty-four lacs (8,400,000) when the weary soul becomes emancipated from matter, and is free to join the Supreme.

There was a spice of humor as well as a vein of sadness in the speaker's words when he explained that "liberation" meant to the Brahmin substituting entire seclusion from the world for 8,400,000 births. Either born of the dilemma is monstrous compared with the free salvation of the cross of Christ.

And how it will be asked whether this philosophy is simply held by a few Brahmins, or is it accepted by the people at large? To which I reply that its teachings have so leavened the thought of the masses of the people of India, that even the most ignorant and degraded are influenced by it. The commonest rustic to whom the missionary carries the gospel will assert that God "is one," "that which speaks in me, that is God." Ask the inhabitants of the remotest village, why he is lame or blind, and his reply will be, "karma," he is suffering from the deeds of a former birth.

Quoting the Brahmin authors and poets to show how this doctrine has infiltrated the national thought, and holding up before his audience the logical conclusion, viz., the thirty-three millions of gods in India, Dr. Wyckoff set forth some of the practical consequences of such a creed — gross immorality.

If all my acts are the acts of God, then it follows that I am not responsible for them, for in all that I do it is God in me that does it. Why the gods of the Hindus are largely personations of evil. Krishna the most popular deity of South India is nothing less than the incarnation of vice. And there is a lower form of worship than that of Krishna, about which I cannot speak for very shame, an abyss into which I would not have you look. Now a stream cannot rise higher than its source. How can a people be pure whose very religion is the fountain of pollution.

And why do I dwell on this dark side of the picture? Why I find on coming to the homeland that a good many people here have a rose-colored idea of Hinduism. Tourists visit India, and see chiefly the large cities that have been built up by the English, and they come in contact with Hindus who have learned our language, and who have been influenced by our civilization, and they come home and say that the bad condition of the heathen has been exaggerated. But they do not see Hinduism as we do, who live and move and have our being among the masses. I wish to assure you that heathenism has never yet been painted in too dark colors. It becomes more revolting, more ghastly, the longer I stay in India. Oh, I can see them now crouching by the myriads before their dumb idols and monkey gods, and never, never, can the picture be effaced from my memory

AFRICA.

The last speaker, Rev. Willis R. Hotchkiss, was a young man of unusual magnetic power and a fine command of English. In that country he has been a missionary, and he was full of his topic.

What the world needs is not angels in heaven, but men and women with angelic spirit down here on earth, for men and women to bring force and influence and power of divine life down into the darkness and ignorance, squallor, dirt, and sin of this earth life. God knows that the mud is deep and the darkness is dense and the sin is appalling, but there is a fountain for the world's purging. The problem before us as Christian Endeavorers is to bring the great supply that God has furnished down to the human need.

In Africa it is manifestly impossible for a handful of workers there to do this great work. Multitudes of men, noble men and women, have done themselves to death in a heroic attempt to compass the impossible. Noble men like Wilmet Brook have cried out of their heart's agony, "The people are too many for me," and laid down their lives. The question for us, as it is the question of every wise pastor in home land, is that of harnessing the native forces to the great work of evangelization.

Describing the missionary's humble home in the rude jungle huts, their few belongings, their simple manner of living, he said: —

For fourteen months I never saw a piece of bread; for two months I lived on beans and sour milk. We eat everything from ants to rhinoceros.

The forces of civilization are working on the dark continent. The shriek of the locomotive is heard through her jungles and across her plains; the throb of the steam propellor is felt in her rivers and great lakes; the tide of commercial life is rising higher and higher, and unless these American Christians whom we are training to-day are trained in habits of industry to meet the oncoming of the tide of civilization, they must inevitably go down as the American Indian has gone down sadly before the advance of civilized race.

In connection with the rum traffic, the Christian Endeavor hosts of the world are going to help us in Africa by putting their veto upon this great traffic. Slavery slew its thousands, but the rum traffic, legalized, government-protected rum traffic, slays its tens of thousands.

I do not ask you to pity the heathen. Pity is a weak thing and spends itself in tears, and then forgets the object of it, but I do ask you with all the strength of your heart that you simply treat Jesus Christ right. Is it right to receive eternal life at those scarred hands, and then give Him the spare change we happen to have left after we have supplied ourselves with luxuries? Is it right to receive Heaven at the price He paid for it, and then give Him in return the odds and ends, the convenient service and the things we can spare and will not miss? We have no right to crucify the colored race or any other race upon the cross of your convenience.

CHAPTER XIX.

Hurrah for the Homeland.

TENT ENDEAVOR, MONDAY AFTERNOON.

"America" was the watchword Monday afternoon, as the audience sat almost gasping for breath under the smothering folds of the tent that seemed to shut out what little life there was in the sultry air.

In his opening remarks Dr. Power, who presided, said that the liquor question reminded him of a colored preacher's questions about the exodus:

"Where was Pharaoh?" "He went under," was the answer. "Where were the children of Israel?" "They went over."

In a few years, he believed, the question would be asked, "Where is the saloon?" and the answer would be, "It went under." And the question would be asked, "Where is temperance reform?" and the answer would be, "It has gone over."

Rev. John Royal Harris, of Pittsburg, the first speaker, to whom Dr. Landrith afterwards referred as "A man from the wilderness whose name was John," rightly stigmatized the saloon as

COLUMBIA'S ASSASSIN.

Columbia with a barkeeper assassin creeping up behind her — the stars and stripes being hauled down and the constitution danced upon by a white-aproned anarchist — this is the picture I show the world. Our republic is sure to fall unless we greatly diminish the drink traffic. This national menace is our greatest danger from the business.

When a charge like this is made, it must be able to stand the test of a world's investigation, the scrutiny of a world's eyes. It is a startling, sweeping assertion. For its support appeal is confidently made to reason and well-known facts. Here is an iron-clad syllogism which no navy of argument can defeat, no submarine error can torpedo:

Major premise: *The safety of this republic depends upon the right kind of a majority.*

Minor premise: *The wrong kind of a majority is being built up by the drink traffic.*

Conclusion: *Therefore this republic is in danger from the drink traffic.*

In developing his major premise Mr. Harris referred to the instability of South American republics. In his minor premise he touched upon the tacit alliance between the red flag of anarchy and the saloon, and the school in law-breaking kept by the saloon. What a scathing arraignment was that when he said: —

Never before has the trade been under such temptation to turn against law through its own proprietors and employees. Such are now banding themselves together against the regulation and prohibition of their own business, and the transition is easy from hatred for anti-saloon laws to hatred for all law. That transition has already occurred very generally. The issue is clearly joined. In some cities this determined opposition to authority has caused even the ministry to debate the question of Sabbath or no Sabbath. Some sovereign states have grappled with this Goliath, have been worsted, and have repealed their own enactments.

Can you measure the effect of this upon the safe majority? Law is like woman's virtue — respect goes with its violation. At one great blow, our enemy will finish his work of overturning our safe majority, if that safe majority allows law to fail in this one case, ceases to oppose, and dwells upon the spectacle. Failure of law? What would happen if it failed in controlling robbery and murder? Who would consider himself safe? And yet this traffic makes most of the robbery and murder.

In all our land, in the most public places, in the most attractive guises, stand a quarter of a million places of business dedicated to defiance of law. There they stand, saying to the passing millions, "We cannot be controlled!" Those millions joke about law's feebleness, throng the temples of anarchy, fraternize with and pay money to the conspiratiors in charge! A quarter of a million temples of Mafiaism or of polygamy, so situated, so submitted to, so fellowshipped with could not transform and dethrone a safe majority half so soon!

Showing how this is still further aggravated by the bribing of voters and the election of pliant tools to the sheriff's office and judge's bench, he pictures the saloon as the most colossal of trusts.

Trusts with ordinary products have taught us how legislation is shaped, and have aroused our apprehension. They are symbolized by an octopus, its feelers taking hold of every function of trade and government. What should depict the whiskey trust? Nothing short of hell given feet and arms, tusks and tentacles, spilling gold and bristling with implements of destruction!

It is trying to pervert the sentiment-making forces of our country. Public opinion is rightly accounted the Samson-locks of popular government. Some Delilah has told this to the Philistines, and they are trying to use the shears! They put up cheap politicians — and some not so cheap — to fulminate against temperance legislation. Committees appointed to study the question are hired to bring in biased reports. Scientific men write alcohol-favoring articles for papers and text-books. Great newspapers are subsidized, and syndicate stuff is run through the press generally, often in editorial columns at opposite sides of the nation in the same day — and in the same words. Preachers, themselves, let fall liberal ideas, and a vigilant press bureau puts them in glaring headlines around the world, and hell enlarges her bed capacity.

Two favorite arguments of lower inspiration are these: Fighting intemperance makes men break the laws; we are making no headway, as there is as much alcohol consumed per capita as there was at the close of the Civil War. Answers are easy, but many are proselyted by such sophistry. The breaking of temperance laws is done by the trade, and magnified by it, to get them repealed. An official in a dealers' association reported $200,000 spent in six months to defeat the law in small towns of Kansas. Fixing the responsibility for broken laws upon the temperance cause is like fining a man for breaking a plate-glass window, shattered by a rock he dodged!

It is true that as much alcohol is consumed per capita as there was at the close of the Civil War, but there are not as many heads consuming it, There has been no failure of temperance legislation where it has been, but a remarkable failure of non-temperance legislation where it has been. Drinking has so increased in "wet" territory that it makes up for all decrease in "dry." This is really our loudest thunder — not theirs.

What would have happened had no education and legislation been done? This shows how dangerous perversions of these sentiment-making forces may be. If many can be turned to such use, our final protection — an appeal to public judgment — is seriously weakened, and nothing worse could happen except the muzzling of platform and press by saloon censorship.

Like one of the prophets of old, Mr. Harris's figure and speech rose to heroic attitudes as he predicted what the end of this would be unless counteracted. His appeal to American manhood to arouse and save the nation from the assassin's blow, rang like a clarion call to arms.

Away with all this mouthing about not being against the man, but against his business! We must be against *him*. He must be saved, but we are under no Christian obligations to fellowship with him, no more than we are with any other murderer of men and nations! Make him an outcast. Let him feel as he walks the streets and peeps from behind his screens, that the mark of Cain is upon him, and that the justice of men and of God is slowly but surely tightening around him. Give the traffic no support. Certainly not by vote, and as certainly not by presence in its dens and money over its counters.

Let not men who scorn Nero for fiddling while Rome burned, drink while America falls! No discord in the ranks — blades of conflict are not sharpened upon each other. The grindstone of experience will whet, and wear away the needless. Jehovah will let no plan devised against His old-time foe come to naught. All our plans and methods will be clods and stones and bridges in the highway, of human progress toward the saloon-less day.

No more important topic was discussed than that which was ably treated by Rev. T. H. Acheson, of Denver.

THE BIBLE AND OUR PUBLIC SCHOOLS.

There are in our land about twenty-two million children of school age — 15,-600,000 enrolled in our schools; and an average attendence of 10,700,000. There are 430,000 teachers for their instruction.

Certain ones tell us when we discuss this question: "You are forcing the issue, and results may be unfavorable to the Bible." Such remarks recall the story of General Longstreet at the battle of Gettysburg. When one of his generals told him he was unable to bring forward the soldiers for an advance against the enemy, the General is said to have replied, "Very well; just let them remain where they are. The enemy is going to advance, and will spare you the trouble." We also think of those old, crude newspaper lines: —

> "There was a young lady from Niger
> Took a ride on the back of a tiger.
> They returned from the ride
> With the lady inside
> And a smile on the face of the tiger."

He gave an interesting *résumé* of the legal status of the Bible in the public schools of the various States. Twenty-one have laws or decisions in favor of the use of the Bible in the schools. Sixteen others sanction it by usage. Only five are adverse.

In our State of Colorado the law makes no decision on this matter. It rests with the board of trustees. Our present honored State superintendent is plainly in favor of the Bible in the schoolroom; but such is the atmosphere about us that not one teacher in ten in our city of Denver reads the Word of God at the opening of the session.

Mr. Acheson believes that all Christians ought to take the position of the National Educational Association, at its meeting in Chicago: " The Bible that made the public schools ought to be taught in them."

The great aim and end of education is to produce character! And to that end there is necessary, for moral instruction, the very highest text-book in the sphere of morals, which is the Bible.

The State's preservation demands the development of character. That our nation have the highest prosperity and prepetuity we need the Word of God in our schools.

Mr. Atcheson quoted Professor Huxley's emphatic declaration in favor of the Bible rather than mental chaos, and cited the conviction of a French boy for murder, whose lawyer exclaimed, "I accuse you atheists who have reared the boy."

His concluding words were: —

And so it is grossly inconsistent if we deny our youth the reading of the ten commandments in the schoolroom, and then in later years bring them into the court-room and sentence them to the Reform School because they have broken those same ten commandments.

A beautiful solo was exquisitely rendered by Mrs. Ray F. Shank, of Denver.

Dr. Clark introduced as a pleasant surprise of the afternoon Mr. Leon P. Hills, of the Philippine Islands, who told how Christian Endeavor began in those islands.

A VOICE FROM THE PHILIPPINES.

I am very glad to have the pleasure and privilege of representing the Philippine Islands here this afternoon. Christian Endeavor over there began by a few words which Dr. Clark spoke crossing the ocean on the steamer three years ago. He fell into company with a missionary, Rev. Leonard P. Davidson, and they talked the matter over and Dr. Clark suggested to him that when he reached the Philippine Islands he started the Endeavorer work there.

No sooner had he landed than he began the work among the American people first, because he had not learned the foreign dialects, among the army soldiers, nurses, and English-speaking people generally in Manila. It flourished from the start, and one of the most progressive Endeavor societies I have ever seen is there to-day.

Mr. Davidson was not content with this, but also started the Endeavor work among the Filipinos, and it has prospered. We held the first Endeavor society organized this century. Mr. Davidson and Miss Pipe organized it on the first day of January, the first day of this century. You know we are where time begins. On the same day the first convention of this century was held in the Philippines ; about thirty Christian Endeavors went up the Pasig River.

Another variation of the programme was the introduction of Rev. Mr. Bradt, of St. Louis, who desired to repeat from Mr. Folk's lips one of the greatest utterances ever made. When he was prosecuting one of the arch conspirators and boodlers of St. Louis he said to the jury: "Gentlemen of the jury, when a man elected to a public office accepts or gives a bribe, he is neither a Republican nor a Democrat, but a criminal, and I prosecute him as a criminal."

St. Louis's Invitation.

This great nation will celebrate the one hundredth anniversary of the Louisiana Territory Purchase next year. It will be the grandest World's Fair ever witnessed by man. They have provided $30,000,000 for this great Exposition, and they have sent their agents to the uttermost parts of the earth, ransacking the highways and byways in order to find the great products of nature and man's art and wisdom, and they bid fair to have everything in the world that will entertain, amuse, and interest, and instruct.

The citizens are putting their homes in order. The churches are enlarging their domain, preparing to give a grand reception to their brethren. I wish to extend on behalf of the Christian Endeavor union of St. Louis, who have raised $200,000 for an Endeavor hotel with an auditorium that will seat 8,000, and on behalf of the State union of Christian Endeavor, a cordial invitation to come to this Louisiana Purchase Exposition, and promise you a hearty welcome, and we shall try to catch a blessing from on high to give to your hearts.

The task of furnishing a recipe for municipal house-cleaning, better than sapolio, Dr. Landrith said, had been overestimated. He wanted Endeavorers to think it was easy enough when they honestly tried. No one doubted, when he had finished discussing,

How Shall We Purify Municipal Politics?

How shall we purify municipal politics? The same as you purify anything else — clean it! Clean it out from within, if you can, and clean it up from without if you must. It is a great task, a tremendous task, for back of the evils of municipal politics the saloon is entrenched, gambling is armed, and boodle is supplied, but the task is over-estimated. Decency has despaired too early.

Selfishness cannot maintain a reliable organization because men who unite for the common weal ultimately fall out for individual weal, and become enemies of each other, and besides, "conscience makes cowards of us all." A Christian coward is an anomoly. If there is anybody in this world who has no right to the white feather or to show one, it is the man who knows God is with him and who has the assurance that one day he will be with God. Vice, political or personal, is a big, braggart liar, but it cannot fight forever against organized good, and that is the strain I want to sing.

Decency can rule in this country, therefore decency ought to rule. United integrity can purify American politics and it must. "But Christians have no business in politics," says the white-aproned, black-nosed individual philosopher who tooks after our political rights. Nobody that is honest has any business in politics; I hurl it back in the teeth of the iniquitous ward boss or the saloon manager or the man who has not more conscience than he has selfishness. You have no right in politics and you have no right out of it.

Going into Politics after the Devil.

When the devil goes into politics or into anything, he says, "Let us alone. What have we to do with you?" But some wise-acre says, "If Christians ought to go into politics there are some Christians who should not, — preachers should not go into politics."

Will you give me a sufficient reason why? I have never discovered any special reason why the preacher is not a man. Sydney Smith said there are three classes of human beings, men, women, and preachers. If a preacher is any thing worth while, he is a specialist in anything that is right. (*Applause.*) Therefore the preacher ought to be interested in making politics right. He has not the right, therefore, to stay out when there is a moral question involved in politics.

You know the story of a boy with his piece of cotton string and a pole and a bent pin, and the old man who came along and asked him what he was doing? "Since it's you that asks me, I will tell you what I am fishing for? I am fishing for fish." No pulpit did anything that did not fish for fish. The chief issue of this country is what we ought to know most about, and that is not the tariff reform but the green-baize door of the saloon. The preacher, as well as every Christian, ought to know that the only issue in municipal politics is right against wrong; that decency and not democracy ought to control in politics.

If you are going to get rid of the bad side of politics you must have integrity. It is the age of heroically being good. A whimsical, nerveless, spineless, lacksidasical church attracts no manly man, and if you want to know why your church pews are vacant, study that sentence a little. Men — and I spell it with a capital M — want to bring things to pass; they want to vote as they pray, and pray as they vote, and pray and vote for decency against squalor and filth. If you are going to clean up municipal politics, demand that politicians be upright, by moral suasion if you can, by legal suasion, if you must, and by prison suasion if there is no other way. (*Applause.*)

The ballot box is the ark of civic righteousness, and that man who touches that ought to die, not physically, but socially. This subject of the ballot box should not be made the subject of jest. I believe the man who steals a ballot is as much a thief as the man who steals a pullet. Let him walk off with a poling list, and he is as likely to walk off with your horse if he gets a good opportunity. It is as mean to steal a franchise as a fortune, and just as mean to do it by trust as by bribery. Public office is a public trust only when it is in the hands of a trustworthy person, otherwise it is a public snap. "I'd rather be right than be President," said Henry Clay, and I've wondered ever since why he was not both. If he lived in the twentieth century he could be. (*Laughter.*)

We are learning at least what we ought long ago to have known; honesty is not only the best policy, but it is becoming the best politics. Politically, as a rule, the upright are indolent. Kingsley said there are three kinds — the good, the bad, and the good-for-nothing. Take care of your boys and reform the drunkard.

That man is a fool and a failure who follows in the footsteps of other folks. Individualism, — that is the secret of all success. This is the individualistic movement. Let us not be like other people, but like Christ who turned the rascals out with a whip He made Himself. It will be hard work but what are you here for. Be an active Christian citizen, and don't you do what you did last election, either. You sold your vote. Oh, yes, you did! You said you were too busy; you could not leave the store, crops would fail if you did not stay at home and plough. You didn't go to the polling place for the price of a day's labor. Don't do that again.

Theodore Roosevelt said what is true — the worst evil in any community is the unenforced law, and the way to get rid of a bad law is to enforce it; and that made him President, and it is going to make him a close race the second time. The people are tired of jobbery and mobbery, and they want the enforcement of the law. God needs men, for times like these demand great hearts, true faith, and ready hands; men whom the lust of office cannot kill, whom the spoils of office cannot buy, men who have honor that cannot lie.

TENNESSEE'S BRACE-UP.

There was once a time we could not get rid of a saloon in Tennessee, though it chanced to be up against a church with four schoolhouses on the other side. We had no rights in the matter. We had to have it whether we wanted it or not.

There come one day a man from the wilderness whose name was John Royal Harris, and that man led us to the point where now eleven towns in Tennessee are as dry as the mouth of the speaker. To-day you can take the train from Nashville and run all the way to Memphis and not get a drop of whiskey. Go the other way to Chattanooga, and not get a drop without going four miles off the railroad. Go to Knoxville and not a drop.

Another reform. Nashville, the first day of January, 1903, had forty wide-open gambling houses and not a saloon that would shut on Sunday unless it wanted to. To-day Nashville has not a single wide-open gambling house, and now no saloon is open on Sunday in spite of the fact that the mayor said it could not be done, a criminal judge was elected to see it should not be done, and an attorney-general was chosen by the people who represented that element. Give us a Joe Folk and the thing could be done in thirty minutes.

The press of Nashville absolutely, without the exception of a single column of a single newspaper in the town of Nashville, stood by moral reform and law enforcement. The sign of the times is that the newspaper can no longer afford to be indecent, no matter who owns it or what party controls it.

Dr. Gilbey C. Kelly, a member of the Board of Trustees of the United Society, preached the first sermon, a little before Christmas, and organized what we call a Committee of One Hundred. Every word of it except the "of" is spelled with a captial letter. Really, we had to have it that way; and this Committee said: "Gentlemen, shut up your old grog shops," and they shut; "Close up your gambling houses," and they would not. But to-day we have five hundred indictments against them and felony indictments against the rest of them are being filed. We got tired of a mayor who said the thing could not be done. We sewed him up in a sack, and threw the needle away, and made him swear he would never be bad in all his life. And now if you have any wish for gamblers' outfits we have a job lot at second hand, worth $3,000, and I am going home to-morrow to be at the bonfire Thursday night. (*Laughter and applause.*)

The delighted audience looked as though they would hug Dr. Landrith, and but for the decorum due such a place they might have carried him off in triumph on their shoulders.

"Now everybody wave a flag or a handkerchief as we come to the chorus," said Mr. Foster, as the audience lustily sang, "Onward, Christian Soldiers," the only fitting song after such an address, "and let it be a sign of distress for the devil."

The audience had scarcely time, after the close of Dr. Landrith's all-absorbing address, to realize that it was oppressively hot, when every one was summoned to self-forgetfulness again by a very piquant feature of the programme — four terse, spicey answers to the question.

WHAT THE UNITED STATES MAY LEARN.

The first to reply was Rev. C. H. Bandy of India, who struck a very happy vein.

Christian Endeavor can teach you something. We have learned that Christian Endeavor cannot live in India without revival spirit. We have organized Christian Endeavor societies there to have them die, and we have organized Christian Endeavor societies to have them live and are to-day marvels in the way of evangelization, and we have learned that there is no such thing as revival spirit unless it is coupled with evangelization.

You get a group of boys or girls, young men together in a Christian Endeavor society, and set them to work to save somebody's soul, each one coupled on to some particular individual to try to save his soul if it is possible, and the way they have prayed for that soul! You have to caution them not to be too personal, not to mention names. I have heard them simbly plead with God to save a soul, and lead that soul to Christ.

You have heard a great deal about evangelization in this convention, and I heard a great deal more in our General Assembly at Los Angeles, but I believe we are fully five years ahead of you in evangelization in India. I attended a mission meeting where we had a whole day of fasting and prayer, and just upon the heels of that day of fasting and prayer we began to see results all around us. We began to revive ourselves. We got our churches and Christian Endeavor societies revived, and we think we can teach you that.

The answer of Mr. Ogawa, of Japan, was very brief and modest, yet charming in its simplicity and disingenuousness.

WHAT JAPAN MAY TEACH.

My friends in Japan are the missionaries and school-teachers. They are very good people. My association with American people being such as it is, when I see you, I love you all. You look to me all like saints. It is one of your writers who told me this truth — when people praise me it reminds me of what I ought to be, than what I am. The people in the United States are looked up to as ideals for our people, and you ought to be our ideals. Many English words are being translated into Japanese, and no word appeals to the serious in Japan as the words Puritan, politeness, hospitality, high thinking, independence. You are looked up to, brethren, and you are thought to be the ideal of the Puritans, and you ought to show what real Puritans are, or will you disappoint our hope?

China's answer came through a woman, Miss Emily S. Hartwell, who appeared on the platform gowned in a beautiful Chinese costume, and who presented some of

CHINA'S LESSONS.

It is with great pleasure that I stand before you to testify that my life was spared in 1900, as the lives of hundreds and thousands were in Central and Southern China, through the courage of two Chinese officials. Upon these two officials fell the duty of transmitting across the telegraphic wires an edict of the Empress Dowager, and they took this edict and they changed the words "destroy" to "protect," and they transmitted to all the viceroys in Central China the message to "protect all foreigners." Dear friends, let us learn from these two Chinese officials who died for foreigners to think more kindly and act more justly for the Chinese who are foreigners in this land.

There was a day when into my father's study came a Chinese with his hand bandaged. Upon inquiry we found he was the only Christian on an isolated island in a little village. A man came to him who demanded that he give a subscription to a heathen procession. He said he was a Christian and could not subscribe to a heathen procession. They threatened him. Finally to convince them he took a knife and with one stroke struck off the tip of his finger, which is the Chinese way of proving that they will not change their mind. We may learn from this one Christian who stood alone in that village, we should be steadfast and immovable for truth, equity, and righteousness.

The fourth, and most peculiarly honored speaker, was Rev. F. J. Horsefield, and never will he forget the day or hour, for a reason that will appear presently. His response was:

WHAT THE HONORED MOTHER MAY TEACH HER FOND DAUGHTER.

We were told that this was an age of being heroically good, and when I see you poor, suffering, sweltering people, I think the speaker's words were literally true. It is an age of heroically being good. You are heroes, every one of you!

I hope you do not think for one moment that I suggested it to the committee that they ask me to speak and tell you what England could teach America. The suggestion did not come from our side at all.

I remember some little time ago hearing of a lonely fellow who had just been married and at the wedding breakfast — which forms a part of our English customs still — he was called upon to respond to a toast of health to the bride and bridesmaid. He was very nervous, unaccustomed to public speaking; didn't know what to say. When he got up on his feet in a perfect fluster, he laid his hand very lovingly on the shoulder of his bride and he began: "Ladies and gentlemen, this thing was thrust upon me." (*Laughter.*)

I can honestly say this thing was thrust upon me. I did not seek to make this speech and I wish I hadn't got it to make.

Here with the Stars and Stripes floating above me, it is a little bit too bad to shake my hand in your face and say you cannot manage your country; come and learn from us! I imagine I was asked to do it because, coming from the East, I was supposed to be a wise man.

I am not talking this afternoon to Endeavorers. They don't need any teaching They are neither ignorant, nor do they lack information, but I am talking to America and I want to speak, not that Americans don't know, about what we English do know, and there is all the difference in the world between the two. When I was asked to do this I was in a state of terrible trepidation, as I am still. I tried to find out what I was supposed to tell these people, and when I asked, all my friends who had ever been to America, what England could teach America, and they told me "nothing!" That didn't help me a bit. And when I got across to this side my first business was to find Dr. Clark, and I felt I would have liked to kick him for having asked me to do such a thing.

There is something we in England glory in. First of all in England we have all the real purpose of life. We do not altogether aim at money-making. There is something of money-making, of course.

And the next is — we have the greatest reverence for holy things. Take your marriage laws. I do not understand much about them, but I saw in a paper the other day that one State was actually contemplating the crossing out of the marriage promise the word "obey." I am glad I was not born to be married in that State. I am very glad my wife is not here, because she might want to copy after that new law. I cannot help but feel the marriage tie is held much more dearly in England than it is in America, — in many parts of this wonderful country of yours.

And then the sanctity of the Lord's day. We love our Sunday. It is a day of rest, and unfortunately it is too true that there is too much worldliness creeping into Sunday life. Still, as a nation, we honor the Lord's day. We rejoice in the quietness and joy of the day he has given us.

Respect for the law, human and divine. I was astonished to hear that one in every sixty-five deaths in the United States during the last year were due to either murder or suicide. In England at least, I think we have a greater reverence for human and divine law than that.

Then my last point must be this: I think in England we do love righteousness.—

SOMETHING NOT ON THE PROGRAMME.

Just as Mr. Horsefield was concluding his remarks, at 4.04 P.M., a sudden puff of wind swayed the tent. The bell was instantly rung by the watchful chief usher, as a signal to ushers and canvas-men in charge to let down the side curtains, which were rolled up for ventilation.

But before they could complete their task a stronger gust filled the huge canvas like a balloon and lifted it from its fastenings. It hesitated an instant as if undecided whether to go on up, or come down, and then slowly careened over towards the earth. Then followed a scene of indescribable excitement and yet of marvellous self-control and almost miraculous deliverance from awful peril.

The tent fell slowly, as a structure of canvas, ropes, and poles, full of buoyant air must. Some one called out, "Don't rush. There is no danger. Get under the seats. Men, hold up the canvas; catch the poles!" The only outcry unless it was the crying of children, was a prolonged "O-oh!" in a ascending scale.

A STREET AMONG THE CONVENTION TENTS, THE UNITED SOCIETY LITERATURE TENT IN THE FOREGROUND.

With presence of mind the eight thousand people in it dodged the heavy poles and dropped down between the seats.

Hundreds of strong arms responded, and never once after the first moment of startled consciousness of danger was there panic or forgetfulness of others. There was no screaming or stampeding or trampling others under feet. The strong and cool-headed helped the weak and hysterical, and in a few moments those first out had formed a rescue corps, and all were extricated from the wrecked tent. and were singing, "Praise God from whom all blessings flow" in the rain outside, devoutly thankful that not one had been seriously injured, though there were, of course, many hairbreadth escapes.

Every one of the dozen or more heavy eleciric light globes was shattered and fell, yet no one was cut by broken glass.

One reporter came back to find one of the great poles lying upon his hat umbrella, and notes, on the table whence he had fled.

Mr. Horsefield said, "I found myself in front of the platform. I cannot remember how I got there, but I am of the impression that an angel carried me. God never seemed so near and precious."

That was precisely the feeling of many. Not once in a thousand times, and only in rare sections where wind-storms come so suddenly, could a strongly built tent like Endeavor thus collapse.

And not once in a thousand times could such a tent fall with no fatality from heavy poles or deadly electric-light wires. Providentially, it must seem, the attendant in charge of the hospital tent foresaw the latter danger in time to telephone to the electric-light works and have the current turned off.

And none but a Christian audience could have faced such a frightful calamity as seemed to impend with such superb self-control and thoughtfulness for others.

Many instances, of surprising coolness might be given. The official stenographer, Mr. J. Cornelius Freund, recorded Mr. Horsefield's last uttered word, "righteousness," and secured his notes for the afternoon.

Dr. Power, who was presiding, said nothing else was so noticeable as that people were reaching out for their cameras to get a snap-shot Like the young woman before whom a young man, about to propose, fell on his knees, when she said, "Don't move; I want to get my camera."

The tent services ended abruptly, but not in confusion. Dr. Breeden's address, cut out by the catastrophe, will be found following. Dr. Clark stood on a seat and announced that the closing meeting, which was to have been in the ill-fated tent, would be held in the four central churches. Christian Endeavor may be shaken up, but it is not easily daunted.

Immediately after the tent had fallen, and while the Endeavorers were singing, it began to rain. In the northeast the sky was black with threatening clouds. In the west the setting sun was casting its rays over the hills, and the storm-clouds became streaked with the bright colors of the rainbow. It seemed like a sign from heaven that God was watching over His children. Again He set His bow in the clouds as a sign of His Covenant.

CHAPTER XX.

Finally and Farewell.

CENTRAL CHRISTIAN, CENTRAL PRESBYTERIAN, TRINITY METHODIST AND FIRST BAPTIST CHURCHES, MONDAY EVENING.

The tenor of the last night's services was that of gratitude because the accident had not marred the closing session of the Convention; and God, in His wisdom, had taught the delegates that He is ever watchful, and can snatch a vast assemblage as that in Tent Endeavor from the very jaws of death.

FIRST BAPTIST CHURCH.

The feature of the meeting at the First Baptist was the closing remarks of President Clark. He took occasion to compliment the delegates, and pronounced the Convention the most successful since the beginning of the Christian Endeavor movement.

"It was not the largest," he said, "but the most enthusiastic. Never before did I see such enthusiasm displayed among the workers of God, as I have the last few days."

I also want to compliment you on your action this afternoon. It was a grand exhibition of Christian courtesy, and one that I will remember as long as I live. I was thoroughly impressed with the order displayed after the accident. Everything was as orderly as possible. There was no ungentlemanly or unladylike conduct on the part of any delegate. It was a great object lesson of gratitude and thanksgiving to our Father in heaven.

CENTRAL CHRISTIAN CHURCH.

Rev. F. D. Power, who presided at the meeting in the Central Christian Church, said the experience of the afternoon was the most thrilling and startling he had ever experienced. He pronounced the accident nothing short of a miracle, and thanked the Heavenly Father for His careful watch over His children, and for His snatching them all from the jaws of death. He remarked that the accident took place as he was about to introduce the Rev. H. O. Breeden of Des Moines, but he was glad that he had the opportunity of introducing the speaker at this service.

WHAT AMERICA CAN TEACH THE NATIONS.

We have heard the messages glad and golden from the sister nations of the world. From old India, land of mystery, home of philosophy, from the land "where Afric's sunny fountains roll down their golden sand," from new Japan, realm of the Sunrise, greatest of Island kingdoms, from the nations of modern Europe, each emphasizing a great truth which America will do well to ponder. May we not paraphrase the words of Shakespeare's Venetian Jew and say "the virtue you teach us we will execute, and it will go well with us if we better the instruction." But we have a message for the nations of the world.

America is the heir of all the ages. It was not in the land of the Cæsars, nor yet in the land of the Saviour; but here in this beautiful, broad land that man was to assert for the first time in the history of our world, his right to life, liberty, the pursuit of happiness, and to worship God as he pleased.

There is not upon the globe an equal area so fertile, so rich, so diversified in its productions. In its whole extent, America is one vast plantation. Its orchards would make principalities, its meadows kingdoms. Was Attica the home of philosophy, Judea the home of religion, Italy, of arts? Then America is pre-eminently the home and sphere of agriculture. Does "Brittania rule the sea?" Then far better does America rule the soil and keep the new gardens of Hesperides, while she guards the granary of the world. But best of all, our marvellous area lies in the region of thought and improvement, the latitude of progress and power. The five great civilizations of the world have been in the temperate zone. And there are here the natural conditions for the establishment, the development, and the perpetuity of the finest type of intellect and character; the noblest institutions; the most exalted civilization that ever blessed and immortalized a race. Is it not true that here in America, the free room of human individuality, what man can do will be done, that what man can be he will become? For ultimate America depends not on gold-lined mountains, or corn-covered plains.

America's watchwords on her banner, "Liberty and Equality," were the text from which Dr. Breeden spoke. Our liberty we purchased with a great price at Bunker Hill and Yorktown, that we might teach the world its value. Equality we wrote in the blood of 360,000 of our sons slain to free a race.

We can teach the nations of the world the dominance of God's hand in history. Indeed, Divine Providence is recognized in our constitution, authorized in our laws, vocalized in our songs, and symbolized in our flag. The revolutionary fathers reaped the harvests of victory with ascriptions of praise to the Lord. To the present day, Congress begins its daily sessions with prayer. He who secured the observance of that custom, while not a Christian by profession, yet appreciated the privilege of calling upon the God who rules among the nations. He, it was, who said: "If a sparrow cannot fall to the ground without God's notice, is it probable that a nation can rise without his aid?" How potent have the words of scripture been in all the great crises of our history.

"Stand still and see the salvation of God," was the message flashed by Abraham Lincoln on one memorable occassion. And when Lincoln had fallen, and a great seething, surging mob bent on destruction, surrounded the World Building, in New York, Garfield appeared at the window shaking a white flag, and thus addressed the multitude: — "Clouds and darkness are round about him; righteousness and judgment are the habitations of his seat." God reigns, and the government at Washington still lives." The first words flashed along an electric wire in America, were the words: "What hath God wrought?" And when the electric cable bound two continents together, and flaming messages of love and hope flew "through the oozy dungeons of the rayless deep," almost the first words were, the divine message of Christmas: "Glory to God in the highest, and on earth peace and good will."

He told his rapt audience how America had taught the world the glory of a national soul, in our great national hymns. Corporations and trusts have no hymns; they have no flags, or sentiment that clusters around emblems or watchwords.

Endowed with a national soul, it has remained for this youngest member in the family of great nations to teach the world the true philosophy of national life embodied in the injunction: "Thou shalt love thy neighbor as thyself." The little unhappy island of Cuba, long in the thrall of tyranny, and wrapped in the sable garments of oppression, reached helpless hands to the civilized nations of the earth in vain for succor. She was "an infant crying in the night; an infant crying for the light, and receiving no answer but a cry."

Then the great heart of America could bear the plaintive cry no longer. But overriding every barrier of tradition and custom, she sent her loyal legions to smite the mailed hand of the oppressor in the name of justice, and liberty, and God. And the "lion and the tower," pale emblems of Castillian pride, was displaced for a season by the stars and stripes, emblems of liberty and brotherhood.

But only for a season did that glorious emblem float in the soft Cuban breezes. Her work of mercy, protection, and love accomplished, the world witnessed an unheard of spectacle — the lowering of "Old Glory," that a free and independent republic might float forever, the Cuba Libre. And shall not we, Christian Endeavorers, pledge our fidelity and love upon the altar of Christ and our country, to keep the flag up to the divine ideal?

If, at a carnival of nations, the different flags of the world should ever be displayed, the observer would see there the flag of noble Victoria, upon which the sun never sets; and the tri-color of France, under which fought the great Napoleon; and the ensign of the strong monarchy of Russia, bearing the stain of persecution upon its escutcheon; and the proud flag of Germany; and the Irishman's banner of green; an little Cuba's five bars; but highest and most beautiful — sweetest and most sacred — will be the Stars and Stripes, Old Glory, the Star-Spangled Banner. May we not prophesy now, in the golden words of another: "And if there are flags in heaven — perhaps there are, who knows — the first of course, will be the banner of the Cross, that was bathed in Calvary's fountain; but just below it will be the flag we love so well."

TRINITY METHODIST CHURCH.

Trinity Methodist Church was full of tender, grateful hearts on Monday night, as the great audience that crowded it thought of the wonderful deliverance from the storm-wrecked Tent Endeavor that afternoon. Instead of Mr. Graff's stereoptican lecture taking the whole evening, a portion was given to short addresses, prayers, and expressions of thankfulness.

Dr. Patterson's voice was deep and almost tremulous as he read the traveller's psalm, introduced the speakers, and referred to the peculiar significance of the circumstances under which they met.

Dr. Barbour said that he had supposed his work done, but when Dr. Clark asked, "Please fill in a little time at Trinity Church, and then speak a few minutes in the open air," as an Endeavor minuteman he had cheerfully obeyed. He spoke feelingly of God's great goodness.

Dr. Doyle, of Philadelphia, followed in the same strain, and then came a season of short spontaneous prayers, two or three at a time often, and warm from hearts yet under the influence of the afternoon's providence.

The roll-call of States, that was to have been in the tent, was carried out as far as possible in each of the four church meetings.

Wisconsin, Pennsylvania, New York, Minnesota, Illinois. and Colorado responded with such magnificent outbursts of their State songs that a stranger would not have guessed that anything had marred the programme.

Missouri, Louisiana, Hawaii, Washington, Texas, and Iowa each had one or more representatives.

"I have come 12,000 miles to this convention," rang out the voice of an Australian.

"I represent a society that meets under the shadow of the pyramids," said a young man.

"They're not all mummies in Egypt," commented Dr. Patterson.

Mr. Makins spoke for the Endeavorers in Nagasaki, Japan.

A voice in the gallery said, "I was a soldier in the Philippines, and the Nagasaki Christian Endeavor Home is all right."

A response from Siam was heard below. Up in the gallery some one shouted, "I represent the Indians."

"Stand up!" cried the audience, and he stood.

It seemed as though the climax had been reached half a dozen times, but when some one said, "There is an Englishman here who spoke so eloquently this afternoon in the tent that he brought down the house," the audience simply let itself loose.

"I still have five minutes of my time left," said Mr. Horsefield, as soon as he got a chance to put in a word.

"Go ahead!" cried some. "You can't raise *this* roof."

Mr. Horsefield showed a small Union Jack that Mr. Foster had picked out of the wreckage of the tent and given him as a souvenir. In another meeting a Convention flag had been added to this. Before he had finished speaking he was handed a small American flag to keep them company.

Perhaps the most picturesque response came from India. Rev. C. H. Bandy appeared dressed as a Mohammedan, and Rev. A. G. McGaw as a Hindoo, and sang several Christian songs in native dialect, and invited the Convention to India in 1905.

The spirit of the meeting was something wonderful. Glad hearts overflowed with expression. The most carefully planned closing meeting could not have surpassed this impromptu one in enthusiasm and impressiveness.

And when a silver thank-offering had been made for the benefit of the Denver committee, but unsolicited by them, and Mr. Jacobs had sung softly and expressively "My Times Are in Thy Hands," a hush of rapt and holy joy rested upon the audience.

A moment, and the lights died away, the snowflakes began falling on the screen in the first view of Mr. Graff's stereoptican lecture. It was a winter scene in Portland, Me., 1882. And for three-quarters of an hour a delighted audience followed Mr. Graff "Around the World with Christian Endeavor."

CENTRAL PRESBYTERIAN CHURCH.

With the awarding of the prize banners and the consecration service, witnessed by hundreds of the Endeavorers and their friends who crowded into the Central Presbyterian Church, the great Christian Endeavor Convention of 1903, in many respects the greatest of the many gatherings held by that Society since its organization, was ended. Auspiciously as it was heralded, auspiciously as it was conducted throughout, more auspicious and impressive were the last closing hours.

Long before eight o'clock, the time set for the evening meeting and announced in the "extras" which the newsboys were calling over the city, the spacious Church was filled with Endeavorers.

Vigorous announcements from Dr. Gray, and much rearrangement on the part of the audience, brought members of the State delegations together.

The service of thanksgiving was opened with that grand old hymn,

"All people that on earth do dwell," closing with "Praise God from whom all blessings flow."

Said Dr. Gray, in introducing the service,

"Some six thousand persons were underneath the tent when it fell, and with the exception of one sprained wrist no injury whatever occurred. When a great tent falls upon six thousand persons, and an ambulance is called, and then there is no use for the ambulance, it is an evidence that God lives, and that He is present with His people. After it was all over, and she had found her way out from under the débris, a young lady bared her arm to her elbow and showed a slight scratch. 'I was standing,' she said, 'where I saw two of those great poles coming apparently on top of me. I lifted up my heart in prayer to God for deliverance, and they came down one on either side of me, and this scratch was the only harm I received.' Now," said Dr. Gray, "I believe that was a direct answer to prayer; don't you?" In one deep, reverent voice the audience answered, "Yes!"

Dr. Coyle then led in the responsive reading of the beautifully appropriate one hundred and fifteenth Psalm, and Mr. Foster, who had been in the accident, led in a fervent prayer of thanksgiving to God for His protection, and for the exhibition of the faith and peaceful confidence of God's children, an exhibition which alone, perhaps, would have rendered the event a blessing. Then, though the remainder of the evening, of course, was full of references to the accident, the praise service closed with the hearty singing of "When all Thy mercies, O My God, my rising soul surveys."

There was great applause when Dr. and Mrs. Clark came on the platform, and also on the appearance of Mr. Horsefield, whose afternoon speech had been so rudely interrupted. Dr. Clark expressed his especial gratitude for the fact that there had been no panic, no disorder, and that even in that severe testing-time it had proved itself a Christian gathering.

HANDS ACROSS THE SEAS

was the topic assigned for the evening in the programme, and actually carried out, though partly in one church and partly in another.

Rev. Mr. Bandy and Rev. Mr. McGaw, two Presbyterian missionaries who have done splendid service for Christian Endeavor in India, appeared in resplendent Hindu costume, and sung in the Hindu tongue a song whose refrain, translated, was, "We bow down at the feet of Jesus." Mr. McGaw then gave geetings from India's 350 millions, and presented an invitation urging the Endeavorers to hold in Calcutta the Convention of 1906 — an invitation that the around-the-world Endeavor tour, if carried out, will make possible of acceptance. Dr. Clark, by the way, announced the first "booking" for the journey, — that of a mother who intended to take her two sons for the sake of the missionary information and inspiration they would gain from the trip.

In introducing Mr. Horsefield, Dr. Clark said he hardly knew whether it was safe to have him speak or not, but the church seemed strongly built and he was inclined to risk it.

Our delegate from England had won hundreds of devoted admirers by his cheery ways, his kindly spirit, his versatile and open mind, and the manliness that characterized his every word. Two Episcopal Christian Endeavor Societies in Denver are promised as one result of his visit.

Mr. Horesfield gave as the message of English to American Endeavorers the watchword proposed by the new president of the British Christian Endeavor union, Rev. W. Bainbridge, "Organize, Vitalize!" and Dr. Clark, while accepting the motto, begged permission to add to it one word, asking Mr. Horsefield to accept it as America's return message, — the key-word of the Denver Convention: "Evangelize!"

As Mr. Horsefield concluded, Mr. Foster, in a happy little speech, presented to him a little Union Jack which he had found in the fallen tent, and preserved as a souvenir for the British visitor.

There followed the greetings from our Endeavor brothers across the seas sent by mail or cable; introduced, however, by a cordial message from ex-Secretary Baer, which was received with warm applause that showed he was by no means forgotten. These messages were from a surprisingly wide geographical range.

GREETINGS.

BRITISH UNION.

Will you please give my greetings to your convention, as President of the British Union? The text is the song to be sung in the land of Judah, "In that day shall this song be sung in the land of Judah; We have a strong city; salvation will God appoint for walls and bulwarks. Open ye the gates, that the righteous nation which keepeth the truth may enter in. Thou wilt keep him in perfect peace, whose mind is stayed on thee: because he trusteth in thee."

Our brethren, the Rev. F. J. Horsefield and Rev. Mr. Campbell, will well represent us.

From Rev. W. Bainbridge,
Sunderland, England.

CHINA.

Personal Greetings.

REV. W. P. BENTLEY, Shanghai.
MISS EMILY S. HARTWELL, Foochow.
REV. J. E. SHOEMAKER, Ningpo.

FROM COSTA RICA.

The 160 members and 80 Juniors of the nine Societies of Costa Rica send greetings to the Christian Endeavorers at Denver. We thank God for the help our societies have been to us in teaching us how to do better work for God, and pray that soon the gospel through Christian Endeavor will belt the world.

On behalf of the Christian Endeavorers of Costa Rica,
Yours sincerely,
S. WITT (signed).

CUBA.

It is our ardent desire that by this bond of union and through the precious blood and love sublime of our Master, we shall more and more strengthen each other. We invoke our Heavenly Father's blessing and guidance in our work for the glory of our Saviour

"Beloved, let us love one another for love is of God, and every one that loveth is born of God, and knoweth God.

Sent by V. Tuzzio,
Manzanillo, Cuba.

ENGLAND.

Personal Greetings.
REV. R. J. CAMPBELL, London.
REV. F. J. HORSEFIELD, Bristol.

GERMANY AND AUSTRIA.

Personal Greeting.
DR. S. S. HAURY.

GERMANY.

By cable.

Raise the standard. Raise the standard as people born from above, especially in your daily duties, just to that point which God would like to have, before the unbelieving and the unevangelized youth to the World's redemption. Christ is victor.

Sent by the Secretary of the C. E. Union for Germany,
    Rev. F. Blecher,
        Friedrichshagen (*Via* Berlin), Germany.

HUNGARY.

Our prayer is that our Lord Jesus Christ may bless Christian Endeavor, not only in Hungary but throughout the whole world. We send hearty salutations to the Endeavorers who will meet in Denver, and while we are thankful for the generous help we have received from our brethren across the ocean, we ask every Endeavorer to pray, and to pray, and to pray for Hungary.

Sent by Prof. A. Szabo,
    Buda-Pest.

INDIA.

They of India salute you. On behalf of India's thousands of Christian Endeavorers, I send you affectionate and grateful greetings. Our cause is making more substantial progress in this Empire than ever before. Blessed tokens of encouragement shine in every quarter of the heavens.

Personally, "Though I be absent in the flesh, I am with you in the spirit, joying and beholding your order, and the steadfastness of your faith in Christ."

Sent by Rev. F. S. Hatch, M. A.,
    72-1 Jaun Bazar St., Calcutta, India.
General secretary of United Society of India, Burmah, and Ceylon.

INDIA.

Personal Greetings.
    REV. C. H. BANDY.
    REV. L. B. CHAMBERLAIN.
    REV. A. G. McGAW, Etah.
    REV. JOHN H. WYCKOFF, D.D., Arcot Mission.

ITALY.

Our first thought has to do with our spiritual solidity with you, brethren, in Christ. As our prayers rise these days to the throne of our common Father in Heaven, we do not forget to what extent we are debtors to the brethren of America for the valiant worker they sent among us, the pioneer of the blessed work, and for the help which they are giving us in this first part of our experience. The gratitude which we feel, added to our love to the common cause, will be a powerful stimulus to vigorous labor on its behalf.

The prayer which we, full of holy enthusiasm raise to Heaven is that the holy cause of Christian Endeavor continues its glorious march throughout the earth for the triumph of God's Kingdom. "They of Italy salute you."
    (Heb. xiii: 24.)

AFRICA.

Personal Greetings.
    REV. WILLIS R. HOTCHKISS.

JAPAN.

One hundred and twenty Christian Endeavor Societies in Japan, the land of the dawn, send through two delegates and eighteen banners their fraternal greetings to the Denver Assemblage.

They flash this message from their sacred Mount of Fuji to the heights of Colorado.

The world is *one* in Christ.
Let the world be *won* for Christ.

(Eph. iii: 20, 21.) Now unto Him that is able to do exceeding abundantly above all that we ask or think, according to the power that worketh in us, unto him be glory in the church by Christ Jesus throughout all ages, world without end. Amen.

Sent by the President of the Union,
  Rev. T. Harada.

JAPAN.

Personal Greetings.
  MISS A. E. GARVIN, Osaka.
  MR. JOHN MAKINS, Nagasaki.
  MR. C. OGAWA, Sendai.

MARSHALL ISLANDS.

I am authorized to send the love of our Society here in the Marshall Islands Training School, the first in Micronesia, '95, and of the Kusaian Society, the youngest, '02.

Sent by the Superintendent,
  C. F. Rife, M.D.,
    Kusaie, Caroline Islands.

PERSIA.

Though as yet we are a feeble folk in Persia, we are laboring together with you in the effort to hasten the coming of the Kingdom by consecrated youthful energy.

Sent by Miss Bertha H. McConaughy,
  Urumia, Persia (*via* Berlin and Tabriz).

QUEENSLAND.

Queensland Christian Endeavor union sends heartiest greetings of brotherly love to the Denver Convention. "Trusting in the Lord Jesus Christ for strength, we promise Him that we will strive to do whatever he would like to have us do." In His name, your co-workers.

Sent for the Executive Committee, by the General Secretary of the union,
  Mr. J. A. J. Ferguson.
    Eagle Chambers, Brisbane.

SCOTLAND.

The Ninth Annual Convention of our union has just been held in Glasgow. At that convention the members of our union instructed me to forward to you as the greeting from our union to the Denver Convention, the message contained in I. Corinthians 16: 13, "Watch ye, stand fast in the faith. quit you like men, be strong." I have very much pleasure indeed in transmitting that greeting.

Sent by the Secretary of the union.
  Mr. Andrew Alston, LL.B.,
    58 Renfield St.,
      Glasgow, Scotland.

SOUTH AFRICA.

The South African Endeavorers assembled in convention at East London, Cape Colony, have desired me to convey to you their hearty greetings and prayerful good wishes for the annual World's Convention soon to assemble at Denver, U.S.A.

We pray that God may grant you a share of the presence and power of the Holy Spirit, and such stimulus and inspiration that the New Year may be one of greater progress than any in the history of the Movement.

It may be of interest to know that this message comes from a body composed of both English and Dutch Endeavorers, who are already realizing on the Endeavor platform that unity of the Spirit in the bond of peace, which is not only one of the fundamental principles of the Christian Endeavor Movement, but the great need of the South Africa of to-day.

In the bonds of Christian fellowship,

Sincerely yours,

MILDRED M. CLEGHORN, *Sec'y.*

SOUTH AUSTRALIA.

South Australia sends greeting to the Denver Convention in John xvii: 22, 23. (And the glory which thou gavest me I have given them; that they may be one, even as we are one: I in them, and thou in me, that they be made perfect in one; and that the world may know that thou hast sent me, and hast loved them, as thou hast loved me.) And prays the influence of the gathering will give a mighty stimulus to Christian Endeavor in the wide world.

Sent by the Secretary South Australian union,

Mr. H. N. Holmes,
    Beaconsfield Buildings,
    King William St.,
    Adelaide.

SPAIN.

"We thank our God upon every remembrance of you." (Philippians, i:3.)
Sent by Superintendent Spain Christian Endeavor union.

Rev. William H. Gulick,
    Biarritz, France.

SWITZERLAND.

Mr. President and dear fellow-endeavorers,

The great Endeavor family has its feast at Denver this year, and our small Swiss Christian Endeavor union would have much appreciated the privilege of taking part in it. Unfortunately it is not possible for us to have the pleasure of making personal acquaintance with so many beloved and prominent Christian workers, neither shall we be able to draw with you from the treasures of experience and knowledge which the Lord puts at your disposal during these days.

But the Swiss Christian Endeavor union cannot let this grand manifestation pass, without sending to the convention a cordial message of its fraternal affection. Our prayer is that the Lord bestow upon the Denver Convention the fullness and the power of His Holy Spirit, and that this gathering may give a mighty impulse for the advent of our King's kingdom.

Yours most sincerely in Christian Endeavor fellowship and love,

CHARLES BRIQUET, *Secretary.*

TASMANIA.

The Tasmania Christian Endeavor union sends cordial greetings. "The Lord bless thee, and keep thee: the Lord make his face to shine upon thee, and be gracious unto thee: the Lord lift up his countenance upon thee, and give thee peace."

Sent by the Secretary of the union,

Mr. John Stranger,
    Mechanics' Hall,
    Melville St.,
    Hobart.

THE VICTORIAN, AUSTRALIA, UNION.

We pray always for you, that our God would count you worthy of this calling, and fulfil all the good pleasure of his goodness, and the work of faith with power.

that the name of our Lord Jesus Christ may be glorified in you, and ye in Him, according to the grace of our God and the Lord Jesus Christ. II. Thessalonians i: 11, 12.

Sent by the Secretary of the Union,
Mr. George R. Hexter,
315 Little Collins St.,
Melbourne, Victoria.

WALES.

Personal Greetings.
Brought by Rev. F. J. Horsefield of Bristol England.

A cordial greeting was received from Mr. John Willis Baer, former General Secretary of the United Society, but in the confusion incident to the destruction of Tent Endeavor it, with some others, was lost.

BRAZIL.

The National union of Brazil sends greetings and desires to express its warm interest in the success of the great Convention at Denver.

At the first National eonvention in Brazil, last November, a delegate was commissioned to be present at Denver, but, unfortunately, is unable to be with you.

Christian Endeavor as an organization is young in Brazil, but not as a fact. We have much to learn of ways and means from our brothers in the North, and we are deeply grateful for the help we have already received, especially for the interest that has been shown by the United Society and the inspiration received from the pages of *The Christian Endeavor World.*

Dear brothers and sisters of the North, you do not really know how hard it is for us in the Southern Hemisphere. Pray for us. May God bless you there at Denver, and in your homes when you return.

R. W. FENN,
Trustee and delegate of the Brazil union.

HAWAII.

(By cable.)

Greetings.

HAWAIIAN CHRISTIAN ENDEAVOR.

FINLAND.

(On a birch-bark postal card.)

The Finnish Christian Endeavor Societies send to their brothers and sisters in America their warmest regards. We wish you well. May the Christian standard always be carried high in your country! May the American Endeavorers always go ahead in the name of the Lord!

We are thankful to you, as from you the Christian Endeavor movement has come to Finland. And on this, your great Convention, our thoughts go to you across the ocean. May God bless you!

Yours in Christ,
EMIL SARBACK.
AINA JOHANSSON.

NEW SOUTH WALES.

Psa. cv: 4. "Seek the Lord and His strength. Seek His face forevermore."
J. NEALE BREDEN.

MEXICO.

San Luis Potosi, Mexico,
June 23, 1903.

My dear Dr. Clark: —

I take great pleasure in presenting to you Rev. James S. A. Hunter, of the Associate Reformed Presbyterian Church, and missionary under the Synod of the same to Mexico, and located in Ciudad del Maiz (The City of Corn), in this State.

As the president of our United Society is not in the country at present, I take it upon myself to name Brother Hunter as fraternal delegate to the International Convention to be held in Denver, July 9 to 13, in representation of our Mexican National United Society of Christian Endeavor.

I know of no other Endeavorer going from Mexico to the Convention, at present. If I hear of others I shall gladly recommend them to your fraternal care.   Very sincerely,

MEDORA B. WILLIAMS
Secretary of the United Society.

Mr. Hunter was to have been heard in person in the Tent, Monday night, but after the storm compelled holding four meetings in churches, much to the regret of all, he, with some other foreign delegates, could not be located when the roll of foreign lands was called.

PARIS.

Dear Comrades: —

A little more than a hundred years ago our forefathers fought together for the triumph of freedom and justice. Our Lafayette devoted himself to the cause of your dawning independence. Your Franklin initiated our people to the manners of a republican democracy. It is not the only time that our two nations have become debtors one to another, for whereas our Declaration of the Rights of man was inspired by your Bills of Rights, on the other hand there are French Huguenot names among those who signed the charts of your freedom.

We, citizens of the French Republic, are proud to celebrate like you, citizens of the United States, the memory of the two great Revolutions by which our two free Republics have been founded. But we are ever more convinced that political emancipation is nothing unless man be free from the yoke of sin and united by the obedience of faith to his Savior and God. Therefore do we rejoice in the admirable work which is accomplished by your Christian Endeavor Societies. They are truly the vanguard of the army of Christ, for, disdaining political ambition, class or party spirit, they are determined to promote the reign of Him who came not to be ministered unto but to minister, and who gave His life for the moral and social salvation of mankind.

Miraculously saved from the persecutions, massacres, and proscriptions, that troubled our country for two hundred and fifty years, few, weak and scattered the evangelical churches of France are still at present in a most critical position. All around them a desperate fight is being waged between clerical domination and superstition on the one hand, and infidelity on the other hand. Obliged as they are to make front on both sides at the same time, against foes that are a hundred times more numerous than themselves, they are continually in danger of being crushed by the onset of the two great rival hosts.

Our Christian Endeavor Societies are also in a much less favorable position than yours. It is your churches that have moulded the manners of your country, whereas the manners of our country have been moulded by the church of Rome. We have not your Sunday. Our children do not grow up in a Christian atmosphere such a yours, and our young ladies do not enjoy such freedom. It is therefore not to be wondered at that the Christian Endeavor Societies of France are still few, and that their organization is still imperfect. But we are convinced that you have put into our hand a first rate tool, which will be most useful in the work of reviving our churches and evangelizing our country. We thank you most heartily for the very efficient help which you have given us, and are convinced that the seed which you have sown will produce plenteous fruit to the glory of our God.

A few years ago our two nations gave each other a testimony of their mutual sympathy, France by erecting at the entrance of the port of New York the Statue of Liberty enlightening the world, and the children of the United States by placing in the centre of the palace of our ancient Kings, the effigy of the gallant soldier who fought for your independence and for our civil and religious emancipation.

Prevented as we are from being present at your convention we, also, French Endeavorers, wish to give you a testimony of our thankfulness and our Christian sympathy; we therefore send you in our place the emblem of our country, the tricolor flag. We know that we put it into the hands of friends. May it wave beside the starry banner and remind you that you have in France comrades and brethren who worship the same God, follow the same Master, and fight with you for the triumph of his reign of goodness, righteousness, and truth.

In the name of the Christian Endeavor Societies of Paris,

JEAN MONNIER, *president.*
HENRI MERLE D'AUBIQUE.

CHINA.

As delegate from the National Committee of the United Society of Christian Endeavor for China, I bring greetings and thanks from the nearly 6000 Endeavorers of that Empire.

In Fuhkien province alone where Christian Endeavor was started in 1885 we have 125 societies with a membership of about 4600. To-night will be presented a banner from the Anglican Endeavorers of Foochow, and I feel that banner should be an inspiration to us all, for since Dr. and Mrs. Clark's visit to Foochow at our All-China Convention in 1900, the increase in the Endeavor ranks of the English Church mission in Fuhkien have been 400 per cent.

Mr. Hinman, the new general secretary you have so generously helped our United Society of China to secure, sends this encouraging word. He says that Mr. Hoste, the superintendent of the China Inland mission says that many in their mission are anxious to start Endeavor societies. Mr. Hinman also reports that an invitation has come from Monkdin, Manchuria, to start Endeavor there. We feel that in the near future is prospect of a large increase in the Endeavor ranks in China.

I bring special greetings and boundless thanks from our National Committee with the hope that you will continue to help us to have a general secretary on the field. I bring greetings for China's first Provincial union, — the Fuhkien Endeavor union; from China's first district union, started last year by one of the Intermediates who presented Dr. Clark with the Intermediate banner in 1900. It pays to begin to train Endeavor workers in the Junior and Intermediate societies.

The English speaking society of the Union Church, Shanghai, sends Phil. iii: 13, 15. "This one thing I do, forgetting those things which are behind, I press toward the mark for the prize of the high calling of God in Christ Jesus. Let us therefore, as many as be perfect, be thus minded."

And I have a message for this great Convention from some of China's Juniors. Another banner presented to-night was designed by an earnest Junior worker, a young man who relinquished a lucrative position as interpreter to the British troops to teach for Miss Posey in her boys' school. He was the first Junior of Central China, and is worthy the honor.

The Junior message is II John i: 3. "Grace be with you, mercy and peace, from God the Father, and from the Lord Jesus Christ, the Son of the Father, in truth and love." Also Hebrews xiii: 1. "Let brotherly love continue."

In closing I invite you all to Foochow in 1906 on your way to the World's Convention at Calcutta. Don't fail to call at Foochow, the cradle of Endeavor in China, and the most scenic and beautiful port in the Empire.

EMILY S. HARTWELL.

New Zealand.

"O Jesus! Grant that we may know,
As we go forth into the world again,
That Thou art just the same where'er we are —
The Mighty One, who strengthens, keeps, and saves
The weakest of his trusting little ones."

W. Cooper,
Secy N. Z. C. E. Union.

Prayer was offered for all these lands, and for our distant comrades in Christian Endeavor.

Then came a scene which six months of the most earnest effort of Christian Endeavor history had anticipated as the climax.

The Awarding of Banners

in the Increase Campaign. These banners had been hung on long wires across the front of the tent only a few hours before the collapse, but they had been rescued, unharmed, from the ruins. One by one Dr. Clark unrolled them, held them up, and presented them to the unions that had so finely earned them.

Proud were the States that graciously accepted the banners so well earned for their increase in number of societies during the past year. But prouder still was President Francis Clark to be enabled to award the banners to the representatives of the great and growing society, which but a few years ago he had founded and consecrated to Christ.

As each of the representatives accepted the banner presented to his delegation, he offered a few words in response, permeated with hope for even greater work in the future. And the successful candidates responded with a verse or song, and were heartily received by the gathering.

Even as the little cohort from Maryland lustily sang their special verse, so did the two representatives from India respond with songs in the Hindoo tongue. The audience didn't understand, but judging from the applause, one would have thought that the auditors were quite familiar with the selection. Or, perhaps, it was the fervor which the singers put in their song and the spirit of the whole gathering, which incited the warm reception.

The charming, delicate banner given by the Endeavorers of Sendai, Japan, was presented by Mr. Ogawa, head of the postal-telegraph society of Sendai, to Colorado, and President Chapman, amid much applause, received it, the great gallery full of Colorado Endeavorers breaking out in their State song, "Colorado for Christ we sing." This banner, like the others that followed, was suspended by broad ribbons that bore the words, "Increase Campaign Banner" and "Fidelity and Fellowship," while streamers descending on either side bore the stars and crescents thus far earned, with spaces for those that are to come.

What a bewilderingly beautiful succession of dainty banners from Japan! Each seemed more dainty and artistic than the last. Miss Garvin, of Osaka, read an eloquent message from President Harada

ONE OF THE ENTRANCES TO TENT ENDEAVOR.

THE GROWTH OF CHRISTIAN ENDEAVOR ILLUSTRATED AT THE
JUNIOR RALLY.

accompanying them. Eighteen banners were sent in all from this "United States of the Orient," and some of the loveliest remain to be given to the States that next reach the ten-per cent increase.

The prize banner, that from Yokohama, went to Ohio, who, through the splendid activity of Field Secretary Hubbell, President Fout, and the other officers, has made the largest absolute gain, the glorious number of 335 new societies since November, while, as President Fout said in accepting the banner, he had in his pocket the names of sixty other societies that have not yet been reported.

The Okayama banner went to Utah, the Kobe Church banner to Alabama, the Kobe union banner to Maryland, and other Japanese banners to New Mexico, Georgia, Missouri, and Wisconsin. Maryland took the opportunity to invite the Convention to Baltimore in 1905 — an invitation emphasized by a telegram received after the tent blew down. Minneapolis and St. Louis also extended invitations. President Withers of Missouri received his banner as "a reminder of the fact that Jesus Christ has never been permitted to do His best with any one yet, and of how much might yet be done to win Missouri for Christ." He handed the banner over to Miss Minnich, the secretary of a district that has gained 144 per cent in the number of societies. President Kirbye, speaking for Georgia, quoted exultantly a jolly little poem that ended:

> There's a fish on every line
> In Georgia.

A characteristically eloquent message from France accompanied a magnificent silken tricolor, bearing the words, *Pour Christ et pour son église.* Remembering the large share of Frenchmen in the population and history of the State, this banner was given to Louisiana.

A splendid Chinese banner was presented to Oregon, the State nearest to China, and the first to gain its ten per cent (it actually has gained fifteen per cent). President Rockwood, in receiving the banner, attributed their success to the inspiration and encouragement received from Mr. Eberman. The same tribute was paid to Mr. Eberman's memory by the State of Washington as it received the brilliant golden banner from South Africa, with its striking design of an open Bible lying upon a native shield and assegai.

China's other banner, the most elaborately and richly decorated of all, went to Indiana, which led the way with 306 societies reported before the first of July.

Hungary sent a very simple but remarkably elegant banner, of heavy silk in three bars of the national red, white, and green, bearing the words, "Magyar C. E." This token from the zealous Endeavorers of Budapest and other Hungarian towns was given to Oklahoma and the Indian Territory, in recognition of their seventeen-per-cent gain.

Germany furnished two banners of strong and effective design, which were welcomed with especial delight. One of them, that from the Saxony Christian Endeavor union, was awarded to the Canadian

Province of Assiniboia, and the other, that displayed a sunburst spring-
ing from the Christian Endeavor monogram, went as far as possible
from the old Fatherland, to the Endeavorers of Alaska. That banner
alone had no delegate present to receive it.

The banner from India was of rich blue velvet, richly embroidered
with red and yellow, bearing the outline of the Empire dotted all over
with Christian Endeavor monograms. This resplendent affair went
to Nevada, which has made the largest percentage of gain, and which,
as the president of the State union said, "has a Christian Endeavor
society in every evangelical church in the State but one, except
the Methodist churches. And all honor to them," he hastened to
add "for they have been a great missionary church in that great
State."

The last banner was from Korea, and was the most remarkable of
all, with its absolutely strange devices, and especially the queerly
twisted design of red and black, which represented the principles of
good and of evil trying to swallow each other. West Virginia received
this unique banner, and President Pollock, in accepting it said that
Christian Endeavor's purpose for the future should be that the red
shall entirely eliminate the black from the Mountain State.

Thus was completed this most interesting ceremonial. It was en-
livened throughout with State songs and other vivacious responses,
it brought to the front many sections of the country, especially the
South, from which we were delighted to hear words of progress and
good cheer, and, best of all, there was manifested no sense of a task
completed, but only of a great task hopefully begun. The ten-per-
cent campaign has gloriously initiated the one-hundred-per-cent campaign, and may God grant a triumphant conclusion in 1912!

Dr. Clark next spoke words of earnest gratitude to all the many
helpers that have contributed to make the Denver Convention in some
respects the climax of all Endeavor gatherings. The local committee
the ushers, the choir, the press, the reception committee, the hospitable
citizens of Denver, — all were given the most heartfelt gratitude.

It is not the idea of a gain in number of societies and members, for which we
all feel so thankful, but the gaining of workers and souls to Jesus Christ at which
we rejoice, said President Clark in his closing remarks.

We are very grateful to God for his aid and guidance through this, the best
and the greatest of the many Conventions that the Christian Endeavor has held.

We wish to heartily thank the ushers who have conducted the gathering with
great skill and the press committee and the press and the hospitable homes of
Denver which were generously thrown open to us.

Dr. Clark also expressed his thankfulness for a brotherly resolution
received from the Colorado Epworth League, and also for the aid
given the Convention by the local societies that bear other names than
Christian Endeavor. The hard-working committee of arrangements
were brought before the Convention at Dr. Clark's special request,
and were given an enthusiastic Chatauqua greeting.

Introducing the members of the committee who, by their untiring

efforts had made the Convention an unprecedented success, Chairman
W. E. Sweet said: —

"It is with keenest regret that we come to the final hour of the Convention.
Your presence is its benediction. It is our earnest hope that you may journey
in safety to your homes, feeling to the greatest degree the inestimable good de-
rived from this Convention, and may 'God be with you till we meet again.'"

The long and earnest applause, following Mr. Sweet's remarks,
plainly showed that he had touched the right chord in the hearts of
the hundreds of delegates.

Last of all, after a thank-offering from the Endeavorers which was
given to help the Convention committee meet the unexpected expenses
attending the fall of the tent, Dr. Gray conducted a solemn closing
consecration service.

When the last strains of "Nearer My God to Thee" had died away
after the consecration service the benediction was pronounced and the
great Convention of 1903 was ended.

OFFICERS OF THE UNITED SOCIETY OF CHRISTIAN ENDEAVOR

TREMONT TEMPLE, BOSTON, MASS.

REV. FRANCIS E. CLARK, D.D., *President.*
MR. VON OGDEN VOGT, *General Secretary.*
MR. WILLIAM SHAW, *Treasurer.*
MR. GEORGE B. GRAFF, *Publishing Agent.*

TRUSTEES.

BISHOP B. W. ARNETT, D.D.
BISHOP ALEXANDER WALTERS, D.D.
REV. JOHN T. BECKLEY, D.D.
REV. W. H. BROOKS, D.D.
REV. HOWARD B. GROSE
REV. P. S. HENSON, D.D.
REV. WAYLAND HOYT, D.D.
REV. J. L. GILMOUR
REV. J. M. LOWDEN
REV. C. F. YODER
MR. GEORGE A. CHACE
REV. CANON J. B. RICHARDSON
REV. C. I. BROWN
REV. N. BOYNTON, D.D.
HON. S. B. CAPEN
REV. FRANCIS E. CLARK, D.D.
REV. CHARLES A. DICKINSON, D.D.
REV. JAMES L. HILL, D.D.
MR. WILLIAM SHAW
REV. J. H. GARRISON, LL.D.
REV. CHARLES B. NEWNAN
REV. ALLAN B. PHILPUTT, D.D.
REV. F. W. POWER, D.D.
REV. J. Z. TYLER, D.D.
PROF. H. L. WILLETT
REV. FLOYD W. TOMKINS, D.D.
PROF. ELBERT RUSSELL
REV. M. RHODES, D.D.
REV. N. B. GRUBB, D.D.

REV. H. K. CARROLL, D.D
REV. GILBY C. KELLY, D.D.
REV. A. C. CREWS
REV. W. F. WILSON, D.D.
REV. E. HUMPHRIES, D.D.
REV. GEORGE E. McMANIMAN, D.D.
REV. W. H. VOGLER, D.D.
MR. JOHN WILLIS BAER
REV. RALPH W. BROKAW
REV. J. WILBUR CHAPMAN, D.D.
REV. TEUNIS S. HAMLIN, D.D.
REV. CLELAND B. McAFEE. D.D.
REV. WILLIAM PATTERSON, D.D.
REV. WILTON MERLE SMITH, D.D.
MR. ROBERT E. SPEER
REV GEORGE B. STEWART, D.D.
REV. HUGH K. WALKER, D.D.
REV. ALEXANDER ESLER, M.A.
PROF. JAMES LEWIS HOWE
REV. W. J. DARBY, D.D.
REV. IRA LANDRITH, LL.D.
REV. SAMUEL McNAUGHER, Ph.D.
REV. W. H. McMILLAN, D.D.
BISHOP SAMUEL FALLOWS, D.D., LL.D.
REV. DAVID JAMES BURRELL, D.D.
REV. RUFUS W. MILLER, D.D.
REV. H. F. SHUPE
REV. U. F. SWENGEL

180

AN ENDEAVOR ENCAMPMENT.

THE COURT HOUSE DECORATED WITH THE CONVENTION COLORS.

OFFICERS OF THE WORLD'S CHRISTIAN ENDEAVOR UNION

REV. FRANCIS E. CLARK, D.D., *President*,
TREMONT TEMPLE, BOSTON, MASS.

MR. JOHN WILLIS BAER, *Secretary*,
156 FIFTH AVE., NEW YORK, N.Y.

MR. WILLIAM SHAW, *Treasurer*
TREMONT TEMPLE, BOSTON, MASS.

The officers of the World's Union serve without compensation, and all contributions are used in the advancement of Christian Endeavor in the world-wide field. Missionaries of all denominations bear cordial testimony to the great usefulness of the Christian Endeavor Society in training the native Christians, and in developing a self-sustaining church membership.

INDEX.

THEMES OF ADDRESSES, SERMONS ETC.

www.ingramcontent.com/pod-product-compliance
Lightning Source LLC
Chambersburg PA
CBHW031546040426
42452CB00006B/204

ALSO BY DAVID ALAN BLACK

Paul, Apostle of Weakness

Linguistics for Students of New Testament Greek

New Testament Criticism and Interpretation

Linguistics and New Testament Interpretation

Scribes and Scripture

Learn to Read New Testament Greek

Using New Testament Greek in Ministry

New Testament Textual Criticism

It's Still Greek to Me

The Myth of Adolescence

Interpreting the New Testament

Rethinking the Synoptic Problem

Why Four Gospels?

Rethinking New Testament Textual Criticism

The New Testament: Its Background and Message

Perspectives on the Ending of Mark

The Jesus Paradigm

Christian Archy

Will You Join the Cause of Global Missions?

The Authorship of Hebrews: The Case for Paul

It's All Greek to Me: Confessions of an Unlikely Academic

Seven Marks of a New Testament Church

The Pericope of the Adulteress in Contemporary Research

*Running My Race: Reflections on
Life, Loss, Aging, and Forty Years of Teaching*